D0776860

MEMORY
PERCEIVED

Recent Titles in Psychological Dimensions to War and Peace

Perpetration-Induced Traumatic Stress: The Psychological Consequences of Killing
Rachel M. MacNair

MEMORY PERCEIVED

RECALLING THE HOLOCAUST

ROBERT N. KRAFT

Psychological Dimensions to War and Peace
Harvey Langholtz, Series Editor

Westport, Connecticut
London

Library of Congress Cataloging-in-Publication Data

Kraft, Robert Nathaniel.
  Memory perceived : recalling the Holocaust / Robert N. Kraft.
    p. cm.—(Psychological dimensions to war and peace, ISSN 1540-5265)
  Includes bibliographical references and index.
  ISBN 0-275-97774-9 (alk. paper)
    1. Holocaust, Jewish (1939–1945)—Personal narratives. 2. Holocaust, Jewish
  (1939–1945)—Psychological aspects. 3. Holocaust, Jewish (1939–1945)—Influence. 4.
  Holocaust, Jewish (1939–1945)—Historiography. 5. Memory I. Title. II. Series.
  D804.195.K73 2002
  940.53'18'092—dc21   2002067303

British Library Cataloguing in Publication Data is available.

Library of Congress Catalog Card Number: 2002067303
ISBN: 0-275-97774-9
ISSN: 1540-5265

First published in 2002

Praeger Publishers, 88 Post Road West, Westport, CT 06881
An imprint of Greenwood Publishing Group, Inc.
www.praeger.com

Printed in the United States of America

The paper used in this book complies with the
Permanent Paper Standard issued by the National
Information Standards Organization (Z39.48–1984).

10 9 8 7 6 5 4 3 2 1

Copyright Acknowledgments

The author and publisher gratefully acknowledge permission for use of the following material:

Poetry excerpt from *The Night Parade* by Edward Hirsch, copyright © 1989 by Edward Hirsch. Used by permission of Alfred A. Knopf, a division of Random House, Inc.

Portions of chapter 1 and chapter 2 that appeared in "Holocaust Memory: Persistent Recall of Extreme Trauma," in *Viewing Psychology as a Whole: The Integrative Science of William N. Dember*, edited by Robert R. Hoffman, Michael F. Sherrick, and Joel S. Warm (Washington, D.C.: American Psychological Association, 1998), pp. 375–398. Copyright © 1998 by the American Psychological Association. Used with permission.

Excerpts of oral testimonies from the Fortunoff Video Archive for Holocaust Testimonies. Used by permission of the Yale University Library.

To my family, present and past

CONTENTS

Foreword *by Harvey Langholtz*   ix

Preface   xiii

Acknowledgments   xxi

1. Revealing Memories: Oral Testimony and the
    Holocaust   1

2. Defining Memories: Patterns of Remembering   17

3. Childhood's End: Memory in Young Children Who
    Survived the Holocaust   57

4. Apprehending Atrocity: Levels of Awareness During
    Prolonged Trauma   91

5. Aftershocks of Traumatic Memory: Disturbing Behavior
    and Beliefs   121

6. Beyond the Aftermath: Lessons of Memory   163

Appendix   187

Selected Bibliography   197

Index   205

FOREWORD

The Holocaust stands as an undeniable example of the most troubling, disturbing, and haunting aspects of human capacity. The notion that a civilized European nation in the twentieth century efficiently, systematically, and relentlessly pursued the extermination of millions of people is a reality with which we are still trying to come to terms. Perhaps we are searching for an explanation that will reassure us that the Holocaust was an isolated event and not representative of the higher ideals we would like to associate with our definition of what it means to be human. But that reassurance does not seem to be forthcoming, no matter how much we wish it would.

In *Memory Perceived: Recalling the Holocaust*, Robert Kraft presents an oral history based on testimonies from Holocaust survivors, permitting the reader to learn first-hand what occurred, not at the level of black-and-white images that factually portray the event, but instead at the personal and experiential level of those who survived it. What emerges is a psychological study that is both rich in detail and as scientifically rigorous as is possible. This is a study of memory, but it is a type of memory that stands apart from other forms of memory. Through 129 testimonies gleaned from hundreds in the second edition of the *Guide to Yale University Library Holocaust Video Testimonies* and from ORBIS records, Kraft pursues a meticulous and structured psychological understanding of the memories of survivors. In order to do this he first develops a scientific approach to conducting this psychological research based on oral testimonies. He then goes on to study patterns of these memories, the special effects on children who survived the Holocaust, psychological levels of awareness during prolonged trauma, psychological effects throughout the lives of survivors, and psychological lessons of memory about the events.

The reader will see that this book certainly does all that is possible to help us become informed from the oral testimonies of survivors. But the fundamental question remains unanswered, or perhaps answered in a way that we find disturbing. Is the Holocaust behind us as a singular and aberrant part of history, or is this behavior part of the human condition? While World War II now takes its place in the history of the last century, does the capacity for another Holocaust remain? How is it possible that since the close of World War II there have been more than 100 wars with a toll of 30 million war-related deaths? How is it possible that during the intervening 57 years there have been more than 50 cases of genocide and mass political murder with a toll of at least 9 million deaths? Pol Pot's genocide in Cambodia during the 1970s, the genocide of Rwanda in 1994, and scores of other such incidents are very disturbing reminders that the capacity for people to repeat the acts of the Holocaust remains with us. Indeed, even during the very week the United States Holocaust Memorial Museum opened in April of 1993 with solemn declarations of "never again," ethnic genocide was being carried out in one area of the European continent, but this time with different perpetrators and different victims. It is also disturbing that the phrase "never again" was not a prediction in any of the testimonies in this study.

By presenting multiple testimonies, integrating these testimonies, and finding patterns of experience, this book takes us to a deeper level than simple words can reach. In chapter 5 Krafts tell us: "There is too much to tell, the extent of shame and grief too great, the ghettos and the camps too alien for others to imagine." He quotes one of the survivor's oral testimonies: "If you want to record the Holocaust, [it's] not just numbers—in the thousands, in the hundreds, in the millions. You can focus on one family, one person, on one particular day." And this focus is what *Memory Perceived: Recalling the Holocaust* has done for us. In these pages we hear the testimonies of some of the individuals who survived the Holocaust, and as we listen we try in a structured and careful way to learn the lessons they have to tell us.

Harvey Langholtz

PREFACE

Winter descends in knives, in long sheets of ice
Unravelling in the sky,
In stuttering black syllables of rain.

Edward Hirsch

This book began in paradox. As I listened to the oral testimony of those who lived through the Holocaust, I became increasingly aware of how much I did not understand. The more I listened, the more there was to know. At the same time, my peripheral vision of world events told me I was not alone. Recent reports in leading journals and newspapers continued to teach the informed public how much there was to learn.

Consider just the past several years. In February 1997, the Secretary of State of the United States found out definitively for the first time that she is the grandchild of Jews who perished in the Holocaust. In the spring of that year, the notorious Fascist group, the Ustaša, reemerged as a political force in Croatia. In the summer, one of the most enduring international stories was the recognition by Swiss banks that they hold tens of millions of dollars belonging to European

Jews who were killed in the Holocaust. An initial list of dormant Swiss bank accounts was first published in July 1997, more than fifty-two years after the end of World War II. That same month an Italian military court convicted two Nazi officers, Erich Priebke and Karl Hass, for their role in a massacre of 300 people more than fifty years earlier.

A sampling of news stories from the summer of 1998 is equally revealing. In August alone, Jewish groups, Swiss banks, and legal representatives for Holocaust survivors reached a comprehensive settlement over assets lost during the war, a Dutch newspaper published recently discovered excerpts from Anne Frank's diary, the U.S. Congress passed a bill requiring federal agencies to release their records of Nazi atrocities, and a major exhibit of Hitler's artifacts opened in Washington, "World War II Through Russian Eyes."

Three months earlier, in the spring of 1998, an international tribunal formed to resolve insurance claims by survivors of the Holocaust. In July, Volkswagen announced it would set up a private fund to compensate slave laborers who worked for the company in 1944 and 1945. In December, General Motors announced plans to investigate the role of slave labor in Nazi-occupied Europe in manufacturing plants that contributed to their own automobile operations. The following May, a consortium of European insurance companies reached an agreement for processing claims on prewar insurance policies. A year later, the French government completed its long-awaited report on property and money illegally confiscated during the occupation, documenting a surprising $1.3 billion of assets stolen from Jews under the Vichy regime. Three months after that in July 2000—fifty-five years after the end of World War II—the German government announced an unprecedented agreement, approving a fund of $5 billion to compensate people who were forced into slave labor by the Nazis. And the news stories continue.

Robert K., who lived through the Holocaust as a young child, explains, "Once in a while I hear someone say, 'Aren't you a little obsessed with the Holocaust?' And my response to that is, 'I think the Holocaust is obsessed with *us*. That the stories follow *you*, no matter what.' "[1] Another survivor, Isabella L., says, "For those who think that it happened long ago, it happened yesterday," referring not only to the painful vividness of Holocaust memory, but to real events in her own life. In January 1945, Isabella and three of her sisters escaped their captors during a death march from Auschwitz. In the violent confusion that followed, the oldest sister became separated from Isabella and her two remaining sisters, and they never saw her again. Many years later, Isabella met one of the women who had helped her at Auschwitz and only then learned of her sister's death in Bergen-Belsen. "Thirty years later, I found out what happened, what really happened to my sister," Isabella says. "So it happened yesterday."[2]

What is not so apparent from the many news reports is that, in addition to shaping the contours of political history, each reported event connects directly to the lives of those who survived the Holocaust—and to their families. Listening to oral testimony reminds us that the stories underlying the news reports are stories of individual lives. In fact, I believe there is a growing desire for the immediacy of individual stories that goes well beyond the world of Holocaust scholarship. Recent films and televised programs attest to this desire. In February 1997, NBC broadcast *Schindler's List*, virtually unedited, bringing in an estimated 65 million viewers, considerably more than the 25 million who saw the 1993 film during its original release. Two months after that, PBS telecast *The Trial of Adolph Eichmann* to a national audience. In the past several years, numerous films have reexamined the Holocaust and its aftermath, including *Anne Frank Remembered, Under the Domim Tree, The Long Way Home, Healing by Killing, The Truce, Apt Pupil, The Devil's Arithmetic, Life Is Beautiful, The Last Days,* and *The Grey Zone.*

My research took place at the Fortunoff Video Archive for Holocaust Testimonies at Yale University. I selected 129 testimonies from a set of nearly 600 testimonies abstracted in the second edition of the *Guide to Yale University Library Holocaust Video Testimonies* and from the Yale University on-line records of English-language testimonies of ORBIS. To carry out a comprehensive, integrative study of Holocaust memory, I needed a large and representative sample of testimonies. Readers should be aware, however, that sampling procedures must be adapted to fit the group being sampled. In studies of people who have lived through mass destruction, standard procedures for choosing participants are not feasible or even appropriate. The sample is always constrained by circumstance. Even so, groups of people conscripted into extended trauma by political and military forces are far more diverse than samples cleanly selected from colleges and universities. In the testimonies I studied, people came from ten different European countries, originally speaking eleven different languages, ranging in age when World War II started from infancy to forty-three, ranging in age when giving testimony from forty to ninety-five. They varied in economic background, level of education, religiousness, language, and culture. For a detailed account of the sampling procedures and complete lists of testimonies and witnesses, refer to the Appendix.

The Yale Archive does not solicit testimony; witnesses contact the Archive if they wish to do so. Each testimony usually consists of a single witness spontaneously recalling events in the presence of two nonintrusive interviewers. In fact, the word "interview" is misleading: The two trained interviewers are there to listen. They begin by prompting the witness to talk about life before the war and, if necessary, they ask about accounts that seem unclear. Witnesses can engage in uninterrupted recall for thirty or forty minutes. The length of most testimonies is between forty minutes and three hours, with a typical length of two hours.

The current interview procedure at Yale University has been in place since 1984. Before testimony is taped, there is a short preinterview on the telephone to ascertain family history and locations of the witness before, during, and after the war. Interviewers then prepare by studying maps and historical documents of the chronology of events, constructing a timeline of events and noting in particular the dates of Jewish holidays. None of this information is provided to the witness; it is simply preparation for the interview. A paradox shows itself with such interviews. The more the interviewers prepare, the less they participate during the taping of oral testimony.

Preparation is carried out quickly. Soon after initial contact, an interviewer calls, and the witness usually gives testimony three to five days after that. During that three- to five-day period, research is completed. For years, witnesses may not want to talk, but when they decide to provide testimony, the Archive acts quickly. In one case, after years of family encouragement to contact the Archive, the wife of a Holocaust survivor finally called the archivist and simply said into the telephone, "Chaim is ready."

During the interview, there are usually four people in the room: one behind the camera, two interviewers, and the witness. Family members may wait out of sight in the control room. Interviewers focus on listening, not asking questions. This focus shows in the methodology of gathering testimony: Witnesses introduce themselves at the beginning of the interview, thereby establishing that they are in charge of the testimony; interviewers do not pursue particular themes; interviewers do not take notes; and there are no time limits. Witnesses speak from memory, and in almost all cases, the interview is the first time for extended recall.

Although there are multiple reasons for providing testimony at a particular time, the main reason is to leave a record so that future generations will know. Each survivor who gives testimony is the agent, not a patient seeking treatment, not a legal witness facing adversarial cross-examination.[3] To give testimony is to remember for the purpose of remembering. Some witnesses do censor themselves, sometimes to avoid painfully shameful acts or to avoid reflecting badly on the Jewish people. Witnesses, however, are motivated by a fundamental desire to tell what happened, and this essential motivation can override tendencies to protect oneself and others from judgment. In one interview I personally observed in 1994, the witness placed a restriction on release of the testimony until well into the next century because he still feared being deported. He gave testimony to leave behind an accurate record.

The book presents testimony as it was given by the witnesses. The only phrase edited from testimony without an accompanying ellipsis is the repeated phrase "you know." The book refers to each witness by first name followed by the first letter of the last name. None of the names have been changed. In those instances when witnesses speak their own last names in the quoted testimony, the last names are replaced with the first letter followed by a double dash. In one case, the witness is a well-known journalist and filmmaker, and his full name is used. When referring to the population of people who lived through the Holocaust, I use the word "survivors." When specifically describing those survivors who gave testimony, I use "witnesses."

Perhaps within five years, testimonies will be accessible over the Internet, and I hope that the integrity of the testimony will be preserved, with each one available for study in its entirety and not segmented into sound bytes. Surely, observers can spend an hour or two listening to an individual's testimony. The 65 million viewers who watched *Schindler's List* uninterrupted on television demonstrated the required willingness and attention.

When I first began the study of oral testimony, I had the experimentalist's desire to quantify. How many people suffer from nightmares? How often? What percentage of witnesses feel split into two different selves? What are the predominant physical ailments and how many people suffer from each? Such analytical questions can be addressed, but they should be deferred until the individuals are more fully understood and larger themes emerge. Initially, quantification trivializes. This book presents multiple case studies, exploring each individual's testimony in depth and then generalizing across the different cases. Inductive analysis of the testimonies produced clear patterns of memory, and these patterns were tabulated as a basis for making qualitative distinctions about the characteristics of memory and its influences.

I studied the testimonies in the third person, as someone who did not conduct the interviews and as someone outside a clinical setting. While studying the testimonies, I was able to attend closely to what the witnesses communicated: their words, their intonations, their voices, and their gestures. By studying videotaped testimony, I did not personally intrude on the contents of the testimonies, and the witnesses themselves were unaffected by my appearance or my mood or my facial expressions or my spontaneous, unintentional remarks or how much time I spent with each testimony.

This book is not a review of the existing literature but an analysis of a new source of information about memory. This source—oral testimony—consists of videotaped records of *extended recall* of personally experienced events. The following chapters organize and synthesize more than 200 hours of oral testimony from 129 separate testimonies, revealing the enduring characteristics of Holocaust memory as well as the persistent influence of memory on the lives of the survivors. As a contribution to psychology, the book integrates measured qualitative analysis of Holocaust testimony into the study of traumatic memory. As a contribution to the study of oral history, the book applies constructs from memory research to the understanding of Holocaust testimony.

Chapter 1 introduces the distinctive contributions of oral testimony to the study of memory, beginning with a description and explanation of the extraordinary persistence of Holocaust memory. Chapter 2 presents a comprehensive analysis of the structure of Holocaust memory. Interweaving quotation and commentary, this chapter allows readers to hear the individual accounts of the past events while apprehending the defining patterns of memory. Chapter 3 sharpens the focus to the special case of those who were young children during the Holocaust. It analyzes testimony from survivors who were between infancy and eight years old when World War II began, disclosing early childhood memory in extremis and laying bare the consequences of painfully truncated autobiographical memory. Chapter 4 provides an unprecedented, retrospective view of the experience of atrocity, exposing an anguished composite of perceptions, thoughts, and emotions. Analysis of the testimony provides an elaborated taxonomy of the *encoding* of trauma and reveals how the encoding process translates into the indelible characteristics of traumatic memory. Chapter 5 documents the behavioral and ideational results of traumatic memory. The chapter analyzes how specific memories of past horrors direct the lives of survivors today, evoking specific fears, invading sleep, altering interpersonal interactions, and ultimately shaping concepts of the self. Chapter 6 closes with an analysis of *memory directives*, the lessons of Holocaust memory that are inherent in the memories themselves. After witnesses record the specifics of memory, after videotape assumes the responsibility of documenting remembered history, witnesses send the messages of memory—not as bridges, but as signals to cross the vast outer space between an unearthly past and the obvious present.

NOTES

1. Tape HVT-318, testimony of Robert K., 1984, Fortunoff Video Archive for Holocaust Testimonies at Yale University.

2. Tape HVT-1270, testimony of Isabella L., 1989, Fortunoff Video Archive.

3. Geoffrey H. Hartman. "Learning from Survivors," in *The Longest Shadow: In the Aftermath of the Holocaust* (Bloomington: Indiana University Press, 1996), 133–150.

ACKNOWLEDGMENTS

Inspiration for this book arose from Lawrence Langer's seminal work, *Holocaust Testimonies*, which explored a field of study even before it was a field of study. Further acknowledgment is due Lawrence Langer for critiquing earlier versions of my chapters.

I express enduring appreciation for the spirited advice and friendly rigor of Joanne Rudof, the archivist of the Fortunoff Video Archive. Her guidance and unflagging faith in my work began in December 1993 when I started my research and continues beyond the publication of this book. She deserves much credit for my education over the past eight years. I am also thankful for the wisdom and foresight of Geoffrey Hartman, project director and faculty advisor for the Fortunoff Video Archive. And I thank Debra Bush, the archive assistant, for her gracious and knowledgeable help.

I am indebted to the generous sabbatical program at Otterbein College and to Patti Frick, the Academic Dean, who patiently supported my research even when its pace seemed glacial. The George and Mildred White Faculty Development Fund and the N.E.H. Faculty Development Fund provided additional opportunities for study at Yale. I thank my colleagues at Otterbein College who supported and advised me, in particular, Lou Rose, Beth Daugherty, Allan Cooper, and Marsha Aman. I am especially thankful for the enlightened pessimism and honest encouragement of Peggy Lobb who carefully read each of my chapters.

Unseen colleagues from around the country were kind enough to review my work and offer insightful suggestions: Eugene Winograd of Emory University, David Pillemer of Wellesley College, David Myers of Hope College, and Jeanne Marecek of Swarthmore College.

At Praeger, I am grateful to Debbie Carvalko, Nicole Cournoyer, Karen Treat, and David Wilfinger for their patience and diligence in bringing about the publication of this book. I am also grateful to Harvey Langholtz, the series editor, for his breadth of experience and his thoughtful support of my research.

My family has encouraged me in many ways. I thank my parents, Allen and Lillian Kraft, for their wisdom, their faith, and their whole-hearted interest in my work. Amy Kolen, a gifted essayist who also happens to be my sister, provided diplomatic critiques of each of my chapters. Those who live with me deserve special recognition for putting up with the petulant disturbances of someone in the house writing a book. I am especially indebted to my wife Virginia Petersen, who read my manuscript more than once and each time provided helpful insights. Though she has been held in the dogged embrace of illness for many years, her graceful efforts to live life fully have inspired everyone around her to keep on working. I give thanks to my daughter Jessica Carew, who read, critiqued, advised, encouraged, questioned, and always motivated. I am grateful to my son Samuel, whose independence allowed me to work long, odd hours and whose peripheral vision discerned the benefit of punctuating my work with ping pong and Indian food.

Ultimately, this entire book depends on the words of the witnesses whose stories were recorded at the Fortunoff Video Archive—survivors of the Holocaust who possessed the courage to come forward and document their memories.

CHAPTER 1

REVEALING MEMORIES: ORAL TESTIMONY AND THE HOLOCAUST

Holocaust testimony violates common assumptions about memory. The testimony transmutes basic concepts of memory, demanding explanations for the persistence of memory and definitions for the distinctive forms of memory that shape human experience. If we observe closely, oral testimony of those who lived through the Holocaust can teach us how people comprehend and remember the most extreme horrors and how the resulting memories of atrocity exert their influence over time.

Holocaust testimony tells us that the most pervasive characteristic of memory for atrocity is its extraordinary persistence. Specific, personal memories can remain vivid for more than fifty years, causing people to cry suddenly, to break down uncontrollably, to become enraged. Memories can intrude unbidden and unwanted and powerfully into the consciousness of the individual. People can clearly visualize events that occurred more than half a century earlier. While recalling, people can become immersed in memorial images, where the outside world recedes and people relive the events of the distant past.

Core memories can remain accurate and unchanged over very long periods of time, though interpretations may change.[1] For those who were young children during the Holocaust, long-remembered emotional trauma from early childhood can lose its influence during middle age, sometimes suddenly. Conversely, emotional shocks later in life can trigger recall of suppressed childhood trauma, though such cases are rare. Over time, memories of long past events can singularly and consistently influence present attitudes and behavior without the person's awareness.

Testimony reveals that several forces maintain the persistence of memory. Clearly, the routine existence of those who lived through the Holocaust stands apart from any other set of experiences, separated in memory by a durable membrane that contains the images of atrocity yet remains permeable. Irene W. says, "There is a . . . division, sort of a schizophrenic division, or a compartmentalization of what happened. And it's kept tightly separated and yet it isn't." Isabella L. states flatly, "I am not like you. You have one vision of life, and I have two. . . . We have double lives that we can't cancel out. . . . I talk to you and I am not only here, but I see Mengele, and I see the crematorium, and I see all of that."[2]

Consider a few phrases that witnesses use: "a double existence," "another world," "a schizophrenic division," "two worlds," "two different planets," "double lives." Almost all witnesses state that they live a double existence. There is a Balkanization of memory, where Holocaust memories and normal memories are assigned to two, sometimes hostile, territories. In most cases, unlike normal personal memories, even of traumatic events, Holocaust memories are not integrated into the survivor's definition of self. They stand apart as defining another self at another time in another place.

Another force contributing to the persistence of memory is the encased emotion that resides within each remembered episode. Emotion is not separate from specific memory. The emotional energy is *in* memory, keeping it alive and powerful. When a witness recalls a specific episode, this emotion can reveal itself unexpectedly and overwhelmingly.

Still another force is uncertainty. Not knowing the outcome of specific events, not knowing what happened to particular people, keeps memories alive. The uncertainty encourages imagination and extrapolation. For many years, some people did not know for certain if their mother died or their daughter or their husband. And even today, there remains uncertainty about how and where people died. The father of Beatrice S. was wounded while fighting in the Russian army. She says, "And I never heard from him again. And, ah, I wrote to the Russian government, and looked for him. And I always look for him. To this day, I always have images of him that he is some place in a hospital, sick and old. And it's been bothering me all the years because I don't know whether he is dead or he is alive."[3]

Finally, memory persists to preserve the existence of those who were murdered. Two years before Paul D. gave testimony, he injured his back. Confined to bed for three months, increasingly despairing, Paul found himself thinking about his small Slovakian town under Nazi occupation and the *shokhet* in this town who was deported and killed when Paul was a child. (A *shokhet* is the person designated and approved by the community to slaughter and dress animals for market.)

> The feeling that overwhelmed me was that there were people who only lived in my memory. And I was the only link to the world, for these people. The Shokhet of Hummene. And the feeling was just so awful. What I did was I called in my son. I was still in bed then. And I said, "What I want you to do is hear about the Shokhet of Hummene, so that you will also remember him." And I told him about the Shokhet of Hummene. And my son said to me, "Okay, I will remember him." And I know he will. I know he will. And my daughter also. She listened. She said, "I will also remember him."[4]

Paul D. and others testify to their memorial responsibility, which they view not as a general monition against forgetting, but as an unquestioned belief in maintaining specific and real representations in memory. Witnesses state that failing to recall the image of a person who was killed allows that person to be killed again.

Before probing further into patterns of memory, it is important to address the difficulty of *learning* about the events of the Holocaust. What is it about the Holocaust and human understanding that may preclude understanding? When Jolly Z. is asked what prevents survivors from talking about their experiences, she replies, "It's unimaginable. You know what? Sometimes I don't believe it anymore. I sometimes ask myself, was it possible? How can anybody believe it if I question it?"[5] Although the focus of this book is on memory, questions of epistemology underlie all Holocaust research intended to teach the events of the Holocaust. How can people come to know the unthinkable?

In virtually all testimonies, witnesses state emphatically that the listener will not understand. After nearly an hour of testimony, Leon H. says, "I can tell you a million stories. But, what good is it? Who will believe? Nobody believes it. Because I don't believe myself. That this kind of a thing could happen. I don't believe it. How could you?"[6] Salomon M. says, "The thing is, to tell day by day ordeal . . . nobody could imagine it. It's not believable . . . impossible even to tell it to anybody."[7] Some witnesses even doubt their own experiences. Renee G. says, "They're right in not believing it, because I myself didn't believe it. I had to go back to Poland to convince myself that this was really me."[8] The witnesses' general point is clear: Regardless of how well-meaning or how knowledgeable or how sincere the listener, unless a person has directly experienced the Holocaust, it cannot be comprehended.

One witness (Leo G.) presented more than three hours of testimony in 1980 and then returned for a second interview eight years later. Even so, during his second interview, Leo G. makes the following statement. "I still believe . . . it can't be told. They might hear it and sympathize [with] it, and believe it, but not understand it. Nobody would understand for the simple reason because it can't be told enough to make somebody understand."[9]

He continues by telling the interviewers that if they listen to him for a while and tell him they understand and have no more questions, then they do not understand. And if they do have questions and say they do not understand, he will tell them more. And if he tells them more, then they will need more questions, and so on. The reasoning of Leo G. invokes the fundamental paradox of learning anything, discussed by Plato in the *Meno*. Learning consists of relating new information to old, assimilating it into prior knowledge. But if information is truly new, by definition, it does not relate to old knowledge and, therefore, cannot be learned.[10]

The Holocaust, according to witnesses, is something truly new and, therefore, unknowable. Yet many people who lived through the Holocaust have found a way to understand enough to tell us what happened during those years. They understand enough to try to communicate their memories to those who were not there. As researchers, then, we can construct an understanding of the events of the Holocaust by observing and integrating the oral testimony provided by these individual witnesses. The Holocaust resists comprehension in its entirety, in the detail, the scope, the intricate cruelty, and the relentless brutality, but the difficulty in creating a full understanding should not lead to resignation or disbelief. For the second generation of Holocaust researchers, it is essential to communicate the memories of those who lived through the Holocaust, teaching what the poet Amy Clampitt calls "the livingness of history."[11]

In testimony given by Claude Lanzmann, he speaks of the eleven years of making the movie *Shoah*. People would ask Lanzmann, "What is your concept?" And he admits, "But I have no concept. . . . If I would have had a concept, *Shoah* would have been a very bad film." He goes on to say that "The building of the film was a step by step process. And you cannot do such a film theoretically."[12] I do not mean to equate my research with the film *Shoah*. What I mean to say is that the *discovery process* may be similar and may, in fact, be similar to all attempts to communicate memories of those who lived through the Holocaust. When studying Holocaust testimonies, we need to generate *initial* conclusions inductively, maintaining awareness of narrative expectations and theoretical perspectives that might limit our understanding of what the survivors are saying. In research with oral testimony, it is important to act as a scribe, observing and recording the testimonies, then building categories of recall inductively. These categories can then be brought into the literature on traumatic memory and in turn, the theoretical constructs in this literature can clarify and sharpen the inductively derived distinctions from the testimonies and help communicate them effectively. The final section of this chapter describes the methods for collecting data and the analytical strategies for interpreting and categorizing the findings.

When students initially try to understand the Holocaust, they invariably construct inappropriate analogies. One pervasive non sequitur is the hopeful expectation about the importance of liberation. Based to some extent on early Holocaust books and movies, but to a larger extent on the application of canonical narratives of abduction and imprisonment, we expect liberation to be an exhausting but joyous release from suffering—a turning point or catharsis—in the survivor's tale. And yet, in one testimony after another, witnesses describe liberation very differently: as a time of confusion, illness, and grief.

We need to pay close attention to metaphor. For example, many witnesses refer to their memory as something massive and heavy and real. Max B. says his memories are a "load" that is "getting heavier and heavier and heavier."[13] Nearly all witnesses refer to their memories as ever-present. Leon H. says, "Everything is in front of me. I can't get rid of it. It's like a screen . . . and everything moves."[14] We should also attend to the survivors' subjective experience of memory and to their own theories of memory, even though the actual patterns of recall may conflict with these intuitive theories.

We need to be aware that difficulties in understanding are not only intellectual. Leo G. describes the emotional conflict in trying to communicate with close friends or members of his family: "If that person listens and understands it, and if he does, it must have an effect on him. Then I figure, then I feel I put my burden on him. And have I got a right to?"[15] Sabina S. describes a version of this conflict turned inward: "I myself say, 'Am I normal?' How could I still live a normal life after living through what I did?"[16]

For a fuller understanding, each testimony must be placed in the context of other individual testimonies. Martin Buber writes in *Between Man and Man* that if we consider the individual alone, then we see that individual as we see the moon, only as an object in isolation. If we consider only the aggregate, then we see individuals as we see stars in the Milky Way, as a large, vague cloud.[17] Only by studying individuals with other individuals do we begin to understand both the personal tragedies and the collective horror. In this way, oral testimony integrates psychology and history: the study of the individual and patterns of the past. Expository collage may be the most accurate form for writing of the Holocaust: irregular shapes placed together, with each witness represented in the context of other individual witnesses, repeated particulars conveying the resonant patterns of memory. Each witness to the Holocaust should be presented as an understandable individual and not as a representative of a generally different class of being. The Holocaust permanently altered those who lived through it, often in generalizable ways, but they and their trauma should be presented as individual, human trauma.

In *The Diving Bell and the Butterfly*, Jean-Dominique Bauby suffers a stroke in his brain stem, leaving him with locked-in syndrome: an active, intact mind locked inside a body that cannot move except for his left eye. Painstakingly, Bauby writes his memoir by blinking the identity of each successive letter in a specially sequenced alphabet.[18] Communication demands patience and discipline both from the teller and the listener. Although the specifics are obviously different, an analogy can be drawn to the communication of Holocaust memories. Witnesses to the Holocaust often find the words to describe particular atrocities, but it takes extraordinary effort to express their emotional and physical suffering: grief, humiliation, betrayal, and hunger. Everyday words seem weak, and many witnesses speak of the need to invent a new language.

In his personal account of Buchenwald, Jorge Semprun believes in words but doubts the listener's diligence: "Language contains everything. You can speak of the most desperate love, the most terrible cruelty." He goes on to ask, "But can people hear everything, imagine everything? Will they be able to understand?"[19] I believe that we *are* able to hear and imagine and understand. Oral testimony allows us to do so. The testimony can teach us how to comprehend large-scale atrocity so that the detailed reality of the atrocity will not transmogrify into myth.

Oral testimony at the Yale Archive communicates the events of the Holocaust directly and personally. Witnesses are not actors; their stories are not scripted. After viewing just a few cases, observers can detect the distinctive strengths of oral testimony: thoughts, emotions, and personal events in vivid detail, information that cannot be gathered from documents or represented in the broad strokes of statistics or even depicted in film. Oral testimony gives a face and a voice to individuals who otherwise would not be seen or heard. Giampiero Carocci in *The Officers Camp* calls this type of knowledge "little history."[20]

How else do we discover the detailed misery of Hanna H., absorbed in thoughts of suicide, thinking about her "beautiful, vivacious, encouraging" fifteen-year-old sister taken away in a selection and killed, the deportation and murder of her father, her young husband shot and dumped into a mass grave, her mother sent to Treblinka, her infant son taken away by the SS, and Hanna running away from each murder? Hanna describes hiding in a rat-infested cellar, crawling under a basin to escape execution by the Nazis:

> Made myself like a snail and I put the basin on the top of me, and I was laying there for the longest time . . . I don't remember how long. I was cold. I was on the black ground, probably filthy from the coal, and I was thinking to myself how will I go out,

looking like this? And then I started to think and how foolish! How stupid! That I am fighting for life that's not worth a cent. I mean, *what for*? Everybody's gone. I have nobody in this world. I have to——. I am preserving my life for what purpose? I should be with them. I should have gone with my husband, although I had no control over because he was in the factory. I could have gone with my sister. I could have gone with my mother. I shouldn't have left. And with the baby. *Why* did I leave the baby? And I decided that if I get out, I will commit suicide, and I had a whole place. I wanted to drown myself. I thought that was the best way to go because they will not find my body and nobody will have fun. But then I started to think, I'm too young to die. Why *should* I die? Why shouldn't I live to see their end? Get some revenge. Maybe—maybe to kill. I was very very hateful. . . . So many lives were taken from me and so young. I didn't even start to live.[21]

How else can we know the thoughts of Martin S. as an eight-year-old boy working in the slave labor camp of Skarzysko? He describes one incident:

I just kept asking, Why? And I couldn't get the answer. I remember, I walked by a spot, and a guard hit me very hard over the head. (He pauses.) After I recovered, because he did put me into a sort of semiconscious state for a few minutes, I turned around and I said, he doesn't know me. I wasn't even thinking of the fact that I was a child. He doesn't know me. I don't know him. Why does he have such a hatred for me? Those things used to gnaw at me. The brutality of killing. There was a clean way of killing, and there was a brutal way of killing. I could not understand the brutality.[22]

Heda K. describes her transport to the Ghetto. "And it took us several days to get to Lodz . . . I don't remember how long. I remember these horrible screams. Because they always——. They used to come from outside in to the wagon, and they slammed the doors and sometimes they hurt people's fingers. . . . They took someone out of the . . . train, and they beat them up. And this was the first time I heard people screaming with pain."[23] The historically inconsequential detail of fingers painfully smashed provides a small opening for observers to enter the horrors of the Holocaust, communicating the detailed, personal reality of the historical events.

Oral testimonies can add to historical knowledge, offering information about victims that cannot be found in any other place. Obscure labor camps and small ghettos where documentation is sparse can be more clearly described. Sometimes oral testimony can identify existing errors. For example, Hoffman and Hoffman describe how oral testimony corrected an inaccurately captioned photograph on display at Yad Vashem.[24] Though oral testimony can serve as a type of historical document, its greatest value is in transforming historical facts into compelling narratives. The amphitheater at the United States Holocaust Memorial Museum fills each day with people transfixed by the testimony of individuals simply remembering selected experiences. In fact, the authors of *The Holocaust Museum in Washington* state that oral testimony "is considered by many as the strongest single exhibit in the whole exhibition."[25]

Oral testimony simultaneously provides an account of the individual tragedies and the enormity of the collective tragedy. Such information is not available any other way. The first reading about cannibalism may shock. Hearing an older man describe in detail the extreme deprivation and desperate reasoning that led people to eat human flesh may leave the observer revulsed, but with a fuller understanding of the events. Max B. describes the suffocating and deadly transport to Bergen-Belsen, standing packed inside a cattle car for ten days: "No water. No food. The lips dehydrated. The lips were cracked." When inmates reached out to scoop up snow from the train, the SS shot them. Those who could still urinate ripped their shirts into rags, urinated into them, and used the urine-soaked rags to wet their lips. Max B. describes his thoughts in the cattle car: "How long can a person live without food?" He reasoned that "animals live on flesh," and there were so many bodies. "We ate the liver from them. . . . We ate the liver to survive."[26]

The Fortunoff Archive for Holocaust Testimonies is especially suited for revealing memory. The interviewing philosophy encourages spontaneous recall. The witness does not speak from notes and does not follow an imposed structure. In fact, many witnesses are more likely to reveal guarded information to a prepared stranger than to friends or even family.

When evaluating research on oral testimony, some may question the representativeness of the sample. Are those who give testimony different? Are they more obsessed, more articulate, more talkative, less likely to have betrayed others, better able to remember events? The simple answer is no. Paradoxically, the Yale collection contains oral testimony from those who did not give testimony. A person who decides, at long last, to give testimony for the first time in 1998 may not have talked at length about the Holocaust for fifty years. Many witnesses are reluctant historians, resisting the giving of testimony until many years after the events.

Insights revealed in Holocaust testimony can apply directly—and unfortunately—to other catastrophic events in the twentieth century. One such catastrophe currently haunts Cambodia, where Pol Pot's unrelenting, murderous devastation in the late 1970s shows itself today in each person who survived the trauma more than two decades ago. Throughout Cambodia, the Khmer Rouge brutally murdered entire communities, decimating the population, and the result now is a country with some of the most severe and pervasive mental health problems in the world.[27] A more recent catastrophe permeates Rwanda. In 1994, Hutus massacred more than 500,000 Tutsis, hacking people to death with machetes or burning them alive as family members looked on. What will be the damage a generation from now as a result of this most recent devastation?

Though oral testimony supports historical data, the analysis in this book focuses not on historical fact, but on the human response to atrocity. This analysis identifies patterns in the responses of human beings who lived through the Holocaust, with the disquieting hope that the findings can be applied elsewhere—to other people who have been victimized by widespread atrocity.[28] The following chapters analyze how memory responds to atrocity—how people remember, comprehend, and ultimately adapt to the horrors of the Holocaust.

A DESCRIPTION OF THE METHODS

In December 1993, I began my study of Holocaust testimony, equipped with a methodological plan but limited by a lack of experience with the painful richness of qualitative research. From the very first day, I was confronted with enduring personal memories that defied quantification and resisted established methods of analysis. The experimental literature on extended trauma offered useful constructs for understanding Holocaust testimony, but it did not provide an organizing, theory-driven framework for studying unconstrained recall of deeply traumatic events. The multilayered complexity of oral testimony demanded the adoption of inductive strategies that were qualitative, exploratory, and hypothesis-generating. In the weeks and months that followed my initial study of Holocaust testimonies, I elaborated and adapted my methodological plan to support a thorough and congruent analysis of the testimonies.

Ultimately, I analyzed more than 200 hours of Holocaust testimony, identifying patterns of commonality in the different testimonies as well as lines of demarcation. My working goal throughout this study was to develop a comprehensive taxonomy of memory for atrocity. To construct such a taxonomy, I studied the characteristics of memory, the experience of remembering, the apprehension—or encoding—of atrocity, the later effects of deeply traumatic memory on daily life, and the lessons of memory. My general strategy was to focus on the phenomenal experience of the witnesses—to listen to their memories and observations about these memories—and to find structure in the remembering. Historically, this strategy is rooted in the inductive methods of ethology and population biology.[29] More recently, it draws on methodologies that have been developed and elaborated over the past decade for the qualitative study of complex psychological phenomena in natural settings.[30]

The Holocaust scholar Geoffrey H. Hartman has observed that the survivor's language in videotaped testimony has "an uncalculated poetry" that stands apart from other poetry and from prose. Each survivor speaks in the distinctive voice of experience. As a result, the communication of Holocaust testimonies gives rise to two different kinds of voices: the experiential voice of the survivor and the engaged voice of the author. To write about Holocaust testimonies, to convey the patterns in the survivors' memories of atrocity, I chose what some might call a paradigmatic voice. This choice allowed me to identify commonalities across many different witnesses without collectivizing the testimonies and without speaking in what Hartman calls a "prematurely unified voice."[31]

Going into this study, I assumed that valid theoretical principles about traumatic memory could be constructed from the oral testimony of Holocaust survivors. I assumed that there would be commonalities in the way human beings respond to extreme environments and that, given the same broadly defined experiences of horror, people would undergo the same kinds of changes in response to these horrors. The defining experiences for these witnesses were trauma over an extended period of time, loss of home and family, loss of freedom, enforced helplessness, physical deprivations and physical pain, the direct witnessing of brutality and murder, and the threat of imminent death. My assumptions taken together led to the conclusion that there are patterns in the witnesses' memories of atrocity, that these patterns can be identified in the testimonies, and that the patterns can be used to construct theoretical principles about memory and its long-term influences.

In analyzing the testimonies, I employed a repeated study procedure, which involved a two-view minimum. I viewed each testimony in its entirety, attending to the general content of the memories, to the observations of the witnesses, and to the distinctive features involved in telling the memories. I then reviewed the whole testimony, focusing on the portions that I annotated during the first viewing, transcribing the words and describing the contextual and extralinguistic features. I then selectively viewed the testimony up to ten more times, detailing the passages I identified during the first two viewings.

While studying the oral testimonies, I recorded the remembered events as well as the witnesses' observations, and I categorized the content and structure of the memories and the process of recall. Categories emerged as I studied the testimonies. Initially, the categories were broad and were structured in terms of lists. Later in the analysis, I organized these categories into higher-level groupings.

My initial categories of analysis included the following: functional characteristics of specific memories; elements that make up specific memories; metaphors describing memory; intuitive theories of memory; observations about the subjective experience of remembering; emotion displayed while providing testimony; emotion described as part of the remembered events; strategies of recall; the organization of the episodes; types of transitions between episodes; inconsistencies within each testimony; assessments of confidence in the accuracy of one's memories; probabilistic terms associated with the remembered events; metamemory observations; speculation about the responses of listeners; descriptions of attention during the remembered events; descriptions of ongoing behavioral, emotional, and attitudinal effects; current difficulties in one's life due to Holocaust memories; clinical sequelae; observations about the self and memory; observations about translating memory into language; gestures and other nonverbal behavior; and the general lessons embedded in the memories.

After categorizing and labeling each of the recorded passages in the testimonies, I tabulated each category. As the analysis proceeded, the number of categories grew and the categories themselves subdivided, becoming more precisely defined and more detailed. For example, in the second category listed above, "elements that make up specific memories," I included subcategories describing the phenomenal experience of memory: visual, auditory, and olfactory imagery, as well as physiological responses. In the category "observations about the self and memory," I identified a new subcategory to include descriptions of experiencing "split selves." For the category "emotion displayed while providing testimony," I recorded each time a witness cried, as well as the duration of the crying. In the category of "remembered emotion," I recorded each instance that the witnesses said they were "numb." In the category of "nonverbal behavior," I noted pauses and timed them. Each of these new subcategories was identified and recorded.

For each testimony, I parsed the transcribed portions into passages that were comparable to paragraphs in a written text. I labeled each passage with the categorical terms that characterized the passage. It is important to note that testimony does not present itself in cleanly divided categories and that several categories of memory can be present in a single transcribed paragraph or even a single sentence. Moreover, external linguistic context (testimony before and after the passage being evaluated) must always be considered—as it should be for any analysis of linguistic material. It is also important to note that the power and extremity of the experiences that created the memories often resulted in witnesses using similar or even identical language—especially in their observations about their memories and about the events. This verbatim commonality was helpful in identifying the patterns of memory.

The higher-level groupings of the categories of analysis became apparent as I examined the categories themselves for superordinate themes. In fact, the chapters reflect the organization derived from these superordinate themes. This chapter summarized the most urgent and ubiquitous observations of the witnesses: the extraordinary persistence of Holocaust memory and the impossibility of others fully understanding what the survivors endured. Chapter 2 presents an in-depth examination of the patterns of traumatic memory and the process of recall.

NOTES

1. The issue of accuracy continues to be investigated and redefined in the experimental literature on personal memory. For an introduction to experimentation and theory on accuracy and memory, refer to *Affect and Accuracy in Recall* edited by Eugene Winograd and Ulric Neisser (New York: Cambridge University Press, 1992). More recently, the 2000 edition of *The Annual Review of Psychology* contains a concise history of research approaches in experimental psychology that pertain to accuracy and distortion in memory, including a section on autobiographical memory. (Refer to Asher Koriat, Morris Goldsmith, and Ainat Pansky, "Toward a Psychology of Memory Accuracy," edited by Susan T. Fiske, Daniel L. Schacter, and Carolyn Zahn-Waxler [Palo Alto: *Annual Reviews*, 2000], 481–537.)

One approach for examining accuracy in oral testimony is to examine consistencies and inconsistencies *within* each testimony. Though this approach assesses consistency and not accuracy per se, it is an important indicator of accuracy. A section in Chapter 2 presents the results of this approach, describing the kinds of information that are difficult for witnesses to remember (e.g., specific dates and durations of events) and the mistakes that witnesses can commit (e.g., incorrectly summarizing the entire sweep of episodes in memory). In addition, the accuracy of Holocaust testimony from child survivors can be examined by comparing their testimony with that of older witnesses who were also present, such as the testimony of surviving parents. This method is employed in Chapter 3 in the few cases that support it. As with other memory-based methods of verifying accuracy, it should be noted that this method assumes the validity of the corroborating (or refuting) memories.

Another approach to assessing consistency involves the comparison of different testimonies provided by the same witness. In this regard, I studied the testimonies of each of fourteen witnesses who provided testimony more than once. The general results of this comparison are described in the Appendix.

In a seminal study, Willem Wagenaar and Jop Groeneweg conducted a quantitative analysis of accuracy and consistency in the memory of Holocaust survivors ("The Memory of Concentration Camp Survivors," *Applied Cognitive Psychology* 4 [1990]: 77–87). They examined the memories of people imprisoned in Camp Erika in the Netherlands during 1942 and 1943. Between 1943 and 1948, twenty-two witnesses were interviewed, primarily in the context of the trials of two camp guards. Between 1984 and 1987, seventy-two witnesses were questioned for the trial of another camp guard. Importantly, fifteen of these participants were interviewed twice, approximately forty years apart (between 1943 and 1948 and then again between 1984 and 1988). Wagenaar and Groeneweg compared the recall of once-interviewed inmates with known facts, and they compared the two sets of testimony provided by the fifteen inmates who were interviewed twice. One main finding of the researchers is the high level of remembering over a period of forty years. The first sentence of the Results Section makes this finding clear: "The most striking aspect of the testimonies is that witnesses agreed about the basic facts, which is demonstrated by a comparison of 55 longer interviews" (80). After noting the "remarkable degree of remembering," the authors then move to a discussion of the specific kinds of errors that witnesses made (80). Chapter 2 picks up this discussion in relation to the patterns of remembering and forgetting revealed in the oral testimony of the witnesses in the present study.

2. Tape HVT-65, testimony of Irene W., Fortunoff Video Archive for Holocaust Testimonies, 1982; Tape HVT-1270, testimony of Isabella L., 1989.

3. Tape HVT-72, testimony of Beatrice S., 1982.

4. Tape HVT-48, testimony of Paul D., 1980.

5. Tape HVT-972, testimony of Jolly Z., 1988.

6. Tape HVT-628, testimony of Leon H., 1985.

7. Tape HVT-253, testimony of Salomon M., 1984.

8. Tape HVT-976, testimony of Renee G., 1988.

9. Tape HVT-977, testimony of Leo G., 1988.

10. Walter B. Weimer, "Psycholinguistics and Plato's Paradoxes of the Meno," *American Psychologist* 28, (1973): 15–33.

11. Amy Clampitt, "What does a writer need to know?" Symposium conducted at Grinnell College, February 1986.

12. Tape HVT-700, testimony of Claude L., 1986.

13. Tape HVT-1125, testimony of Max B., 1988.

14. Tape HVT-628, testimony of Leon H., 1985.

15. Tape HVT-158, testimony of Leo G., 1980.

16. Tape HVT-623, testimony of Sabina S., 1985.

17. Martin Buber, *Between Man and Man*, translated by Ronald Gregor Smith (New York: Macmillan, 1965), 205.

18. Jean-Dominique Bauby, *The Diving Bell and the Butterfly*, translated by Jeremy Leggatt (New York: Knopf, 1997).

19. Jorge Semprun, *Literature or Life*, translated by Linda Coverdale (New York: Penguin Books, 1997), 13–14.

20. Giampiero Carocci, *The Officers Camp*, translated by George Hochfield (Evanston, Illinois: Northwestern University, 1997), ix.

21. Tape HVT-285, testimony of Hanna H., 1984.

22. Tape HVT-641, testimony of Martin S., 1986.

23. Tape HVT-99, testimony of Heda K., 1980.

24. Alice Hoffman and Howard Hoffman, "Reliability and Validity in Oral History: The Case for Memory," in *Memory and History*, edited by

Jaclyn Jeffrey and Glenace Edwall (Lantham, Maryland: University Press of America, 1994), 123. The photograph was labeled "Gardelegen, a concentration camp in which 150 inmates were killed." Based on the oral testimony of the second author, it was determined that the photograph was not of Gardelegen; it depicted a barn near Hannover into which Nazis herded prisoners, then burned them alive, shooting to death any who tried to escape.

25. Jeshajahu Weinberg and Rina Elieli, *The Holocaust Museum in Washington* (New York: Rizzoli International, 1995), 72.

26. Tape HVT-94, testimony of Max B., in Max and Lorna B., 1980; Tape HVT-1125, testimony of Max B., 1988.

27. Philip Shenon, "Cambodia Can't Shake the Legacy of Madness," *New York Times* 12 March 1995: 3.

28. My working assumption is that people have only a limited number of ways to respond to atrocity. Given the same broadly defined experiences of horror, people will undergo the same kinds of changes in response to this horror. The defining experiences include trauma over an extended period of time, loss of home and family, loss of freedom, enforced helplessness, physical deprivations and physical pain, direct witnessing of brutality and murder, and the threat of imminent death.

29. The inductive and descriptive methods of ethology and population biology are an appropriate point of departure for analyzing and categorizing open-ended recall of personal events. In the chapter "Ways of Searching and the Contents of Memory," Marigold Linton describes the application of these methods to the ecological study of memory. (Refer to *Autobiographical Memory*, edited by David C. Rubin [New York: Cambridge University Press, 1986], 50–67.) An informative discussion of the inductive methods used in constructing and validating biological taxonomies is presented in *Waiting for Aphrodite* by Sue Hubbell (New York: Houghton Mifflin, 1999).

30. Qualitative approaches in psychology and other social sciences have been developed to interpret and act on complex data in natural settings. The book *From Subjects to Subjectivities*, edited by Deborah L. Tolman and Mary Brydon-Miller (New York: New York University Press, 2001), presents multiple strategies for conducting qualitative research in psychology, describing theoretical perspectives, specific methods, examples of qualitative research, and challenges for future researchers.

31. Geoffrey H. Hartman, "Learning from Survivors," in *The Longest Shadow: In the Aftermath of the Holocaust* (Bloomington: Indiana University Press, 1996), 133–150.

CHAPTER 2

DEFINING MEMORIES: PATTERNS OF REMEMBERING

Through oral testimony, witnesses to the Holocaust record their individual memories, spontaneously recalling past events, unconstrained by time and expectation. The testimony preserves and documents specific incidents of atrocity as well as the persistent influence of these remembered atrocities on the day-to-day lives of the witnesses. Listening to these testimonies teaches us about the specific memories of each witness; continuing to listen reveals the emergent themes that characterize Holocaust memory in general, with the particulars of remembered experience coalescing into essential qualities of memory. In order to communicate the oral testimonies in writing, this chapter interweaves quotation and commentary, allowing readers to hear the individual accounts of the horrors while apprehending the resonant patterns of memory.

The primary unit of testimony is the *episode*: a discrete event with a start and a finish, a small story. If constructed, the episode is usually a narrative—although it can be impressionistic—and the episode may be placed within a precisely described spatial layout. The basic elements of the episode are *vivid perceptual images, deeply felt emotions,* and *physiological experiences*. These basic elements are then used to construct the episodic testimony. Martin S. precisely summarizes the structure of his thinking: "Episodes, not time. Time seemed to have stood still. I just know episodes. Specifics. That comes back to mind repeatedly." Clemens L. agrees: "Only very highly charged, painful memories are with me. Specific memories."[1]

MEMORY PERCEIVED

When remembering, all witnesses state that they have strong and vivid images, with some referring to their memories as paintings, photographs, or movies. Alex H. says, "For when I look at my children, my grandchild, and I remember what happened to children like them, sometimes there comes a picture before my eyes, and it is so real that I could touch it." Renee G. says, "A mixture of feelings and memories come back that's like a painting. I wish I could paint." Sally H. relates a specific episode about a young woman who was pregnant as they were being forced to walk twelve kilometers to a train station: "I can remember the color of her coat, the curly hair. . . . She was tall. She had curly black hair. She had a very pretty round face and she had terribly swollen feet, at the time. She wore a trenchcoat. . . . If I would be a good artist, I would draw a picture of her."[2]

The visual memories are experienced fully, retaining the status of perceived reality at the time of the events. When Frieda J. was three and a half, her father was taken to the main square of her ghetto and hanged. Her family was forced to watch. When the interviewer asks Frieda, "You have an image in your head of your father being hanged?" she counters forcefully, "Oh, it's *not* an *image*. It's very real. This I remember very distinctly. We had to watch. . . . So, it's not really that much of an image. It's a very *real scene*." Irene W. reveals the same livingness of memory when explaining her reason for rejecting counseling after the war. "I did not know how anyone can change that reality for me," she says. The reality Irene speaks of is memory.[3]

Each episode is constructed from perceptual images, with the interpretation of the images being a separate process. Sometimes this separation is directly apparent; the visual image remains intact, unchanged, even though the interpretation changes. Sally H. tells of a boy at the Skarzysko labor camp who stole a belt from a machine so that he could use the leather to cushion his wooden shoes. The boy was then hanged for his crime, and Sally was forced to witness the hanging—along with the other inmates. She describes her memory:

"At the time, I thought it was a *man* because I was young. The older I get, the younger that face looks. It was a *boy* . . . and we had to watch this. . . . We had to watch that boy being hanged." The visual image of the face stays constant; the understanding of the image changes over time.[4]

When episodes are put together, perceptual images and bodily experiences are used as basic elements. During her first three days at Auschwitz, Eva B. says there was nothing to eat; on the fourth day there was some soup. She then states, "There was water, yeah. I don't remember being thirsty." In other words, Eva accesses her clear and distinct memory of a physical sensation to determine the availability of water. Martin S. describes getting up very early in the morning to begin slave labor at Skarzysko: "I remember dark. It was always dark. And then you'd get something hot, and I'm sure it was coffee." Martin retrieves the core images of dark and hot, then uses these images to generate what he tells.[5]

Core images from episodic memory overlay on the present. Mary E. says, "It is part of me. I look at things differently . . . I look at my grandchildren differently. Because I *see* the other children, what happened to them. I see it . . . I see the other children. I see the child they took away from the mother. I never forget." Hanna F. states, "You [are] constantly with it. You sit and you watch a movie. You sit at a play. And it comes back to you. (She gestures in front of her eyes.) It's right in front of you."[6] In addition to making direct reference to perceived memories, the testimony itself is filled with visual descriptions. Irene W. describes what she saw at Auschwitz, after being selected for work on the Canada Kommando unloading transports:

> We came to a place where there were literally mountains of clothes and things belonging to people. Mountains of shoes and mountains of glasses and huge hills of breads and cookies and every kind of luggage, everything imaginable that people took with them, and it was all dumped on the ground in front of the barracks. And you literally had to look up as you would at a mountain.

As Irene remembers what she witnessed from her barracks, her gestures coincide with her description: "You look out the window, and it was never a clear view. Day and night, people sat or walked and marched into the ovens. Just day and night . . . I recall standing by the window and looking out and seeing the thousands of children and mothers and grandmothers."[7]

When witnesses recall, they state clearly that they recall in the language they use now, not the language they spoke at the time. What does this suggest? The core images are not *in* language and can be described in any language. Sometimes witnesses do remember words in other languages, but these words are reported as auditory images. Perceptual images are primary, visual as well as auditory and olfactory. For example, Renee G. describes the liquidation of her small ghetto, providing mostly auditory images. She remembers looking out her "port hole" and seeing her grandfather and grandmother:

> I never saw them again. . . . I heard people yelling, screaming, and crying. They [were] shooting. And a whole town [was] crying. . . . I heard a child crying and then I heard a shot and there was no more crying. . . . It was a terrible thing to hear a whole town cry. And it was very loud and frightening, and little by little, we heard it quiet down and finally fade away completely. And there was complete silence.[8]

Many testimonies tell of the persistence of sound. Bessie K. describes an incident in the Kovno Ghetto: "They took all the dogs, because they were 'Jewish dogs' as they called them, and they put them in a synagogue, and they burned them alive. And to this day, I always hear the screaming from the dogs."[9] Lorna B. is similarly haunted by sounds:

> There was something that I . . . will never get rid of 'til the day I'll die. When they came in to take the children, that was in 1942. They came and took out just . . . the children of the homes. And if they took them out in the day, the screams and cryings, everyone was crying. They took out the children. We had so many children, small ones, beautiful children, in our courtyard. They took them away. But when they came in the night, in the stillness of the night, you heard the screaming, and the crying, screaming of the parents. It still sounds in my ears.[10]

To describe her arrival at Auschwitz, Isabella L. draws on olfactory images: "We arrived to some insane planet, the kind of which no one has ever seen. It was—the sky was black, thick, smelly, stinking, smoke, the burning of human fat."[11] While Chana B. recounts the moment her father was called for forced labor, she physically reexperiences the bodily sensations from that time:

> And suddenly it was declared, and I heard it, and I was with my father. And my mother was cooking somewhere, and I remember running, trying to find her. (She breathes loudly.) Sometimes, I still can feel the————. (She pounds her heart with her fist.) *Beating* of the————. (She stops to calm herself.) I found her, and she said goodbye. And that what she last saw him. I too.[12]

MEMORY RELIVED

While providing testimony, witnesses sometimes appear immersed in visualizing the events, where the outside world dissolves and the witness is back in the past. When a person is fully visualizing, or "back there," as the witnesses often say, the images are conveyed in raw form, unstructured, and testimony can seem incoherent to the listener. Lawrence Langer's *Holocaust Testimonies* provides a compelling account of this immersion in memory.[13] In terms of subjective experience, "back there" refers to a level of consciousness similar to hypnagogic sleep, with the images of memory possessing the fierce vividness of dreams. As with watching a movie, where the observer experiences being in the scene while simultaneously maintaining a disconnected awareness of the surrounding theater, the witness experiences a loss of self within the immediate environment and an immersion in the past, only vaguely aware of the present.

After an hour of testimony, Jolly Z. says, "I'm sure we are guided by inner needs to see or to deny things around us. Um, but, um. (She shakes her head and looks down for five seconds.) I lost my thought. I'm back there again. (She gestures backward with her finger.) . . . I'm just back there." Jolly is asked what she sees when she is "back there," and she replies: "Mud. And just gray, and mud. (She shakes her head.) Mmm, bodies. (She sighs.) Oh, I know what I was trying to say." During this testimony, Jolly loses the present, slipping fully into the horrors of the past. She describes the experience of being *back there*: "I feel myself to be there. I see the mud around me. I smell it. Smell is very important. I smell it. I see the bodies, dead and alive. I'm there. I see all the details. I'm there. I'm very visual. I'm there. I see the sun or the rain. I feel the wet clothes. I'm there." Jolly explains that she is "seventeen or eighteen" years old when she submerges in this memory, a different self than now:

> I'm not here. . . . I don't even know about myself now. I'm there . . . somebody else talks out of me. . . . You see it's not me. It's that person who experienced it who is talking about those experiences. And maybe that's what I am referring to. Because *I* am there. It is that part of me. Not now.[14]

In *The Remembering Self*, the cognitive psychologist Ulric Neisser states that "memory is always dual."[15] That is, the individual experiences the present self being aware of the past self experiencing the world. However, with survivors of trauma, the phenomenal experience of memory is not always dual. At times, the person enters a different world of memory and is *back there*. The testimony becomes elliptical, impressionistic, and not in narrative form. In *Holocaust Testimonies*, Langer clearly defines the two levels of memory in those who lived through the Holocaust, labeling them "common memory" and "deep memory." With Holocaust testimony, common memory presents a structured narrative account of the monstrous events of the past, as seen by the present selves, drawing upon deep memory, but displaying a lexicon of chronology, logic, and narrative convention. Deep memory is the unstructured, emotional reliving of the events—the raw material of our common memories.[16] In *Unchained Memories*, Lenore Terr suggests that these two different memory systems actually begin with our earliest development. Deep memory is with us as infants to record perception, emotion, and response. Later, with language, narrative or common memory emerges.[17]

For most of us, long-term memories are unavailable, not because they are stored and locked in a separate area of the mind, not because they are actively repressed in the subconscious, but because they are in a form that we cannot consciously experience—a form that is not linguistic or perceptual. These processed long-term memories are represented in cryptic, abstract, and propositional codes that are not comprehensible to consciousness. To reexperience these memories, we must actively search for them, then translate the coded memories into a form that can be consciously experienced. Theories and terminology are legion in theoretical psychology for the nature of these long-term memory codes. (Recent theories refer to them as *neural nets, propositional lists, connectionist networks, schema representations*, and *feature vectors*.[18]) The problem haunting those who lived through the Holocaust is that their long-term traumatic memories are *not* stored in an abstract and inaccessible form. Rather, the memories are all too accessible to conscious experience, in the form of perceptual images, emotions, and bodily sensations that are always there or easily roused.

Hanna F. appears to go into deep memory while describing an episode at Auschwitz. When inmates died during the night, they were taken out of the barracks and dumped onto a pile of bodies. One night, Hanna had to go to the latrine, which meant walking past this pile of corpses. She says, "And the rats were standing and eating the people's faces, eating. They were having a———. (She stops and does not finish her sentence. After thirteen seconds, she abruptly begins again.) Anyway, I had to do my job. I was just looking [at] what's happening to a human being." During the silence in her testimony, Hanna appears to be immersed in the image, caught in deep memory, reliving the events. Other witnesses experience the same immersion into the altered reality of atrocity. Myra L. interrupts her own testimony to comment: "I'm talking a little incoherent because these things, these things. I'm coming back to the transports from the ghetto." Bessie K. explains: "When it comes to me to start talking about it, right away, I step into the camp."[19]

Contemporary theory needs to assimilate the inherent duality of memory. Without theoretical recognition of this duality, apparent contradictions will persist. For example, a wealth of literature in experimental psychology demonstrates the fallibility of memory: Distortions, intrusions, and even fabrications can occur for events that we have directly experienced.[20] Expectations prior to the events and suggestive questions afterward can alter our memories. And yet, juxtaposed with these repeated demonstrations of memory's malleability is the contradictory finding that memory for traumatic events can remain unchanged and painfully accurate for many years. In fact, one prominent researcher found "no published accounts in the scientific literature of intrusive traumatic recollections of traumatic events in patients suffering from PTSD [post-traumatic stress disorder] that had become distorted over time."[21] How do we reconcile this contradiction?

Other inconsistencies arise from studies of people who suffer from PTSD. Traumatic events can be remembered with exquisite clarity, or they may not be remembered at all. Moreover, some survivors of trauma are able to recall and describe their experiences dispassionately, without showing signs of distress, while others break down uncontrollably.[22] Many people are helped in therapy by talking about their unpleasant memories, while others are not helped at all.[23] How do we explain these mixed results?

MEMORY DIVIDED

To account for significant errors in memory, cognitive psychologists have put forth a well-supported theoretical approach known as *constructivism*: Memory is not a representation of worldly events, but rather a reconstruction rooted in our existing knowledge about the general kinds of events we are experiencing. We form new memories by interpreting worldly events through the lens of past experience and then reformulate these interpretations into coherent narratives. In this view, memory is an active, changing process, and errors in memory are natural consequences of this process. Constructivism, however, fails to acknowledge the intense accuracy of memory for trauma and the contradictory results in those who have suffered. And ultimately, constructivism fails to answer its own fundamental question: If memory is constructed, from what is it constructed?

A new theoretical approach is now emerging to resolve inconsistencies in the findings on memory, beginning with the assumption that memory exists very differently at *two separate levels*. At one level, memory represents the *original phenomenal experience* in the form of images, emotion, and bodily sensations. Later, these original memories are integrated into an interpreted, *narrative construction* of events, creating memory's second level. In a seminal article written in 1977, memory researchers Roger Brown and David Kulik posit a "flashbulb memory" for highly consequential events such as the assassinations of President John F. Kennedy and Martin Luther King. According to the authors, this flashbulb memory is "fixed for a very long time, and conceivably permanently, varying in complexity with consequentiality but, once created, always there, and in need of no further strengthening . . . the *memory* is not narrative and not even in verbal form, but represented in other, perhaps imaginal, ways."[24] Although these authors focus on culturally significant events, such as political assassinations, their findings can be directly applied to personal memory. Oddly, while the term "flashbulb memory" quickly migrated into the vocabulary of cognitive psychology, the discovery of a fundamentally different level of memory remained unnoticed for more than a decade.

More recently, different pairs of terms have been introduced in the literature on memory that reflect two distinct levels of memory. Flashbulb memory corresponds to "deep memory," to be distinguished from "common memory." It is "situationally accessible" memory as distinguished from "verbally accessible" memory.[25] The underlying concepts represented by these terms parallel the well-known distinction in research psychology between "implicit" and "explicit" memory: implicit memory is a representation of experience that influences behavior without conscious awareness; explicit memory can be readily brought into consciousness and can be experienced as verbal description.[26] To formalize this conceptual distinction, Valerie Reyna and her colleagues have recently proposed what they call "fuzzy-trace theory," which posits "verbatim" memory and "gist" memory. Verbatim memories are vivid, perceptual representations of the original phenomenal experience. Gist memory is in the form of language, summarizing verbatim memories. Fuzzy-trace theory describes the inherent discontinuity between these two levels of memory, and perhaps most clearly resolves the contradictions in the research findings. Distortions, errors, and intrusions do occur, but they occur within gist memory, not within verbatim memory. Verbatim memory endures, free of distortion and resistant to assimilation.[27] People who have lived through trauma may recall their experiences dispassionately by calling upon gist memory, not verbatim memory, though they may receive little therapeutic benefit by doing this. Those who pass through the membrane separating gist and verbatim memory will experience the vivid images, strong emotions, and physiological sensations of the original events. In different sources, this visceral level of memory has been referred to as "deep" or "flashbulb" or "situationally accessible" or "implicit" or "verbatim" memory.

To reduce confusion among the interchangeable terms for each level of memory, I refer to the two levels of memory as *core memory* and *narrative memory*.[28] Core memory is the representation of the original phenomenal experience in the form of perceptual, emotional, and physiological experience: visual images, sounds, smells, tastes, emotions, and bodily sensations—as vivid and compelling as dreams. Narrative memory is constructed from the images in core memory, shaped in accordance with narrative conventions and conveyed primarily in language. Narrative memory calls upon existing knowledge to organize the images in core memory, forming coherent representations designed to communicate with one's conscious self and with other people. Those who give oral testimony about the Holocaust often draw on narrative memory to tell of the horrible events, and the testimony is structured and coherent. Sometimes, though, when describing a scene, the witness may be drawn into core memory, losing contact with narrative memory, immersed in the hypnagogic past in a state referred to as *back there.*

A fuller understanding of Holocaust memory can be achieved by applying the idea of memorial duality to the following question: What is clear and what is unclear in Holocaust memory? Vivid perceptual images, strong emotions, and physiological experiences make up core memory of the episodes, and core memory accurately represents phenomenal experience. In *White Gloves*, John Kotre eloquently advocates the position of reconstructive memory, yet he admits that recall "is capable of producing trustworthy memories if it is allowed to proceed without interruption." He goes on to say that if witnesses are not forced to provide answers, "their recall will be virtually error-free."[29] That is, if witnesses are permitted to recall freely, testimony will accurately reflect the representations in memory. If interviewers ask specific questions, then the answers to these questions may or may not be accurate depending on their relationship to the original core images. If the questions allow the witness to access *core images*, study them, and then translate the images into words, then recall will be accurate. If the questions allow the witness to access *narrative memories* that were originally derived directly from core memory, then recall will also be accurate. More often, however, answers to specific questions will be uncertain and incomplete because the answers do not reside in the original core images. If questions do not retrieve core images or primary information in narrative memory, witnesses may simply say they do not know, or they may guess, generating approximate or inaccurate answers.[30] By listening for hesitation or probabilistic terms or summary descriptions, observers can discern—and so can the witness—what was known at the time of the events and what was interpreted later.

Consider the testimony of Renee G. After liquidation of the larger Losice ghetto, Renee went into slave labor as a young teenager in a smaller work ghetto. She was the youngest in this ghetto, and as many young teenagers did, she worked diligently to justify the food and shelter she received. One of her tasks was to fold clothes into small, tight bundles. She describes one incident:

> At one point, I bent down because I found a picture of my family, so I must have stopped to look at it and all of a sudden I heard a big whip over my legs and I just remember the *sting* of it. And I just froze for a minute and got up and stood straight. . . . I was probably by that time, completely bereft of emotion . . . sort of half-dead, not here and not there . . . and I just stared at the German into the face. I remember *big, red face*. I would probably recognize him today.[31]

In this single passage, Renee G. reveals both core memories and interpreted narrative memories. She clearly remembers the "sting" of the whip, and she clearly remembers the German guard's "big, red face" from core memory, but the statement that she "must have" stopped to look at the photograph indicates that she is *constructing* a reason for getting caught not working. The reason for the uncharacteristic pause in her work is not part of the originally retrieved core memory. It is constructed and not based in core memory.

Remember also that if the original interpretation of events is faulty in some way, memory will accurately represent this faulty interpretation. Direct perception is accurate, though the original interpretation of the directly perceived events may be incorrect. For example, Jolly Z. insists incorrectly, "They put a chemical in our food so that we did not menstruate later. There was a chemical in our food and we did not have menstrual periods." Adele W. draws the same conclusion. "And you know how we suffered until we got back our periods. We were————. They gave us some certain pills to lose our periods. . . . I was very, very skinny, but I was like a balloon. Blown up. Because we didn't have our periods." These witnesses remember accurately that their periods went away, but they misinterpret the reason and accurately remember this misinterpretation.[32]

Inaccuracy can also occur when the original images in core memory are translated into narrative memory and then shuffled with images from other core memories. The inferences drawn from the inappropriately mixed images will lead to inaccurate recall, even though the elemental images themselves are accurate. For example, witnesses remember places vividly and in detail, and they remember people, but they may not reliably put people in the correct places. A witness may correctly remember a particularly sadistic kapo, and the witness may also remember a specific scene within a different camp, but if the two core images are translated into narrative memory, then spliced together, that witness will place the Kapo in the wrong camp, and narrative memory will be mistaken.[33] (A Kapo is a concentration camp inmate with special privileges, appointed by the SS to be in charge of a group of inmates.)

Another major category of information that witnesses do not remember in detail is temporal. To begin, human beings in general do not directly perceive specific categories of time from the natural environment, so memory is not designed to retain these specific categories. To be sure, in normal life we have access to watches and calendars, but in the deprived world of the Nazi labor camp, there was little specific information about times and dates. Anna K. is blunt: "We didn't have a watch. We did not have a calendar. We didn't have anything. We lived."[34] Long after the events, witnesses may not remember the specific months or even the years during which the events took place. Temperature *is* directly perceived and can be held within core memory to be used for inferring the general time of year. Though the design of memory does not encourage retention of temporal specifics, it does allow witnesses to remember sequences of events in the correct order. An analogy can be drawn to the perception of distance: Most people have considerable difficulty accurately perceiving and labeling absolute distances, whereas they can easily detect relative distances of objects in the natural environment—which objects are closer and which are farther away. Similarly, witnesses do not remember the precise times and dates of events, but they do remember their chronology.

The duration of events is not remembered, and witnesses are aware of its absence. For example, Mary E. describes walking back to Poland after liberation: "I don't know how long. I have no idea. I have no value of time, how long it took, days or weeks." While telling about the death march from her labor camp, Millie W. admits, "The time is something————. (She hesitates.) I can't remember how long." Violet S. tries to describe how long she waited at a brick factory before being transported to Auschwitz: "I would say, month, two months. Maybe two months. Don't take my word for it, because I'm————. I really don't know if that is so." Eva B. describes being transported out of Auschwitz after one week: "Then we were given a piece of bread and a piece of margarine and a piece of salami for the trip. . . . The trip was something else again. . . . I don't know how long that took any more. I've forgotten that." She clearly remembers her food, but not the duration of the transport.[35]

Individual, personally experienced episodes are vividly remembered; larger groupings are constructed. Therefore, witnesses may be inaccurate when trying to aggregate and summarize collections of episodes in their own direct experience, suggesting that traumatic memory is organized in short sequences of distinct episodes and not integrated into larger, hierarchical structures as has been suggested for nontraumatic personal memory.[36] For example, Celia K. tells of hiding in a small hole beneath a barn, where she was later joined by her younger sister. Their brother, who was fighting in the woods with a group of partisans, gave Celia a gun and told the two sisters never to let themselves be caught alive by the Germans or else they would be strung up and tortured. Celia states emphatically, "I had such love for that gun." She would talk to the gun, saying, "I love you. You're my everything." When the gun was later stolen by the partisans, Celia says, "I was so frightened. I was so distraught about it. I was crying so much because it meant being caught alive by the Germans." Earlier in this same testimony, however, Celia states succinctly that she was "like a stone," emotionally numb throughout the war. She says, "Never did I cry during the war." Yet, in a different segment of testimony within a different episode, she remembers crying bitterly when her gun was taken away.[37]

Celia K. is representative of most witnesses, proceeding from one episode to the next, unaware of the specific episodes to be revealed later in the testimony. Core memory is organized in sequences of encapsulated episodes, like beads on a string, with different episodes from the same location close together in a sequence. Different sequences of episodes may be tied to one another by thin, connective strands that are *chronological and geographic* or *thematic* or *rhetorical*, but communication between episodes on different sequences may be poor. Moreover, an episode too distant from the one currently being related remains hidden from narrative memory's myopic vision until the testimony moves within visible range of that episode.

STRUCTURING MEMORY

The organization of narrative memory for trauma is not tidy, though there are patterns of recall. Memory is predominantly organized as a series of individual episodes, with each episode maintaining its integrity. Episodes number in the hundreds, possibly the thousands, detailed and encapsulated. The images within the episodes are clear, but the associative tissue that connects the episodes is not. Heda K. describes this: "I can see pictures like in a movie. . . . I can see details, but there is no connection." As a result, witnesses are often unable to anticipate how much they will remember. Alina Z., for example begins her testimony with modest expectations: "And I remember not too much because I lost a lot of memory, especially the numbers, yes? I'm trying hard to remember whatever I could." More than an hour later, however, when talking about her life in the Warsaw Ghetto, Alina announces: "I remember a lot."[38]

Each episode is separate, with thin narrative strings connecting the episodes and with episodes clustering within a particular location. Irene W. states, "It's been a long time, but I think of the whole period as a series of traumatic events."[39] Most witnesses adopt a strategy for telling these episodes, with the most frequent strategy being chronological and geographic. Witnesses provide testimony that is an ordered series of loosely connected episodes, staying within a place and then moving through that place by episodes, sometimes by season, trying to recall all the events in that place and during that season, before moving on to the next location.

After witnesses draw upon core images to describe an atrocity, they often make abrupt transitions in their testimony, summarizing or changing the subject in an apparent effort to maintain a normal narrative flow. After faithfully recounting the episode, they become suddenly aware of the demands of the narrative. Violet S. describes her first morning at Auschwitz, grafting a chronological ending onto the ineffable:

And mind you, we saw these chimneys, the flames coming out of them, burning, and we thought it was factories, we gonna be working, it was like almost a comfort to us that it———. We gonna be working there. Looks like factories with these huge chimneys sticking out and the flames coming out. But there was also an odor which you didn't question it. So, Saturday came.[40]

Sabina S. similarly strives for continuity. Before the Nazi occupation, several young Ukrainians attacked and terrorized Sabina's family.

First, she tells of the events, then she tries to move along in a normal narrative flow:

> I recall one evening, my grandparents, they lived next door to us in a small house and they invited us over for dinner. It was Friday evening and we were sitting at the table having dinner. And all of a sudden we hear like an explosion, and what happened? The windows were smashed. And a few young Ukrainians jumped in with branches from trees and just started to hit us over the heads just because we were Jews. . . . So they came in and they were trying to kill us, I guess, or hurt us, or whatever, so they hit my head. Later on, I realized it was split open because we ran out and I slid against the wall, and with my father we went to a stable and my wound was open and . . . the blood was coming out. But, of course, you wouldn't go to a doctor because you're Jewish and they're going to report you or whatever. So all night long I lie———. I was in a stable on the hay sleeping and bleeding with my father. Next morning we came back, we came back to my grandfather's house and there was a tremendous stripe of blood (she moves her hand across her head.) from my head wound, and we all gathered and tried to resume our life as much as we could.[41]

In the last sentence, Sabina exhibits no change in her intonation and no pause, just an abrupt normalizing summary.

Abraham E. uses the same narrative strategy. He and his brother were selected for slave labor, then returned to their home, only to find the house empty and their family gone:

> I never forgot, coming home, me and my brother lying down on the sofa, not stopping crying. My parents, my brothers, were taken away. I couldn't stop crying. What is going to be? Why? For what? What have we done? I couldn't stop crying until midnight. And the next day, we had to go back to work.[42]

In Skarzysko, Esther W. worked a machine that made bullets. She describes one incident:

> One day the three of us were called, taken away from the machine. Brought into a shed and . . . were beaten. We had to bend

down (she gestures) and were beaten by one, and two officers were standing and waiting and looking, while we were beaten. And when it came to me to be beaten, unfortunately I made in my pants or whatever, and they stopped. From fear, I urinated. I'm not ashamed to say it but———. (She cries.) Because they claimed it was sabotage. They found some things which were not good and, it's a funny thing, I'm not crying because I was beaten, but the humiliation. Then, the three of us were———. (She pauses.) Just one second, I will compose myself. I'm all right. All right. After that we were paraded through the factory because we committed—what did I say before? (An interviewer replies, "Sabotage.") Sabotage, yes. And we were brought back to the machine, and life went on.[43]

Narrative memory draws on language to structure and communicate core memories. Holocaust memories deviate so radically from shared experience that language cannot adequately convey them, and Holocaust witnesses frequently refer to the insufficiency of language. Consider the attempt of Isabella L. to describe entering Auschwitz: "And we arrived in this land of unbelievable chaos, of screaming and dogs barking and SS and shootings and watchtowers and smoke and stench and skeletons walking about. It was———. It's indescribable. There would have to be a new dictionary made to describe these things. There are no words in the dictionary to describe it." Mary E. agrees: "I am like a person from a different planet because we don't have a common plot for it. We don't have a common language . . . it's no use." In a seminar on the Holocaust at her synagogue, Mary confronted her rabbi: "In your wildest imagination, you would never have known if I described one hour we stood attention in the concentration camp. You are trying to figure this out?" Beatrice S. tries to describe the horrors; then stops: "I see, people screaming, ah, they couldn't believe it, that it was happening. (She hesitates.) I mean—it was—like———. (She pauses, appearing resigned.) I don't know how to tell you." Others recognize the insufficiency of words, yet persist, despite the confines of their lexicon. Samuel B. says, "I know that it is terribly difficult to tell about these things, I mean, we are here in a world of such a different reality that it is extremely difficult to relate through words or through knowledge of facts . . . yet I am absolutely convinced. And this is why I have accepted to tell about these things. You have seen it is not a very easy task."[44]

In particular, words appear most inadequate when portraying the alien nature of the betrayal, shock, terror, humiliation, hunger, and grief that witnesses endured. In fact, the entire act of giving testimony is recognized as a constrained form of expression. Though the Fortunoff Video Archive at Yale University places no time limits on testimony, nearly all the witnesses give testimony for less than three hours. Lorna B. evaluates the unseen constraints:

> In two hours, it's awful hard to bring out. . . . Too many years, you go back and forth, one time to another. One thing brings to another. And, it escapes you. A lot of things escape you, because . . . really if you want to talk, you can talk for days. Only about one day in Auschwitz, or one day in Bergen-Belsen. You can talk and talk and talk and never be able to really bring out the real feelings we had.[45]

David K. is blunt: "How can you cover a five-year period of time in three hours?"[46] Testimony ends not because witnesses have no more to recall; rather, it is often the accumulated pain that stops testimony.

Near the end of their testimonies, witnesses frequently state that they omitted information, that they "missed a lot of things."[47] When witnesses warn the listener of missing events, they directly imply that they are aware of a larger set of information unaccounted for. Even those who have completed books about the Holocaust sense the urgency of missed events. After publishing *Survival in Auschwitz* in 1958 and *The Reawakening* in 1963, Primo Levi believed he was finished writing about Auschwitz. Nearly thirty years after his first book, however, Levi published *Moments of Reprieve*, stating that, "a host of details continued to surface in my memory and the idea of letting them fade away distressed me."[48] Leon H. gives insight into this problem. "I can tell you a million stories. But, what good is it?" Later, he says, "Every day, every hour, there is something to tell." Leon W. agrees: "To go on, every day life in the ghetto, it would be———. I probably could stay here for twenty-four hours about little incidents, what was happening."[49] This testimony brings to mind "Funes the Memorious," a story by Jorge Borges in which a young man is thrown from a horse and left paralyzed for the remainder of his life. Funes lies in a darkened room and proceeds to develop his memory, which becomes so prodigious that it ultimately records everything. The improbability of this accomplishment is highlighted when Funes describes to a visitor the events of the previous day: To do so consumes twenty-four hours.

In Holocaust testimony, memory is selective, with many events not recalled; what distinguishes Holocaust memory are the events that *do* endure in memory, fully alive and painful, as if they happened yesterday. In an effort to convey as much as possible, within the limits of cognitive endurance and emotional stamina, many witnesses begin almost immediately telling about the events of the Holocaust, skipping over their prewar childhood. One witness starts her testimony, "And my name is Violet S———, and I was born in Czechoslovakia, Beregzaz, in 1928, May first to be exact. And, well, I'm here to talk about the horrible things that happened to me in my life." Another witness begins by saying, "My name is Abe L———, was born in Zhar, near Vilnius, Lithuania, and I went through the Holocaust. That's what we're telling about here. And let's start it."[50]

EMOTIONAL MEMORY

Specific episodes in memory contain powerful emotion. The emotion is within each memory, constituting an essential force that maintains the existence of the episodic memory. There are numerous instances where the telling of a specific event produces sudden grief or anger—and the emotional experience is not related to the loss of family or friends. To the observer, the emotion can seem abrupt and unexpected, but the observer soon realizes that the emotions are unleashed with the disclosure of a specific episode in memory.[51]

Alex H. provides twenty-six minutes of testimony with no display of emotion, including a description of how his brother was taken from him during a death march and murdered. He then relates a specific episode that took place in the slave labor camp of Langenstein. He was desperately hungry. Sleeping on the floor next to him was another camp inmate who looked to be quite old. "We just got our ration of bread, and he was already so sick that he couldn't eat that bread. And I was laying next to him, waiting that he should die, so I can grab his bread." After twenty-six minutes of testimony in a low, flat voice, with slow pacing, and modulated rhythm, Alex H. cries for the first time during the interview.[52] Nearly one-half hour into his testimony, Martin S. shows emotion for the first time:

> As a matter of fact, I trained myself to be very brutal, very cold.
> And often times, I have—(pause)—some. (He turns and ad-

dresses the interviewers.) I guess I can't ask them to turn this off can I? (An interviewer replies, "If you like.") No. No. Keep it running. It should be documented. I sometimes think I was made too inhuman—. (He stops and looks away.) Because I didn't care about anybody else. (He pauses again.) And that was the very early lesson I learned. That when you were given your piece of bread. You hide it. You don't let————. And if a man is begging you for a piece, I did not give it up.[53]

The observer realizes in later testimony what Martin S. does not say explicitly here: As he tells of this lesson in self-preservation, he is recalling a small set of specific episodes.

After nine minutes of flat, dispassionate description, Sally H. tells of a specific incident in the ghetto when a rabbi is humiliated and tortured. "It was horrible. . . . They were pulling his beard, and blood was coming out. And no one would help him." She then cries, abruptly and unexpectedly. Mary E. tells of walking in the ghetto where, "They were liquidating a hospital. . . . They were throwing babies on a truck. And putting blankets and stamping with their feet to make more room. (She looks down and stops, incapacitated by pain. After a time, she begins again.) They were burning people alive." Leon H. describes an SS man who took a living, breathing infant by the legs and slammed it into a brick wall, then tossed it onto a truck with other dead bodies. When describing the murder of the infant, he mimes the movements of the SS man. He appears to be reliving the episode, visualizing it. Then, he cries.[54]

Witnesses can become suddenly angry. Judith G., a young survivor of the Vilna Ghetto and Riga, explains: "The scars are there. You don't talk about it as much. You don't discuss it. But when you think about it, there is a great emotional charge that carries forward."[55] One example of this is in the testimony of Clemens L., as he describes hiding in a convent near the end of the war:

I remember my mother coming to visit me on Sundays. I remember one time she came to visit me, she brought me an egg. (He pauses, becoming emotional.) I seem like I'm more sad *now*, thinking about it, than I was then. But to bring a goddamn—to be thankful for a fucking egg is really preposterous to me. It really pisses me off, to think about it that way. But, I must have been eternally thankful to get this one fucking egg.[56]

The abrupt coarseness of the language seems out of character for this witness, and the anger appears to erupt without warning.

Leon H. gave testimony in 1985, forty years after the end of World War II. After testifying for more than two hours, describing one atrocity after another, Leon concludes: "Angry all the time. Face looks angry. I don't know how to straighten my face out." He tells of his mother who was partially paralyzed from a stroke, though she still worked in the Lodz Ghetto, weaving rags. One day, two SS men broke into their apartment and demanded that she tear up the floorboards so they could search for valuables. She was physically unable to do so quickly enough, so the SS brutally kicked her, and she died soon after. "Kicked her so hard, she hardly could breathe," Leon says. "That was my anger!" His face shakes, and he cries. Then he stops.[57]

Some witnesses can anticipate the oncoming torrent of emotion. Hanna F. describes walking long distances every morning from her barracks at Auschwitz to fields where she and other inmates harvested beets and corn. Every day, there were beatings and torture on the way to and from the fields. All the guards were armed, and if a guard decided he disliked a prisoner, he punished her. Hanna stops her testimony and says, "I cannot go into all the details that you want. Some of them are very gruesome, and I don't———, I really cannot go back so far. It hurts." (Hanna slowly draws out the word "far.") She tries to continue, attempting to describe the terror inflicted by the guard dogs: "If they let them loose, they ripped people to pieces, ripped your clothes, depends how you were able to———. (She pauses.) Must I go back to those things? I would rather not."[58]

When witnesses cry while giving testimony, they often apologize to the interviewers, indicating that they cannot control the pain of the memory and that the specific episodes are the source of the emotion.[59] A common pattern in the testimony is for the witness to start slowly, almost soporific, but as more and more episodes are related, recall becomes more energetic, more animated, more insistent, as if the release of energy from specific episodes accumulates, leading to a generalized, overall increase in energy. In a larger sense, opening specific memories may release lasting emotional disturbance, especially when an extended sequence of episodes has been recalled. Emotional shocks persist after the testimony ends, producing anxiety, sleeplessness, and in some cases, prolonged depression.

In the Fortunoff Video Archive, there is a set of testimonies from fourteen witnesses who provided testimony more than once; in twelve of these cases, the repeated testimony was separated by seven to nine years: The first testimony was in 1979 or 1980, the next in 1987 or 1988. The initial testimony was the first time witnesses talked about their experiences at length, approximately thirty-five years after the end of World War II. A comparison of the repeated testimonies presents a view of constancy and change in memory and the aftermath of testimony itself—the results of extended and detailed remembrance of personally experienced, traumatic events.

All witnesses say that giving testimony is profoundly distressing and that they are surprised at the strength of the effects. Sally H. describes her first testimony as "scary" and "very painful" and then says, "Took me quite a while to come down from that interview. . . . You dig up memories you want to bury." Daniel F. evaluates his first testimony: "Ach, do I remember! Terrible. . . . I didn't realize that it's going to just take me to the depths of depression for months. I didn't realize it." Eva B. agrees: "When I did the first tape here, I didn't expect to get as upset as I did get. . . . I can't [couldn't] imagine what the reaction would be." She looks despairing. "It was much more alive in me and much more burdensome to me than I had realized. I really thought I had it good and buried and it wasn't going to ever come up again or bother me again." Hanna F. states that she needed to be tranquilized afterward because of the powerful emotion released during her testimony. In fact, little is remembered from the testimony itself except this pain. Dori K. succinctly summarizes this result: "I remember very well how I felt. And I remember the interview. But I don't remember, really, what I said."[60]

The witnesses theorize that the pain is caused by the length of the testimony, the concentration on a long sequence of events. Daniel F. explains: "It's the segment. It was a lengthy, in-depth kind of thing, where I felt that I was back there. And I was depressed for quite a while afterwards." He says, "Your mind starts to focus on a particular segment of time, and you're trying to pick out all the events in that segment of time. And then after the interview finishes, you continue trying to find pieces of memory of those events."[61] Though a subset of traumatic memories remains painfully active, other core memories lie dormant, below the surface of consciousness. The cognitive psychologist Marigold Linton draws a similar distinction with normal memories between "what pours out of memory and what can be elicited."[62] Accessible with effort, these dormant memories can be the most threatening to the survivor, and awareness that such memories exist contributes to a reluctance to give testimony. Once retrieved into consciousness, these memories contribute to the chorus of torment.[63]

Witnesses are often surprised at how many specific episodes they are able to describe. David K. says, "I kept remembering things that I didn't remember . . . until I started talking about it." Alan Z. explains that giving testimony is different from talking about past events primarily because of the level of detail and that it is the detail that brings forth emotion. Lengthy testimony can revive dormant memories of horror, which can remain active long after the testimony ends, creating new emotional disturbance. Dori K. says "It was the first time I had spoken at such length. . . . It was a very painful experience." Indeed, Martin S. worries that his dreaded nightmares will return because of memories reactivated during testimony. Renee G. says that her first testimony was the first time her memories came out "full force." She explains. "It was almost like a release of emotions, with tension and fear and crying." By saying "almost," Renee carefully qualifies the process of release; there was tension and fear and crying, but not catharsis. Eva B. describes the testimony as, "something I needed to do to get it out of my system. I hope. I hop*ed*. (She corrects herself.) I don't know that I ever will really get it out of my system, but at least, to live with it more peacefully."[64] Does giving testimony release energy, diminishing the power of memory? Or does testimony strengthen the memories through repetition? Perhaps both, simultaneously. Nature provides no appropriate metaphor. The memory seems a self-generating source of energy—the memory burns, consuming the thoughts of the witness, but not itself, burning the witness without diminishing the fire. Specific memories release emotional disturbance in the form of nightmares and depression, especially when an extended sequence of episodes has been recalled.

PERMEATING MEMORY

Each witness describes indelible memories of specific events, memories that are not retrieved per se, but are always present, insistent, and unchanged. Salomon M. summarizes: "Memories are there all the time. All the time." Eva B. is similarly concise: "It's going to be there until the day I die . . . as painful as it is today."[65] Jacob K. elaborates:

> The tortures days and nights. It's something that we have. It's in our mind. You can't forget that. . . . I couldn't even tell you,

describe one day in the Ghetto. I don't want to live with that pain. But, it's there. It's there. It *forms its own entity*. And it surfaces whenever it wants to. I go on a train and I will cry. I will read something and I'll be right back there where I came from. And I can't erase it. I'm not asking for it. It comes by itself. It has formulated something in me. I'm a scarred human being, among human beings.[66]

Sally H. says, "So those things stay with you. It's something you don't forget. You see the trucks. You see the babies. You see the screaming mothers. You see hanging people. You sit and you see that face there. It's something you don't forget." At the end of this testimony, Sally says, "It's with me constantly. . . . I cannot be alone. . . . I have to do something. . . . My mind is just terrible." In testimony eight years later, she reiterates: "It never goes away. Never goes away. Just always there. (She waves her hand in front of her eyes.) . . . I will probably take it to my grave." She concludes, "Fifty years, whatever difference, it's always on your mind."[67]

In a halting manner, Zev H. speaks of digging mass graves and witnessing the methods used by German soldiers to extract gold from those who were killed. He ends by describing an indelible image of atrocity:

We have to dig a big, big hole. And all the deads, stripped, naked, they put in there. And one of the German SS, they have a———. They used to take out the———. They used to look for teeth, golden teeth in this. And they used to look for golden rings. Take off, if they cannot get out, cut off. If the teeth doesn't go out, they used to take a———, some kind of iron piece . . . they used to knock it out from the dead. And throw them in. Throw them in. Then—this was in the Ghetto—then they took me once to clean up some———. Where all the Jews were taken out. And—. (He pauses.) And they———. I cleaned up there. There was, and not far from us, in a different way, small houses, and there was a baby crying. Was three-years-old baby, maybe two or three, I don't remember. I don't know. And the German was with us. He was SS man . . . and he went in, and he took out the child and he threw the child to the fence, and the child stopped crying and fell down, but its eyes were open. And this nightmare recurs to me all the time. All the time.

(Zev shakes his head.) And he went there stomped with the feet
. . . but the eyes were still open.[68]

Pincus S. speaks in general terms of the persistence of memory:

> Let me tell you something, you wouldn't believe it. There isn't
> one hour in the day, what I don't remember things. I can laugh,
> and I can do everything and anything, everything. Still it's every-
> thing, it comes to mind. . . . You cannot forget. Especially dur-
> ing the night, if I go to sleep and I can't fall asleep. The whole
> story goes by, again and again and again. And nothing you can
> do about it.[69]

Hanna F. says, "I don't remember what I did yesterday. . . . I can put
my washcloth in the refrigerator. But the other days, the other years,
and the weeks, and everybody else, is right in front of me. I go to
sleep with it. I get up with it." Sally H. concurs: "I could be in a
room with a hundred people. And if I sit quiet, it's just like a pano-
rama, with all that stuff coming to my head." Chana B. says, "Your
memories just crowd in so much that so many pictures that you just—
——." She sighs, then gestures with both hands to her head. Her
testimony ends abruptly.[70]

When Isabella L. and her family arrived at Auschwitz, her youngest
sister was killed immediately, and the youngest surviving sister blames
herself. According to Isabella, the surviving sister is tortured with
guilt because she thinks she told Mengele that her youngest sister was
only thirteen: "So, one went to her death, and the other has been
suffering ever since." Isabella concludes: "For those who think that it
happened long ago, it happened yesterday."[71]

Leo G. is the only one of seven children to live. He says, "It's
always in the back of your mind. Everything. How can you? How can
you enjoy yourself? It's almost a crime against, against the people that
you lost, that you can live and enjoy yourself." Although Leo married
and raised children who are now married, he qualifies his present life:
"You cannot fully get out of your mind, that something missing. . . .
Enjoyment is cut 'til the end of my days. I just can't get out of myself." Leo explains that the two worlds coexist without being reconcilable:

It should stay that way. It has to stay that way. There's no way of changing . . . unless somebody just without mind or brain, can just lock himself, shut himself out the past. I wish it were possible. How can any thinking person do it? . . . You come at night, you just wake up in a sweat and you don't know where you are. And the whole thing is right back there and not remote."[72]

In *Moments of Reprieve*, Primo Levi writes, "Without any deliberate effort, memory continues to restore to me events, faces, words, sensations, as if at that time my mind had gone through a period of exalted receptivity, during which not a detail was lost."[73] In oral testimony, Celia K. agrees: "There wasn't one thing that I lost. I remember every episode in the Ghetto, and in the woods, and with my family. Nothing is lost. It's very clear." Celia says that on a daily basis the episodes come back. "And I remember those things. It's just they do not go away. They're just like it happened, yesterday." Leo G. concludes, "It's an ongoing thing. It never leaves you. You think years going on and you will finally lay things at rest. . . . How do you escape it?"[74]

Witnesses repeatedly state that present events in the world act as reminders of past horrors. Salomon M. says that seeing a blanket reminds him that he had no blanket. Seeing food not eaten reminds him that food was the most important thing in his life. Beatrice S. speaks of her grandmother: "She was sick, and she couldn't go. And they burned the house with her in it. So, whenever I hear people talking about their grandparents, I see my grandmother's house burning with her in it." Reports in newspapers and on television summon past atrocities. Leo G. says, "You do open up a paper and you do listen to the radio and you watch it and it hits you from every side, and everything is constantly back. Your mind walks back and names and places and faces, and then you translate all this to your family." Sabina G. says, "Any little news, political news, can disturb me. And can bring thoughts: What's going to be? How it's going to be? Will we, will we have it again?" Jolly Z. was troubled by President Reagan's visit to Bitburg, and for weeks she was physically sick, the first time since the war. She concludes that Holocaust memory does not pale, "especially when it is triggered by something." When those in the United States and Europe belatedly learned of the genocide in Cambodia, witnesses reacted. Edith P. says, "When I learned about Cambodia, I went into a depression. It pains me terribly that the world has not learned." Martin S. describes his reaction to the movie *The Killing Fields*: "The thing just I can never get out of my mind is this inhuman, inhuman treatment. . . . My God, nothing has changed." Leon H. summarizes: "If I look at you it reminds me of something. If I look at world, reminds me of something."[75]

In testimony given in 1994, Josephine B. talks about the commemorative reminders from the world:

> Well, if you live in Holland, you're always involved, whether you ask questions or whether you don't. . . . When we had another . . . special year, five or ten years, twenty-five or whatever . . . that sort of awakens the problems. And then I also have— that I've done this now for the last three years. I just can't stand Commemoration Day. So, on the fourth of May, it's commemoration, and on the fifth, it's liberation. So, I just leave the country. Because it's too much. They write so much about it."[76]

Sometimes, events in the world tap into the well of unbearably painful core memories, suddenly and without mediation from narrative memory. When this happens, Holocaust memories can flood into consciousness, unwanted and unrestrained, with responses that are unavoidable and physical. Celia K. speaks of uncontrollable reflexes; Martin S. talks of being conditioned like Pavlov's dogs. According to these witnesses, the connection between worldly events and memory exists at a level deeper than controlled consciousness. Sally H. tells, in cryptic phrases, about a panic attack she suffered while visiting the Holocaust museum in Detroit. When she saw the flame in the Museum, she became disoriented and frightened, and then she panicked and ran. Celia K. is clear about the extent and power of her memories. "I keep on just, not rehashing it, I'm not looking for it. It just automatically keeps on coming to me. And somehow everything is vivid, very much alive, very much." Celia relates a recent incident. A bonfire had been built to burn some garbage in her backyard. Unfortunately, the fire vividly retrieved the memory of her cousins who were burned alive in a small synagogue. "I became so hysterical. Was screaming nonstop. I could not stop. . . . I was screaming until my jaw came out. I could not put my jaw back in. And I could not control myself." Celia then had to be restrained.[77]

Though some memories remain constant and disturbing, many witnesses describe their memories as "worse now"—stronger and more distressing rather than less so. Near the end of his testimony, Abe L. states:

> But the worst of all, certain people, for some reason, some reason, certain figures, certain people is in you, in your brain. Certain people, they stay with you and they can't get away, they can't, they just can't get away. Anyone, if he thinks, he sees the hole in his heart, is—is not getting smaller, is getting bigger. And the Holocaust itself, I thought when years go by, passes by, these will go away. We will have forgotten. No way. It's getting closer. The Holocaust is getting nearer, and not farer [*sic*]. It's getting nearer. And this is————. And anyone tells you, well, it's over, it's gone, and stuff like that; no way. It will never go away until the end of time.

Abe continues: "You just can't get away. *They* just don't go away! The people, the people don't go away, the people. Children, children, especially children . . . the children, unforgettable. I'd like to finish, if you don't mind please. I'd like to cut it off. It's enough. It's enough. It's too much. Too much."[78] Isabella L. says, "It's much harder now. I feel my head is filled with garbage. All these images and sounds. And my nostrils are filled with the stench of burning flesh." Eva B. agrees: "It's going to be there until the day I die. . . . It's *more* painful; it's *more* alive rather than less so."[79]

The puzzled observer wonders how memories can be worse forty to fifty years after the events occurred. Witnesses try to explain the experience of worsening memories. During her second testimony, Sally H. says, "Maybe because we have children, we have grandchildren, and things did not change. . . . Then you recall even more vivid the things you went through because one was too young at the time to realize the terrible things." She concludes, "Time makes it even worse."[80] In fact, there is little change in the memories themselves—in the contents or the intensity. Memory has not grown in strength; it appears constant. Changes in the thoughts about one's memories are experienced as changes in the memories themselves. What changes is the interpretation of memory, after looking back over the terrain of normal life and recent world events and realizing the implications of the past atrocities. The images remain, but the memories are more horrifying.

The healthy distraction of raising children, establishing friendships, carrying out civic responsibilities, and building careers directs the attention of Holocaust survivors toward the challenges of normal life. The power of distraction is most evident when it diminishes. Leon W. explains why the torment of memory is worse: "I think about it more now, maybe because I get older . . . I think a lot about it. Too much I think." Now, Josephine B. wonders simultaneously about her future and her postwar past: "So here I am. I have twenty years to live, and I don't know what to do with my time." Alex H. says that for many years after the war, he was so involved in the fight for a new existence that he did not think about the past. Beginning with no family, no schooling, and the wrong language, Alex says the daily fight to establish himself used all his energy. In fact, he suppressed his time in the concentration camp until three years before he came in to give testimony. He describes the result of accomplishing his goals: "My past is starting to haunt me. . . . And I feel so depressed, very often. That I actually feel that I————, very often feel that I lived long enough." He speaks softly and slowly, looking down.[81]

Eva L. elaborates on several reasons for memory's pain:

The older I get, the more memories are haunting me. I keep asking myself, why, what is it? Is it fate that I am here, of the whole family, of the whole wonderful culture, only I am here from a whole family? I wasn't a strong person, or I wasn't a big hero. Is it fate? Was it meant for me to be? And I constantly ask, I keep on asking myself the question, here. Nights that I am up and I cannot sleep, I try to see my parents. It's kind of like, so many years, the picture's fading away and I won't remember them. Comes a holiday, I try to copy, and remember how it was at home. I can never copy, but I try to remember. It's getting harder, it's getting worse with age. I sit and I work, and I think about things that I went through and I wonder: How is it possible that I was able to live through this? Is it possible? How can anybody————. How can I tell to anybody that story, that would believe, if I myself cannot believe that I was there and I was able to live through a horror like this and yet come here to this country and have a family and live a normal life, more or less, a normal life, and bring up my children a normal way? And I wonder and I lay awake. And when I lay awake I relive lot of things. I think when I was younger, it was easier because I was occupied with the children. I was busy with them. And I try, I try to push away those thoughts, but now they come more often, and it . . . haunts me."[82]

A fading happier childhood, a decrease in worldly distraction, and the constant, laser clarity of the remembered horrors combine to worsen the torment of traumatic memory. Eva works at remembering the faces of her parents and the rituals of Jewish holidays, but these general personal memories formed during normal times and based on repetition are not strong enough to endure. Memory for normal events strengthens only when refreshed with thought or action, yet these events were simply not repeated enough to endure. Prevented from re-creating past rituals as they were in the world, Eva endeavors to reconstruct them in her thoughts, but the faded images of these comforting rituals lack the singular emotional and perceptual vividness that severely traumatic memories possess. She has no difficulty remembering the atrocities that followed, and she can no longer distract herself from these memories.[83]

Consider now an elaborated outline of one person's life, a life that is not unusual for a young Jewish adult struggling to survive in Poland during the early 1940s, with the exception that this person lived. Myra L. was born in Lodz in 1919. Her entire family perished during the Holocaust, one by one: her father, her sister, her mother, her older brother, and her younger brother—along with aunts, uncles, and cousins—all died. In April 1940, the Nazis evacuated the Jews in the city of Lodz and forced them into a small area that was to become the Lodz Ghetto. During the evacuation, each person could take only what could be carried. Myra's younger brother was grabbed and beaten for the crime of walking a short distance on a forbidden street. The Germans picked up her older brother to clean out all the apartments in a large building, and afterward, "He was very much beaten," says Myra, because he did not clean the building the way the Germans wanted it done.

Many of the old and the sick were kicked and whipped to death as they walked to the ghetto. What was left of Myra's family stayed in one small room. Food was scarce. They had to find work or else they would be transported to Auschwitz. Myra was fortunate to obtain a job as a nurse in the ghetto hospital, where she worked until the ghetto was liquidated. In the hospital, Myra and the other nurses had to watch as SS guards threw dead and dying patients out the window into wagons to be carted away. She describes one incident involving the father of an infant. "One man, a young man, came in, a newborn baby there. He stole the baby into his coat, inside, and tried to get out with the baby, but a German caught him, took the baby and crushed up against the wall in the father's presence. (She gestures.) The baby fell apart on the floor. These are the vivid things I can remember."

Myra continues:

> I also remember one thing different from that. Food was rationed and we had very little. We were hungry. We acted like animals. . . . For survival . . . one mother held her, I think, a five-year-old child under the mattress for five weeks, dead, in order to receive that ration of food for the child. After five weeks she couldn't anymore. But, can you think of a mother holding a dead child under a mattress in order to get a slice of bread and a little potato for that? These are the things that worked on me more than anything else. And this was the ghetto.

In September 1942, people found out that the Germans were going to take away most of the remaining Jewish population, in particular, old people, sick people, and children. Myra's sister married and had a little boy who then went to a ghetto orphanage when her sister died. The young nephew heard that the SS were coming to the orphanage the next day and managed to find Myra's room in the ghetto. He pleaded with Myra to take him in, but she and her brothers decided against it because they thought he would have a better chance of survival in the orphanage. "And I remember his eyes. (She cries.) . . . He was so small because he couldn't grow much from the food. He was nine and a half. He went back. We never heard of him." She completes the episode:

> And the worst part, a lucky part maybe, but was worse for me now. When the SS man came and we had to go down, I decided I would be dressed in my [nurse] uniform. Maybe it would help . . . and the SS man says, in German, "The nurse and her family on this side." We all figured it's good. . . . I said this was good because I worried about my brothers, but I cannot live with the

thought of my nephew, because would he be with us, he would be saved. Was my family. "The nurse and her family."

In March 1943, after prolonged hunger, Myra's older brother lay dying. She sold a dress in exchange for four ounces of fish liver oil as medicine. She then gave the medicine to her older brother, even though her younger brother begged her for it. Her older brother died soon after. A few weeks later, her younger brother also died. Before he died, Myra says, he spit up pieces of his lungs. She thinks that maybe she could have saved her younger brother if she had only given *him* the medicine. "You know these feelings. . . . Maybe it would help him. I doubt it. I mean I know it couldn't. Four ounces of something can't help him. But it's the thought of it." Myra then describes the death of her mother, which occurred before her brothers died. "I was sitting with my mother, day and night, for the two weeks, next to her bed (in the hospital). And one evening . . . she says to me, 'Go home. Sleep one night at home.' . . . I went home and I came back and she was dead. That night . . . the one night I went home, she was dead."

The ghetto was liquidated at the end of August, 1944, and Myra was transported to Auschwitz. "Twenty-four hours we were traveling, lying one on top of the other one . . . in cattle trains." She describes her arrival. "We undressed completely. (She gestures.) They shaved us, totally, everywhere, completely. And this is the way we had to wait." She hid passport pictures of her family and she hid a brooch in the insoles of her shoes. The brooch was an antique, with emeralds. She went by the SS men, during the selections, naked, holding her insoles. She went through three such selections the same way: naked, shaved, without shoes, holding the insoles in her hands. If they had examined her hands, she would have been shot. She waited in Auschwitz for three days, shivering, with one piece of thin clothing.

Myra was then sent to a slave labor camp in Freiberg, near Dresden, where she and her fellow inmates worked twelve hours each day as metal workers at an airplane factory. Because she was big, she had to work extra hours, and because one guard did not like her, he beat her, once knocking out her teeth with a brick. It was not too long before Myra realized she would soon starve to death, so she gave away her valuable brooch to a Jewish Kapo in exchange for a specific request: six weeks of extra potatoes and extra food for extra work.[84] (She says the request had to be "reasonable.") She began to feel better because of the extra food. In the middle of April, in 1945, the Germans evacuated the camp, and the inmates were once again packed into cattle trains. This time, however, the German soldiers abandoned the transports, and American soldiers eventually liberated the prisoners.

After slowly recovering from typhus, Myra is left with no family, no friends, no community to return to, no home, and a crippled body. But she retains one thing: memory. She has memory of prolonged, excruciating, and complete trauma; memory of her parents, her brothers and her sister, along with her aunts, uncles, and cousins who died. In this way, she moves through the remainder of her life.[85]

DEVELOPING CATEGORIES

The presentation of oral testimony in written form gives rise to a fundamental trade-off between the amount of quotation and the amount of commentary. To be sure, quotation and commentary must be balanced, but what is the appropriate balance? My strategy was to let the witnesses speak for themselves, while I organized the testimony into different categories. My decision was to allow the organization itself to provide the framework for explaining the processes of traumatic memory. Given the broad perspective of more than 100 testimonies, it was possible to identify categories that clarified the commonalities across the experiences of the different witnesses. And yet the process of discovering inductively derived categories and integrating theoretical constructs was far from straightforward.

During the analysis, categories could emerge and prove unreliable. For example, one observation in the literature on autobiographical memory suggests that when people are remembering events with strong emotion, there may be a switch from past tense to present tense.[86] I tabulated this shift, but ultimately did not report it because the shift by itself was not a reliable indicator of strength of emotion. Given the overall complexity of unconstrained recall, it could certainly be the case that such shifts are not associated with increased emotion. It could also be the case that this particular analysis was complicated by the fact that English was not the first language for any of the participants in this study. Many of the witnesses, especially older witnesses, showed consistent patterns of usage with verbs based on the syntactic rules of their first language and not on the syntactic rules of English. Tense and number, in particular, were affected. Therefore, some linguistic analyses proved inappropriate by themselves as diagnostic indicators of memory effects. Overall, however, complications presented by the linguistic diversity of the witnesses could be resolved by combining different kinds of analysis and by using more obvious indicators.

Another suggestion in the literature on autobiographical memory is that a change in perspective from first person to third person can be an indicator that the memory representation has been transformed from an immediate, subjective point of view to a constructed, objective view. Again, this particular syntactic change may have been complicated by the intrusion of consistent patterns of speech from other languages, especially with older witnesses. However, it may also be the case that changes in narrative perspective do *not* reliably indicate changes in the representation of memories. The witnesses in this study who displayed fluency with the syntactic rules of English showed no predictable relationship between narrative point of view and vividness or elaboration of memory. Moreover, with regard to perspective shifts, I should note that my research on naturally occurring errors in everyday personal memories has revealed no significant correlations between perspective shifts and other memory variables, such as corroborated accuracy or rated vividness.[87]

One potential limiting factor in an inductive analysis of oral testimony is that categories identified early in the inductive process might obscure the detection of new categories. To minimize this early-results bias, it was necessary to view each new testimony in its entirety with an exploratory attitude. For example, during the course of analyzing the characteristics of memory, it became apparent that child survivors displayed different kinds of memories from adult survivors and offered different observations about their memories. In an effort to explore these differences more comprehensively, I selected a sample of testimonies from child survivors to discover the characteristics of early traumatic memory and the development of these memories. The following chapter presents the results of analyzing the memories and the observations of child survivors.

Notes

1. Tape HVT-1091, testimony of Martin S., 1988; Tape HVT-1315, Clemens L., 1990.

2. Tape HVT-210, testimony of Alex H., 1983; Tape HVT-976, Renee G., 1988; Tape HVT-1154, Sally H., 1989.

3. Tape HVT-191, testimony of Frieda J., 1980; Tape HVT-65, Irene W., 1982. In many excerpts in this book, I use italics to indicate words and phrases that the witnesses themselves emphasize in their oral testimonies.

4. Tape HVT-3, testimony of Sally H., 1979.

5. Tape HVT-1, testimony of Eva B., 1979; Tape HVT-641, Martin S., 1986.

6. Tape HVT-260, testimony of Mary E., 1984; Tape HVT-971, Hanna F., 1987.

7. Tape HVT-65, testimony of Irene W., 1982.

8. Tape HVT-5, testimony of Renee G., 1980.

9. Tape HVT-206, Bessie K. in testimony of Jacob and Bessie K., 1983.

10. Tape HVT-1126, testimony of Lorna B., 1988.

11. Tape HVT-1270, testimony of Isabella L., 1989.

12. Tape HVT-92, testimony of Chana B., 1980.

13. Lawrence L. Langer, *Holocaust Testimonies: The Ruins of Memory* (New Haven: Yale University Press, 1991), 17–18.

14. Tape HVT-972, testimony of Jolly Z., 1988.

15. Ulric Neisser, "Self-narratives: True and False," in *The Remembering Self*, edited by Ulric Neisser and Robyn Fivush (New York: Cambridge University Press, 1994), 8.

16. Langer, *Holocaust Testimonies*.

17. Lenore Terr, *Unchained Memories* (New York: Basic Books, 1994).

18. For a concise listing of different models, refer to Mark L. Howe and Mary L. Courage, "The Emergence and Early Development of Autobiographical Memory," *Psychological Review* 104 (1997): 499–523.

19. Tape HVT-18, testimony of Hanna F., 1980; Tape HVT-299, Myra L., 1984; Tape HVT-206, Bessie and Jacob K., 1983.

20. Refer to the following works of Elizabeth F. Loftus: "Memory for a Past That Never Was," *Current Directions in Psychological Science* 6 (1997): 60–65. "The Reality of Repressed Memories," *American Psychologist* 48 (1993): 518–537.

21. Bessel A. van der Kolk, "Trauma and Memory," in *Traumatic Stress: The Effects of Overwhelming Experience on Mind, Body, and Society*, edited by Bessel A. van der Kolk, Alexander C. McFarlane, and Lars Weisaeth (New York: Guilford Press, 1996), 282.

22. Chris R. Brewin, Tim Dalgleish, and Stephen Joseph, "A Dual Representation Theory of Posttraumatic Stress Disorder," *Psychological Review* 103 (1996): 670–686.

23. Daniel Siegel, "Memory, Trauma, and Psychotherapy: A Cognitive

Science View," *Journal of Psychotherapy Practice and Research* 4 (1995): 93–122.

24. Roger Brown and James Kulik, "Flashbulb Memories," *Cognition* 5 (1977): 85.

25. Brewin, Dalgleish, and Joseph, "A Dual Representation Theory of Posttraumatic Stress Disorder," 676.

26. Daniel L. Schacter, "Implicit Memory: History and Current Status," *Journal of Experimental Psychology: Learning, Memory, and Cognition* 13 (1987): 501–518. Daniel J. Siegel, "Memory, Trauma, and Psychotherapy: A Cognitive Science View," *Journal of Psychotherapy Practice and Research* 4 (1995): 93–122.

27. Valerie F. Reyna and Allison L. Titcomb, "Constraints on the Suggestability of Eyewitness Testimony: A Fuzzy-Trace Theory Analysis," in *Intersections in Basic and Applied Memory Research*, edited by D.G. Payne and F.G. Conrad (Mahwah, N.J.: Erlbaum, 1997), 157–174.

28. The term "verbatim" applies specifically to language and does not describe the powerful images, emotions, and physiological experiences of the memory representations underlying constructed memory. The term "core" encompasses the characteristics of these representations, specifically referring to the most basic and activating element in a structure. In computer science, *core memory* refers both to the fundamental memory representations and to the actual physical materials supporting these representations. The term "narrative" characterizes how people structure episodes in personal memory for communicating with oneself in silent remembering and for communicating with others to tell the events of the past.

29. John Kotre, *White Gloves: How We Create Ourselves Through Memory* (New York: Free Press, 1995), 42–43.

30. Willem A. Wagenaar and Jop Groeneweg examined testimony given by former inmates of Camp Erika in the Netherlands, testimony given for the purpose of judicial proceedings. ("The Memory of Concentration Camp Survivors," *Applied Cognitive Psychology* 4[1990]: 77–87.) They found that witnesses were more accurate when they were spontaneously recalling facts than when they were prompted by direct questions. One example cited by the authors involved non-Jewish witnesses recalling the fact that the Jewish prisoners were housed in tents, whereas non-Jewish prisoners were housed in barracks. Twelve out of thirteen (ninety-two percent) correctly remembered this fact spontaneously. With those participants who were specifically asked about living conditions for Jewish prisoners, only fourteen out of twenty-five (fifty-six percent) answered correctly. No specific suggestions were made, and the questions themselves—though directed—were open-ended. Therefore, the mistakes were not due to specific retrieval-based distortions

in narrative memory. Rather, the mistakes may have come about because the answers to the questions were not in narrative representations derived from core memories, and the witnesses only had general knowledge about the camp to make informed guesses about the answers.

31. Tape HVT-5, testimony of Renee G., 1980.

32. Tape HVT-34, testimony of Jolly Z. and Rosalie Z., 1979; Tape HVT-213, Adele W., 1982.

33. In their study of former inmates of Camp Erika, Wagenaar and Groeneweg identified mistakes involving the attribution of crimes to the wrong guard. That is, the witnesses remembered the guards and they remembered the crimes, but the two pieces of information were shuffled in narrative memory. In general, when the same kind of event is repeated, details for a specific incident may be blended with other, similar incidents—even atrocious ones. To forget one murder among many supports the notion of schematizing memory for similar events, though the events themselves may be highly traumatic. (Refer to "The Memory of Concentration Camp Survivors," *Applied Cognitive Psychology* 4[1990]: 77–87.)

34. Tape HVT-1115, testimony of Anna K., 1988.

35. Tape HVT-260, testimony of Mary E., 1984; Tape HVT-134, Millie W., 1981; Tape HVT-1650, Violet S., 1991; Tape HVT-1, Eva B., 1979.

36. Ulric Neisser, "What Is Ordinary Memory the Memory of?" in *Remembering Reconsidered*, edited by Ulric Neisser and Eugene Winograd (New York: Cambridge University Press, 1988), 356–373.

37. Tape HVT-970, testimony of Celia K., 1987.

38. Tape HVT-99, testimony of Heda K., 1980; Tape HVT-2045, Alina Z., 1993.

39. Tape HVT-65, testimony of Irene W., 1982.

40. Tape HVT-1650, testimony of Violet S., 1991.

41. Tape HVT-623, testimony of Sabina S., 1985.

42. Tape HVT-579, testimony of Abraham E., 1985.

43. Tape HVT-2609, testimony of Esther W., 1994.

44. Tape HVT-1270, testimony of Isabella L.; Tape HVT-260, Mary E., 1984; Tape HVT-72, Beatrice S., 1982; Tape HVT-618, Samuel B., 1995.

45. Tape HVT-1126, testimony of Lorna B., 1988.

46. Tape HVT-2741, testimony of David K., 1994.

47. For example, in Tape HVT-869, Josephine B. says, "I don't think I'll ever look at it [the tape], but if I would, I probably see that I missed out on some things. You leave———. You got the layout of the sort of things, the general impression, and that the only things that worry me a little bit is I want to give you exact picture." The following testimonies present clear examples of witnesses talking about missing information: Tape HVT-299, Myra L., 1984; Tape HVT-1125, Max B., 1988; Tape HVT-971,

Hanna F., 1988; Tape HVT-623, Sabina S., 1985; Tape HVT-158, Leo G., 1980.

48. Primo Levi, *Moments of Reprieve* (New York: Penguin Books, 1987), 9–10.

49. Tape HTV-869, testimony of Leon H., 1985; Tape HVT-2, Leon W., 1979.

50. Tape HVT-1650, testimony of Violet S., 1991; Tape HVT-1394, Abe L., 1990.

51. In the chapter "Perspective, Meaning, and Remembering," John A. Robinson outlines two general explanations for the recall of emotional experience based on the representation of emotion in memory. The first states that information about emotion is a part of the overall cognitive representation of an event in personal memory. The emotional information must then be decoded and described in order for the emotion to be reexperienced by the rememberer. In fact, this approach is similar to that of William James who conjectured that emotions cannot be directly revived from memory, but must be re-created. The reliving of emotions during a particular event follows retrieval of memory for that event and subsequent thoughts about the memory. A contrasting approach discussed by Robinson begins with the idea that emotional experience involves complex states consisting of physiological arousal, perceptual representations, knowledge, and evaluation, with different representational systems for each type of information. According to this *multiple systems* approach, reexperienced emotions can be the direct result of accessing an implicit emotional representation, separate from any constructive process. (For more information, refer to Robinson's chapter, "Perspective, Meaning, and Remembering," [199–217] and the chapter of Sven-Åke Christianson and Martin A. Safer, "Emotional Events and Emotions in Autobiographical Memories," in *Remembering Our Past: Studies in Autobiographical Memory*, edited by David C. Rubin [New York: Cambridge, 1995], 218–243.)

Kent D. Harber and James W. Pennebaker discuss a schema-based explanation for the *source* of emotions—and their persistence. According to this explanation, emotions arise when there is a conflict between our expectations and our direct encounters with events in the world. Emotions then function to direct attention to the unsuspecting schemas so they can be restructured to accommodate the discordant events. When expectations are realigned to account for the violating events, the emotions dissipate. If the disparity between schema-based expectations and remembered experience remains unresolved, the emotions will persist. (Refer to Kent D. Harber and James W. Pennebaker, "Overcoming Traumatic Memories" in *The Handbook of Emotion and Memory: Research and Theory*, edited by Sven-Åke Christianson [Hillsdale, N.J.: Erlbaum, 1992], 359–387.)

52. Tape HVT-210, testimony of Alex H., 1983.

53. Tape HVT-641, testimony of Martin S., 1986.

54. Tape HVT-3, Sally H., 1979; Tape HVT-260, Mary E., 1984; Tape HVT-869, Leon H., 1985.

55. Tape HVT-1879, testimony of Judith G., 1992.

56. Tape HVT-1315, testimony of Clemens L., 1990.

57. Tape HVT-628, testimony of Leon H., 1985.

58. Tape HVT-18, testimony of Hanna F., 1980.

59. The following testimonies present examples of unexpected crying—and apology. During her second testimony (Tape HVT-976), Renee G. describes how her younger brother desperately pleaded for a hiding place to save his life. She then surprises herself when she begins to cry: "I didn't think I would cry today. *Sorry.*" Josephine B. (Tape HVT-869) describes how her father escaped to England during the war and how the family was reunited afterward. When she talks of the reunion, she unexpectedly cries: "And then he was there. And he had a suitcase with him. I always———. I mean I love that in my memory. Big suitcase. And there was a pair of shoes he had for each of us." Josephine then begins to cry, and says to herself, "Stupid," for breaking down. Zezette L. (Tape HVT-100) discusses how she never talks with her brother about the Holocaust. "He knows I went back to Auschwitz. He cannot talk. He knows that I now talk, and forgive me. (Zezette begins to cry.) I don't—I don't usually become———. Thank God, learned not to cry this way. But, I guess I'm talking a little more than usual." In more than thirty testimonies, witnesses cry and then comment that they are surprised by their emotion.

60. Tape HVT-1154, testimony of Sally H., 1988; Tape HVT-978, Daniel F., 1988; Tape HVT-1, Eva B., 1983. (Note that there are two separate testimonies from Eva B. on Tape HVT-1, the first in 1979 and the second in 1983.) Tape HVT-971, Hanna F., 1988; Tape HVT-969, Dori K., 1988.

61. Tape HVT-978, testimony of Daniel F., 1988.

62. Marigold Linton, "Ways of Searching and the Contents of Memory," in *Autobiographical Memory*, edited by David C. Rubin (New York: Cambridge University Press, 1986), 50–67.

63. Dormant memories that witnesses are aware of must be contrasted with the totality of memorial absence that *repression* entails. Repression can be defined as *the inability to recall a distinctive personal event that is generally agreed upon to be consequential even after repeated prompts to remember.* Repression is not simply forgetting, nor is it the failure to recall a specific horrible and consequential incident in the context of numerous similar incidents. Using this definition, I have identified four documented cases of repression, one of which I present in Chapter 4. It should be noted, however, that the study of oral testimony is not well suited for uncovering repressed memories. Simply put, if witnesses are repressing important events, by definition

they are unable to describe these events in testimony, and the repression remains concealed.

64. Tape HVT-2741, testimony of David K., 1994; Tape HVT-284, Alan Z., 1984; Tape HVT-969, Dori K., 1988; Tape HVT-1091, Martin S., 1988; Tape HVT-976, Renee G., 1988; Tape HVT-1, Eva B., 1983.

65. Tape HVT-253, testimony of Salomon M., 1984; Tape HVT-1101, Eva B., 1988.

66. Tape HVT-206, Jacob K. in the testimony of Bessie K. and Jacob K., 1983.

67. Tape HVT-3, testimony of Sally H., 1979; Tape HVT-1154, Sally H., 1988.

68. Tape HVT-622, testimony of Zev H., 1985.

69. Tape HVT-163, testimony of Pincus S. and Sylvia S., 1980.

70. Tape HVT-971, testimony of Hanna F., 1987; Tape HVT-3, Sally H., 1979; Tape HVT-92, Chana B., 1980.

71. Tape HVT-1270, testimony of Isabella L., 1989.

72. Tape HVT-158, testimony of Leo G., 1980.

73. Levi, *Moments of Reprieve*, 11.

74. Tape HVT-970, testimony of Celia K., 1987; Tape HVT-977, Leo G., 1988.

75. Tape HVT-253, Salomon M., 1984; Tape HVT-72, testimony of Beatrice S., 1982; Tape HVT-977, Leo G., 1988; Tape HVT-287, Sabina G., 1984; Tape HVT-972, Jolly Z., 1988; Tape HVT-107, Edith P., 1980; Tape HVT-641, Martin S., 1986; Tape HVT-628, Leon H., 1985.

76. Tape HVT-869, testimony of Josephine B., 1992.

77. Tape HVT-1154, testimony of Sally H., 1989; Tape HVT-970, Celia K., 1987.

78. Tape HVT-1394, testimony of Abe L., 1990.

79. Tape HVT-1270, testimony of Isabella L., 1989; Tape HVT-1101, Eva B., 1988.

80. Tape HVT-1154, testimony of Sally H., 1989.

81. Tape HVT-2, testimony of Leon W., 1979; Tape HVT-869, testimony of Josephine B., 1992; Tape HVT-210, Alex H., 1983.

82. Tape HVT-71, testimony of Eva L., 1982.

83. Contributing to perceived changes in memory is the process of life review. Discrete changes in the life cycle intersect with remembered losses, and memory asserts itself. In Tape HVT-72, Beatrice S. says, "I think of my parents all the time. It seems the older I get the more I miss them. And I missed my parents when I was growing up, as a teenager. And I missed my mother very much when I was getting married." When the youngest child of Martin S. reached ten, he was relieved: "Thank God, she had me longer than I had my father." About the graduation of his daughter, Martin says,

"You cannot imagine the emotion that I felt, that she had me until she graduated . . . because I always felt the loss of my father [at age eight] and literally struggled since then." This is in Tape HVT-1091. Witnesses are also aware of the loss in their parents' lives. In Tape HVT-2680, Leo B. says, "I don't know, it drives me crazy when I think of my mother. How she never lived to be———, to have a grandchild."

84. Most of the Kapos chosen to be in charge of a group of inmates were political or criminal prisoners, but some were Jewish inmates.

85. Tape HVT-299, testimony of Myra L., 1984.

86. David B. Pillemer, *Momentous Events, Vivid Memories* (Cambridge, Mass.: Harvard University Press, 1998).

87. Robert Kraft, "Revealing Mistakes in Personal Memory" (paper presented at the annual meeting of the Psychonomic Society, New Orleans, November 2000).

CHAPTER 3

CHILDHOOD'S END: MEMORY IN YOUNG CHILDREN WHO SURVIVED THE HOLOCAUST

Testimony from witnesses who were young children during the Holocaust discloses early childhood memory in extremis, laying bare the persistent effects of prolonged childhood trauma. Their testimony forms a memorial écorché, revealing the underlying structures of traumatic memory as well as the patterns of influence arising from a childhood irretrievably lost to atrocity. Witnesses who were between infancy and eight years old when the war began provided the testimony for this chapter, recording their specific memories of early childhood during the Holocaust.[1]

Almost all of the children who lived through the Holocaust were hidden for some time, partially protected by adults. At times, these children had to escape in fear to other locations that could afford limited protection. Some children hid with adopted families or in orphanages and convents—partially visible. Some children assumed different identities and religions, living carefully as other people. Others hid in cramped, dark spaces—sewers or attics or holes—rarely breathing fresh air. Still others were concealed in barracks during the day while the adults went off to slave labor, returning to the children at night. A small number of children managed to elude death in Nazi camps, such as Auschwitz and Bergen-Belsen.

Periods of Personal Memory

The study of memory in child survivors begins with necessary distinctions about the age of the child during the Holocaust. Based on the clarity, coherence, and stated influence of the remembered events, the testimony divides age into three general groupings: infancy to two, two to five, and six and older. Most events that took place during the first two years of life do not result in retrievable memories, though shards of traumatic memory do remain accessible from the second year of life—between eighteen months and two years. Traumatic events occurring between the ages of two and five can create enduring memories that are vivid and extended, but disconnected from other memories. Though these isolated memories from early childhood persist, the beginning of a clear and continuous stream of memories occurs later, between the ages of six and nine.

A second distinction, related to age, pertains to the structuring of autobiographical memory. Older children, teenagers, and young adults have three distinct periods in autobiographical memory: before, during the Holocaust, and after. *Before* is sometimes idealized. Younger children have only two periods in autobiographical memory: during the Holocaust and after. With severely traumatized children, their first extended memories are of terror, separation, pain, hunger, and death: the foundation of one's memorial self.

Consider the testimony of Frania R. who was seven years old when the war began. Asked if she can remember any encouraging moments in Lodz, Poland, she replies, "For me, not. I don't remember even knowing a better life." Her description of liberation emphasizes this point:

And the thing I recollect very vividly is a Russian [soldier] coming up when I came . . . out of the bunker . . . and he cut my Jewish star and he said, "You are free." I didn't even understand. What does he mean, "free"? What am I doing here? And then my parents started celebrating . . . However, there was another shock with us, with my mother. When she brought me a banana, which was about a month after liberation, I started eating it with the *skin on*. And she started crying, because in our house, we did have bananas before the war. And we did have oranges and watermelon. And I wanted to eat the banana with the skin. She just broke down. She realized then how much I have missed and have forgotten even how to eat.[2]

Frania looks down, and her testimony ends abruptly.

Those who were older children and teenagers during the Holocaust can have clear and continuous prewar memories that are pleasant. Born in Krakow, Poland, in 1924, David K. recollects his childhood home: "Krakow is a beautiful historical city. It is so beautiful that to this day despite all the sad experiences, I retained a very strong attachment to it. . . . Life was very, very nice for me. My childhood was nice, very pleasant. I only have pleasant memories." Henry S., also born in Krakow around the same time, has similar memories: "Now, being an old man, I had my best, my happiest times in Krakow. . . . It's still a beautiful city. And I still have very fond memories of it, too." Born in June 1926, Meir V. says, "I have very vivid and pleasant memories of Vilna. And at this point, I almost have a romantic view of it. It meant so much and still means to me. The imprint of Vilna exists until this day." Esther W., who was born in Lodz in 1929, states concisely, "My childhood and my memories were very good." Each of these older children have enduring memories of a childhood self before the war, a self that is grounded in a place and accompanied by pleasant memories.[3]

In contrast to the pleasant early memories of older children, younger children lack this coherent concept of self in childhood. For very young children, prewar memories are out of focus or not visible at all. Clemens L., only two years old when the war began, struggles to remember *before*. "Maybe I have a moment of a glimpse of my father in the kitchen. But it's hard to say whether it's something I created or it's something that *was*." When Clemens tries to recall the specifics of his prewar childhood, he says he faces "a wall," and memory is blank. His explanation: "I think I was so terrified that I was in a daze. I think I was in a daze. And only very highly charged, painful memories are with me. Specific memories."[4]

In young child survivors, the beginning of the remembered self consists of clear, disconnected memories of fear and suffering, which then serve as the basis for the present self. Consider the first memories of witnesses who were very young. Frieda J. says that her earliest awareness of impending horror occurred when she was a little more than two years old—in late 1939: "I remember not being allowed to play on the street, on the sidewalk. I remember patrols." Frieda then describes the two specific and extended memories that anchor her childhood: being visciously attacked by a German Shepherd dog and watching her father dragged from her house and hanged in the public square.

> Well, I was attacked. I was one of these very friendly little girls. ...What I didn't know was that it [the German Shepherd] was trained to kill on command. And many of the guards that patrolled the neighborhoods at the time, it was just great sport to see how many we could maim or injure and whatever, so I was attacked by the dog. But for some strange reason, the guard that gave the command withdrew it, so that I wasn't killed. I would have been. I had a great big gash on my scalp. (Frieda draws her hand across the top of her head.)

She continues:

> One of my vivid recollections is of the day————. I remember my father was ill. I remember that at the foot of the bed there was a sort of a Parson's table, I suppose, that I was sitting on. And I remember my mother combing my hair.... My father is in bed and I remember the bursting in the room of what now, of course, I know were Nazis in uniform. I remember my father being dragged out of bed. I remember being all of us led out. I remember my mother, my baby brother, screaming. I was crying, but it's as sort of a still life. And then I remember the gathering on the square and my father being made an example to the town. And he was hanged. And of course, we all had to watch it.[5]

Nadia R. was born in 1938 and later moved to the ghetto in Bratislava, Slovakia. She says, "Since there was no previous memory of mine, I thought this was the *normal way*. I wore the yellow star of David on my clothing and . . . I was very much alone." She was later deported, which she remembers vividly:

> Among the strongest memories are these trips. . . . Always, always they took us in the night, under lights, with the barking German Shepherds and the barking guards . . . I was just holding on for dear life to the hand of my mother not to *lose* her. This

was one of the most frightening things which . . . stayed in my mind.[6]

Menachem S., born in 1938, describes his earliest extended childhood memory—a German soldier in the Krakow Ghetto threatening to shoot him to death, along with his father: "I was about four and a half years old, and I was sick. I had an inflammation of the inner ear. I was in terrible pain." Immediately after curfew ended, Menachem and his father went out to the doctor:

Was this German soldier. I can really see it even today. . . . The German soldier raised his rifle and pointed his gun at us. Raised it to fire. You could hear. You can see it, matter of fact, hear the click of the breech, when it was loaded. And I can still hear my father crying, in a very high-pitched voice, "Nicht schießen! Nicht schießen!" "Don't shoot. Don't shoot. The curfew's over." And this guy was a German soldier. (Menachem looks down.) He stopped. He looked at his watch and it was four o'clock, so he lowered his rifle, and we were allowed to go. But, anyway, this is my———. Going back, this is my first vivid memory, really.[7]

For children born within two years of the war, as exemplified by Frieda J., Nadia R., and Menachem S., the remembering self begins in uncertainty and terror, and it is this self that anchors the developing child.

TRAUMATIC MEMORY AND THE DEVELOPING CONCEPTS OF SELF

Some child survivors integrate their past actions into their present self-concept. Smeared sketches of early childhood form an abstract backdrop for clear memories of a deprived and tormented youth, ultimately creating a self-image based on the years of torment and the desperate actions taken to survive. Viewing past actions today, through the lens of adulthood and in the light of normal life, these young survivors judge themselves harshly. Guilt, shame, and self-loathing may result.

When children make adult decisions—life and death decisions—as children, they do not have the wider perspective of adults. They live in an enclosed world, seeing only their own actions, unattached to larger spheres of control. From this station point, children perceive responsibility for their own actions, condemning themselves for reflexive decisions that lead to inevitable tragedy. When younger children are unprotected by adults, surviving on their own, they may judge their actions—and themselves—based on the results of these actions and not the conditions in which they took place. If they are in the care of parents or older siblings, they may blame these family members, at least for a time.

What is the effect of integrating anguished, shameful personal memories from middle childhood into one's self-concept as an adult? At age eight, Martin S. began slave labor in Skarzysko, proving his right to exist on a daily basis by operating several machines that tooled bullets. Suffering from mortal fear and gnawing hunger, Martin's relentless productivity each day earned him a chance to avoid death. At the time he gives testimony, Martin is in his mid-fifties. He goes to Houston frequently on business trips, and in Houston, he says, sometimes there are cockroaches in his hotel room. He tries to smash the cockroaches with his shoes, but he always hesitates. He says, "I see one dodging, I see *myself*. I can't bring myself to kill it." In later testimony, Martin judges himself: "I often wish I could be otherwise. I don't like myself. Oh (he shakes his head), I don't like myself at all."

Why does Martin evaluate himself so harshly? The answer lies in his childhood memories of slave labor at Skarzysko. Martin has assimilated episodes that defined his labor-camp self—hungry, selfish, and terrorized—into his present definition of self. That is why he perceives himself in the cockroaches he is trying to kill in his hotel room, and that is why he does not like himself. When asked if he sees himself today coexisting with his self from before, his answer is unlike that of any adult survivor: "I don't really think I can separate the two," he says. "They seem to be intertwined."[8]

Martin offers two specific episodes that illustrate his self-loathing. While under attack, he and other inmates fled in a hail of bullets. A young man fell in front of Martin, and instead of helping, Martin kept running. When he looked back over his shoulder, he happened to see someone else at the young man's side. He says, "I hated myself for it then. It's those things that gnaw at me all the time." Later, he describes the aftermath of an air raid at Buchenwald that dropped concussion bombs. "A man [was] laying there without limbs, and that comes back in dreams. . . . A man had his limbs blown off and he begged me to crush his skull because he knew he wasn't going to survive. (Martin grimaces, and his voice breaks.) And I couldn't do it. And I can't forgive myself. He died anyway. Why didn't I make it easier for him?"[9]

In stark contrast is Nat G., in middle age during World War II and more than ninety-five years old when he gave testimony. In 1942, Nat searched for a place to hide his six-year-old twins—a daughter and a son, but within the Nazi's cruel Hobson's choice, he was not able to hide his son, so he had to decide between a hiding place for his daughter or no hiding place at all. His daughter went into hiding and lived; his young son was murdered. When the war began, Nat was in his mid-forties with the perspective of a middle-aged adult; it is clear to him that the Nazis made all the decisions and maintained complete control, enforced by terrorism, troops, and machine guns. His words convey pain and grief, but no guilt.[10]

As a result of no remembered normality before the war, as a result of the painful abscess early in life, those who were young children during the Holocaust mourn the loss of childhood. Josephine B., imprisoned at age nine in the concentration camp of Westerbork, says, "*Westerbork*. Even mentioning the name is a trauma. . . . It's very difficult. It spoiled my youth." She continues, "And that's what I think is the worst thing, the one that I regret. I mean, if you miss all your youth, you never make up for it."[11]

Martin S. discusses "terrible resentment" about the loss of his childhood to Skarzysko and Buchenwald. Forced to quit school in kindergarten, Martin was illiterate after being liberated at age twelve. Evicted from the society of childhood, he cannot participate fully in the lives of his children today. While trying to tell stories with his family one evening, his wife asked him, "Don't you know these fairy tales?" He did not. Karl S., born in 1934, similarly rediscovered his loss of childhood when trying to play with his own children: "I did not at the time feel I am missing anything. It's only in retrospect, now that I'm married and I have three children and have trouble relating to them, playing games, or knowing any games."[12]

The privations are often phrased in specifics that serve as metonymy for the cavernous loss of childhood. Sabina S., born in 1931, explains: "It's the minor things like riding a bicycle. I used to see kids riding a bicycle and I would say I don't know how to ride a bicycle because I was occupied by the Germans, and we were persecuted.

And I would envy people. Even today, I envy people that are swimmers. I had no chance to learn how to swim because I was not allowed to be a free person." Josephine B. says, "I'm very interested in tennis. And I like sports . . . and I missed a lot of it in my life." Many young survivors are haunted by the absence of toys and friends. Clemens L. says, "One of the saddest things for me about childhood is that I cannot recall a toy." Later in the testimony, Clemens restates his loss: "I have no memory of any toys. . . . I lost my childhood. I lost birthday parties." Karl S. says, "I realize that I did not have toys and did not have friends." He continues, "The earliest I remember interacting with children, playing with children, was in 1946 in a displaced person camp in Germany." He explains: "It's not that I don't remember. I just didn't have any friends."[13]

Young survivors are often unaware of memory's influence. Traumatic memory, fragmented in early childhood, engenders symptoms that may be difficult to detect—and are delayed. Martin S. describes the difficulty: "I used to say after the war, 'Thank God it didn't affect me.' But, oh my God, it made its mark on me, in many things that I do." Later he says, "I just couldn't bring it to the surface. Things that pain me, things that make me act on a daily basis. Things I do sometimes to my children, which is purely a reaction to what happened to me in the war, they don't understand."[14]

Robert K. says, "There are some other things I learned that I think take a while to take shape, and I think that it's something that's not talked about at all." Karl S. agrees:

Many things don't come out to the surface until a long time afterwards. The behavior of many of those that survived or even young people like me who did not—don't recall too much presently, we may have in us certain qualities, our modes of behavior, that affect our lives very deeply, that will come out in time.[15]

With adults, many Holocaust memories are ever-present, but with very young survivors the influence of extreme trauma early in life may show itself only after many years, reawakened by events in the present. After the first daughter of Menachem S. was born, he went on a buying binge, spending 200 Israeli pounds on toys for his daughter (today's equivalent of more than 1,000 U.S. dollars), proudly displaying the gifts—including an electric train, which he now recognizes was an unusual gift for a newborn. At the time, his wife pointed out that it would take years to play with all the toys, but Menachem countered: "What's wrong with a child having toys?" He admits, "It took me a long time to realize what I was doing. I was finally buying toys for *myself*."

Contributing to the desire for re-creating a lost childhood are memories of growing up suddenly, metamorphosing from a young child to an adult in a matter of months. As a five-year-old, Menachem S. was alone on the streets, scrounging for food, avoiding capture, and struggling to find shelter. He assesses his early childhood: "To me it's serious, although it sounds like a joke. But at that point I was like seventy years old. I was a real old man. I was *short*, but I was *old*."[16]

Hilda S. describes the experience of being a middle-aged woman encased in the body of a teenager. As a child during the war, she was hidden in an orphanage in Brussels to escape deportation. After the war, after immigrating to the United States, Hilda began high school:

> I was like a Martian coming to Earth as far as I was concerned. My experiences were so different from the other kids . . . because I felt that they were all like little children and that I was a very mature individual at the age of sixteen. I probably felt like a fifty-year-old woman after all I had gone through . . . I had matured. I had done it without parents. I had done it on my own.[17]

Renee G. lost her childhood in hiding and her adulthood later in life. "I do not feel my age," she says in her testimony. "To this day, I think I'm trying to recapture a certain time, maybe five years of my youth, and . . . within me I feel like a little girl or a teenager." She compares her past older self with her present younger self: "So, *that* was my old age. *Now* I'm young."[18]

One form of re-creating childhood is to hope for and then imagine the return of one's dead parents. Paul D. saw his father for the last time in the fall of 1944 as he was marched away with a small group of men. Paul says, "We never saw my father again. He was taken to— outside of the town, and he was shot. I don't know how I know this but I know that he was shot in a lime quarry. That was that. But I kept looking for him. When the war ended, I kept looking for him." Clemens L. immigrated to the United States when he was twelve. He tells of a fantasy he held for many years: A guest lecturer would visit his school, and Clemens would walk up to the man, suddenly recognizing him as his own father. "It shows you the power of his absence," he says.[19]

In connection with the loss of one's parents, a powerful *birthday effect* can assert itself in child survivors, linking specific benchmarks in the development of their own children to empathy for the corresponding loss their parents suffered. At age eight, after Kristallnacht, Hilda S. and her brother were abruptly sent from their home in Frankfurt to a state orphanage near Brussels. In her testimony, Hilda says, "When my oldest daughter was eight, the age I was when I left home, I had a real tough time. (She cries for the first time.) I was always very . . . obsessed with what my mother went through. Sending two children away." Hilda then speaks of a similar birthday trauma one generation later. "My granddaughter is eight, and *again* I relive all that, without really talking about it. And so while on the one hand I never felt close to my parents, on the other, I couldn't detach myself from what they went through."[20]

With an intense focus on surviving during the Holocaust, children quickly transformed into adults. After the war, after reuniting with parents, the premature adult was required to become a child again, creating a struggle between reviving the poorly formed child self and maintaining an untenable, precipitant adult. During such a struggle, the tectonic plates of identity shift and consequential events can disappear into a temporal crevice between the horrors of the war and the personal rebuilding afterward. These consequential events can remain unseen for many years until a later emotional shock jars them loose. Consider the testimony of Jacqueline R.:

> I want to backtrack how I got involved in recalling my past and coming to terms with those experiences in the past. And what triggered it was my father's death. He died in 1982. And I was in terrible shock. I couldn't believe it. And all the years prior to his passing away I denied the Holocaust. I denied what happened to me. I didn't want to think about it. I buried it.[21]

Just after the war, when Jacqueline R. was twelve and a half years old, her biological parents asked if she wanted to live with them or the Swiss parents who adopted her during the war. She forgot this dilemma completely—the question and her decision—until the mid-1980s, after the death of her father catalyzed the examination of her childhood.

For those who were traumatized as very young children, fragmented core memories may be difficult to specify, yet teeming with powerful emotion. Karl S. summarizes the ominous dormancy of childhood trauma: "I personally feel I believe I am a successful professional in my field, as a technician. But as a *person*, as a *Jew*, I feel I'm sitting on a *volcano*." Robert K. also refers to an underlying explosive force: "What we learned was *rage*." Later, he says, "I don't know where—how all that takes shape. What surprises me is that we're able to contain it."[22]

One child survivor expresses her enduring rage with a repellent image:

Some of us are more damaged than others. But all of us are damaged. Because of what the Germans did. And personally I will never forgive them. I *hate* them all. And if you wanted to drop an atomic bomb on Germany, I'd have no problems. Which is———. I know it's not *fair* and even Elie Wiesel has said they're not responsible. The younger generations are not responsible. You can't hold it against them. But I don't feel that way.

Another child survivor expresses a similar idea, saying that he does not fear nuclear war, concluding, "If I go, let the rest of them come along."[23]

David Boder's book, *I Did Not Interview the Dead*, was the first to present testimony from Holocaust survivors, its appropriately jarring title a blunt reminder for future researchers that the most frequent response to Nazi terror was death—and that testimony comes from the living.[24] This cold fact is especially important in the study of child survivors. Although the survival rates for European Jews in general were low, the annihilation of Jewish children was a special focus of the Nazis. As many as one and a half million Jewish children in Nazi-controlled Europe were killed—ninety-four percent. Upon reaching a concentration camp, most Jewish children were immediately sent to their painful deaths. Of the one million Jewish children living in Poland before the war, only five thousand survived, a fact that translates into a shocking percentage: more than ninety-nine percent of these Jewish children were killed.[25]

Of the small number of targeted children who managed to live through the Holocaust, many did so by being sent away from their homes and hidden. Consequently, each of these children endured separation from the family. As Hanna G. states in her testimony, families were "ripped apart like paper."[26] When children were extracted from their families and hidden with others, it was always torturous for the parents and disruptive for the children, but the enduring effects of these separations varied, depending on the conditions of separation and the conditions in hiding. When describing his own experience as a hidden child, the psychology professor Shlomo Breznitz addresses the formidable issue of distinguishing different categories of trauma in children. He outlines the physical and emotional suffering that he and his sister endured while hiding in an orphanage after their parents were deported to Auschwitz: "We were hungry, but we were not starving. We were cold, but we were not freezing. We were alone, but we still had hope that our parents would come back."[27] Testimony from Holocaust children reveals three factors that shaped the enduring effects of these necessary separations: the age of the child, how the child was prepared before the separation, and the treatment of the child in hiding.

With respect to the age groupings outlined at the beginning of this chapter, the testimony from child survivors shows that if children were between infancy and two years when they went into hiding, there is little memory of the separation itself. If these children were cared for adequately and their physical needs were met, then memories of their hidden childhood may be less destructive to the developing self than the memories of older children or those hidden in harsher conditions. If children were between two and five years old when separated, the effects of the separation depend on the children's preparation for hiding and their treatment in hiding, both of which can include helpful deception. If the children were six and older at the time they were separated from their families, they can possess a well-formed schema for normal family life, and the separation itself can lead to enduring traumatic effects.

Annette G. was six years old at the time she went into hiding. In comparison to other hidden children, Annette presents an extreme example of how the separation from family can rupture one's development, creating a split within the self. Annette was taken away from her twin brother and her parents and hidden alone for many months in a damp, rat-infested cellar. Due to her age and her harsh treatment in hiding, Annette's separation in early childhood remains the dominant theme in her life. She describes the split from her twin brother:

> I would have rather died together with him than have to be separated from him. Because he was my sole companion. I had really no other companions. . . . My whole structure was revolved around him. That was my structure of my life, from the day I was born until the age I was six. . . . I never felt like I was a whole human being after that, myself. I never felt like I belonged anywhere. Because he was my structure. He was my——. Everything was with him. . . . We were never separated for the first six years of our lives. . . . It was like a living death. I was living a living death. Right there in that cellar, I was dying.[28]

More than forty years after the war, Annette says that she has not recovered from this abrupt and shocking separation, and she still does not understand why she was placed in hiding without her twin brother. She questions: "When did I begin to understand? I'm still trying to put the pieces together. I still haven't. I have not put the pieces together. . . . I'm still looking for the truth. And I don't know if I'll ever find it."

Both of Annette's parents survived. Her difficulty in understanding why she was hidden arises from an inability to assume the perspective of her parents—even now. Details of her testimony suggest that part of her self remains frozen as a six-year-old in the cold, damp cellar where she hid. She refers to the cellar as a "dungeon." She deifies her mother and vilifies her father, blaming him—and not the Nazis—for the separation from her twin brother and the resulting misfortunes. Her choice of words, the Manichaean conceptualization of her parents, the attribution of choice to her father, as well as her appearance in the videotaped testimony all indicate emotional development arrested in early childhood.[29]

For Donald W., born in 1939 in Amsterdam, the remembered experience of separation and hiding is less tormented than for many other hidden children. His age, his preparation for hiding, and the support of his new family combined to generate less emotional disturbance. Donald's father was sent to Westerbork and murdered, but Donald cannot recall his father. After a well-planned deception, Donald was separated from his mother and infant brother at age three and placed with a well-to-do family in Amsterdam, a family that was devoted and caring. Memories of this loving adopted family form the basis of Donald's childhood. "I was three years old," Donald says, "when I first remember anything about the war because this is when I was taken by the underground . . . to my foster parents. And this is really my first—my only—recollection. I really do not remember my father leaving, other than that he wasn't there." He goes on. "I know that I was kept busy, and I asked for my mother . . . but I was over-whelmed with toys . . . and days went by, and it became my family. . . . And you start living with people, and it becomes part of your life . . . you start to forget. . . . And things became normal." Unlike hidden children who lived in more deprived conditions, Donald has child-hood memories that include toys and young friends.

To protect the children and themselves from being captured by the Nazis, adult caretakers sometimes used games to encourage children to remain quiet during hiding. The strategy worked by placing dan-gerous actions within the context of the familiar, deceiving children to behave so that they might survive. (The 1998 film, *Life Is Beautiful*, illuminates this strategy through disjointed fantasy.) At age three, while Donald W. was in hiding with his Dutch foster family, the SS raided and searched the house. He explains:

> The German soldiers did come in the houses. And there were raids. And I remember one time, we played hide and go seek, and I was in a shed underneath the stairwell. And all I was told really was that we were playing a game. I could hear people walking around the house, but never knew that I was really being hidden for any other purposes than, other than there was a game. Because I was just too young for that. And the raids came and they went. And, of course, all this was at the risk of those people's lives. If they would have found me, we would all be killed. But I was too young, of course, to know all that.[30]

The experience of a game with imperceptible horror hovering be-yond the walls of concealment can be contrasted to the direct edu-cation of pounding terror when in hiding. Sabina S., age ten, tells of her constant fear as a child in the ghetto, when German soldiers broke into people's rooms to kill them: "And we heard above us the Germans yelling, searching for us and looking for us. . . . You couldn't breathe. You couldn't talk. You were always afraid they were going to discover you. So there was always that fear. That they're there to kill you. And, as a child, it made a terrible impression."[31]

If children were very young and not in physical pain, there was a tendency for them to translate threatening situations into the familiar on their own. Mostly unaware of the horrors beyond their immediate experience, very young children—between the ages of three and six—might interpret dangerous activities as adventure. When he was four years old, Paul D. says he convinced his mother to let him escape to Hungary where the Jews were safer than in Slovakia:

> This I remember very clearly. (He smiles.) I convinced her that it was a good idea for me to go. She was very ambivalent about that. And, I guess, I remember telling her, trying to convince her that this definitely would be a safe place for me. But all along, I really————. What I wanted to do is have the adventure of a train ride, because I knew I would be going on a train . . . I wanted the adventure. I didn't think that this would last for a very long time. I just—it just sort of felt like a fun thing to do.[32]

While being deported, the family of Dori L. had to ferry across the Dniester River, and Dori remembers thinking of the boat ride as an adventure. While in a labor camp, his early childhood interpretation admits only the immediate, in one case forming a pleasant memory of playing with another child within the larger context of extreme deprivation:

> I remember once sitting on the bank of the [Bug] River, our feet dangling in the water and she told me that you can eat grass. And that's how people can live. And she picked up some grass and ate it. And I followed it and picked some grass and ate it too . . . and there's a certain quality of sunshine, and summer time, and almost a vacation to some of the days in camp. . . . I was sitting on the river bank, with this little girl, and tasting the grass.[33]

For almost a year, Karl S. hid in the barracks of a labor camp while his parents went off to slave labor. After escaping with his parents from the labor camp, he hid for more than a year with his parents and others in a hole dug out in a barn. Karl says he did not feel afraid: "No, I would say it was more like playing hide and seek. No,

I did not, I did not see any atrocities. I don't *recall* seeing any atrocities. I was not hungry. I was the only child. . . . To me, it was a game."[34]

If children were discovered in hiding, they were either murdered immediately or sent to the Nazi camps. Miraculously, even some of the children who were sent to the camps survived, and they too showed evidence of interpreting and adapting to daily deprivations and routine atrocities through their understanding of games. The following is an excerpt from Hana Hoffman-Fischel describing the rehabilitation of these children after the war:

> Among the small children, we had great difficulties. . . . If . . . we did not pay attention, they then played life as they experienced it. They played "camp leaders and block leaders," "roll-call" with "caps off"; they played the sick who at roll-call became faint and in return received beatings, or "doctor" who deprived the sick of their food rations and who refused them help if they could not give him anything. Once they played "gas chamber." They made a ditch into which they shoved one stone after another. The stones represented the people who entered the crematorium, and they imitated their cries. They consulted me, wanting to know if I would show them the way a chimney had to be installed.[35]

For those young children who did manage to stay in hiding, the strategy most beneficial to protect them from physical harm may also be the most effective in diminishing the torment of memory. Taking advantage of children's myopic view of outside events and their natural willingness to participate in the risk of games reinterprets the remembered intrusions of a threatening world.

One consequence of separation and hiding is the radical changing of identities, often through expedient religious conversion. Assimilating different religious identities, sometimes repeatedly, confounds immiscible beliefs and rituals within the childhood self. As children fled from one hiding place to another, they embraced the liturgy of each new religion as a source of comfort and constancy in a violently shifting world. Rachel G. moved many times, memorizing a different name and different cultural heritage with each move in order to avoid capture. She was repeatedly instructed, "Forget what was the past." She describes this life of religious conversion and disruption:

I went to mass, and I loved it, by the way! (She laughs.) Because it was life with other people. I wasn't running anymore. I was settled—a little bit . . . and I was very happy there. But then for [some] reason, it started all over, and I had to keep on going from one place to another. Now why they wanted a seven-years-old child, I will never understand.[36]

Religious identity was even more complicated for Jacqueline R. Born in France in 1938, she was sent away to the indifferent safety of Switzerland. Her Swiss foster parents were pious Protestants living in a primarily Catholic town, but their Protestant church conducted services in German, so Jacqueline did not attend. Instead, she was placed in a kindergarten taught by nuns in the Catholic Church. She says her Swiss parents "would undo at night whatever the nuns did during the day, what they did not approve of." Jacqueline elaborates: "But little did they know how fond I grew of the nuns, and all the ritual. We would pray on arrival. We would get on our knees. We would pray at lunch time, when we go home for lunch. We would pray when we come back. Well, and we learned songs. Anyway, they were wonderful."

On Sunday, Jacqueline went to Catholic Mass in the morning, then to the other side of town to a Protestant Sunday school. During one of her trips to Sunday school, she was confronted by a rabbinical student who then told his rabbi about her. Jacqueline's foster parents eventually met with the rabbi who told them that she needed to go to synagogue. After that, each Sunday Jacqueline went to Catholic Mass in the morning, then crossed town to a Protestant Sunday school, then took a train to meet with the rabbi for training in Judaism. At age six, she wanted to be a nun; at nine, she stopped going to church altogether.

For Jacqueline R. to be Jewish meant betrayal of her Christian parents, accompanied by shame, guilt, and anger. She summarizes her conflict and confusion: "It's been painful for so long because it was so hard to let go without feeling that I was betraying them. . . . I wanted to remain true, to remain faithful, both to my *own* parents . . . and to my Swiss parents, to all the people who had shown love and kindness to me. So, I tried to, I think, straddle both . . . worlds." She elaborates:

I was very angry at my [biological] parents for not giving me this background that they had received. And I slowly have been kind of filling in the gaps. I don't go to synagogue regularly. I've never belonged to one. But, I've gone to synagogues that have this outreach program. . . . I started to learn Hebrew, which has helped me to identify most closely with being Jewish, because as a child for a long time, I was ashamed of being Jewish and ashamed of being ashamed. And it's only in recent years that I've been able to rid myself of this shame, embarrassment.[37]

After denying their religion, many young children became profoundly reticent about reacquiring their original Jewish identity.

After the war, the young child's foundling memories of separation and fear were overlaid with images of the displaced persons (DP) camps, orphanages, and hospitals—places of relative safety but also places of flux and confusion. Clemens L. spent part of the war hiding in a Catholic convent. Changing religious identities early in his life both informs and confuses his self concept: "In the convent, I was a good Catholic. I fit in. I did all the right things, kind of automatically. I think I was sociable kid. . . . When I was in a DP camp, I became religious [as a Jew] and that was very strange because I was just a Catholic." Today, Clemens is troubled by how malleable he is, describing himself disparagingly as a chameleon: "That shift from one to the other . . . puzzles me and disturbs me. I was adaptive, but at the same time, I feel it's like sometimes hard for me to find out who I *really* am. What am I?"[38]

David Pillemer writes of the prescriptive quality of these early memories, stating that they provide messages for future behavior.[39] Distinct events that anchor the remembering self project their lessons for the remainder of one's life, providing a touchstone for future beliefs. Young children who were hidden remember that *changing identities meant survival*. They often speak of dying and rebuilding, using newer memories to construct the present self. The directive of early memory is to blend, to change—completely and quickly, leaving these children without a thematic set of core images to define their younger self other than change itself.

THE CONFLATION OF THOUGHTS AND MEMORIES

With time and conscious effort, painful thoughts about specific memories can transform, and suffering can diminish. In her first testimony in 1980, Edith P. struggles with her present attitudes about her German tormentors. Should she hate them? Should she forgive them? During the last six minutes of her first testimony, Edith talks through her tears, thinking about this personal moral dilemma. Her second testimony eight years later reveals no such emotion. Edith has resolved the struggle: she ignores her German tormentors. Her memories remain strong, but the cognitive conflict about her attitude is resolved, and with that resolution, the emotional pain arising from her thoughts diminishes.[40]

For those who were young children during the Holocaust, memory and thought can become conflated. With these young survivors, early memories about one's family can become enmeshed with later thoughts. These early memories do accurately represent events during childhood, and witnesses can distinguish what they directly experienced from what they were told, but when combined with years of suppression, narrative memory and speculation can intertwine. The testimony of Dori K. illustrates both the conflation of cognition and memory *and* the potential for change in those who were very young— if the torment later in life arises from extrapolating a constructed past and not from specific memories. With Dori K., emotional distress as an adult triggered a reexamination of core memory, which, in turn, allowed her to separate remembered atrocity from thoughts of what might have been.

In testimony given in December 1979, Dori reveals that she suppressed her grief for her murdered father, only recently becoming aware of her emotional pain.

> It was an absolute blow to me. To realize that many of the feelings I've had all these years. Many of————. That it had been with me for years. I just————. I suppose I wasn't ready. Or I was scared. Or I was repressed. Or it just seemed to have taken a tremendous emotional shock to sort of jar me loose. . . . I think I hate the Germans. I think for years I felt my father abandoned me. And I think I might have been very angry at *him*.

In 1979, Dori finally begins grieving for her murdered father, and underlying her grief are thoughts—not specific memories—about what must have happened to him. At the end of this testimony, she says, "I think most of my life . . . has been spent trying to forget it. Trying to lead a normal life. Trying not to think of that man in a concentration camp. (Her voice grows louder.) Trying not to think of human beings beaten. I can't keep thinking about it!" Dori breaks down, crying uncontrollably and holding her face in her hands.[41]

Eight years later in January 1988, Dori K. provides testimony again. Extraordinary change has occurred in her posture, her expressions, and her demeanor. She looks and sounds like a different person. She explains what brought about this change. After her first testimony, she traveled to Belgium, where she discovered more about her own life in hiding and learned what she could about her father, playing "detective," and retracing her childhood years. During this visit, Dori obtained details and documents about her early life and her father's last years, which then began the process of "letting go" of her memorial responsibilities. No longer is she the only means of preserving her father and her former life: There is the place and there are documents. Dori was able to change perspective, reconciling herself to the fact that there will be events she will never know. She admits, "I think about it still. I think about it every day. . . . But it's held in check . . . I don't feel so torn." In her second testimony eight years later, Dori reveals that her most recent struggle with memory entailed giving up the constructed images of her father that she "fastened on." She concludes: "By now they're all gone. By now all that is gone. It really is. The waters have closed above it (the thoughts of her father). I don't feel anything about it anymore. I don't feel as if I ever knew him."

Dori's clear memories of her own experiences in hiding between the ages of three and six are still painful, but the powerful thoughts about her father are gone and, with them, some of her emotional pain. As a child survivor, Dori K. was able to diminish her torment, even when so many older survivors cannot, because the immediate source of Dori's emotional pain was not specific memory, but rather *thoughts* about the suffering and death of a father she never knew. Documents and places—and Dori's own videotaped testimony—now assume responsibility for remembering her father.[42]

Core memories in the very young can be accurate, with segments of memory pieced together incorrectly.[43] Clemens L. talks about the convent where he hid, starting when he was five years old, from the middle of 1942 until 1945. Clemens asserts, "I remember a wrong sequence, which my mother corrected." His memory is of a bishop who took him on a train to the convent, which his mother arranged. According to Clemens, the bishop concealed Clemens's face because of his curly hair and dark eyes that would identify him as Jewish. "I had the memory that he covered my face up with scarves (he gestures), put a hat on me on the train and took me to the convent, hiding me," Clemens says. "But my mother told me though that *she* took me to the train to the convent, not this bishop." It turns out that Clemens was covered up and that the sequence of events and the meaning of the episode are accurate, but he inserts the bishop in place of his mother in the sequence, a type of error that can be termed *person displacement.*[44]

Dori K. was an infant in Belgium when World War II began, and she eventually went into hiding at age three. In her first testimony, Dori remembers her mother visiting her while she was hiding on a farm:

> My mother was very worried that I'd forget who I was and that I would forget I was Jewish or would forget her. And so, when she came, we used to go to the outhouse. (She smiles and laughs a little.) That's where we spent the whole afternoon in her visit, in this damn stinking outhouse. Because that's where we could be alone.

As described earlier, a few years after giving this testimony, Dori K. visited the farm where she hid, back in Belgium. The outhouse was still there, but it is not where she met her mother. In testimony eight years later, Dori says, "You see I had remembered my mother coming to see me, and we would be in a small enclosed place. And I had assumed it was the outhouse. Although I didn't smell an outhouse smell." In fact, she and her mother went to a toolshed in the back of a small store owned by the older son of the farmer who hid her. To construct narrative memory, Dori retrieved accurate images from core memory—the outhouse and the visits with her mother in a small, cramped room—and overlaid one image on the other like double-exposed film. The reconstruction is sensible; she was alone with her mother in a small space, so she displaced the visits to the structure that was nearest to the house, which happened to be the outhouse. In written text, the phrase, "damn stinking outhouse," appears strong and confident, but the videotaped testimony looks and sounds as if Dori is remembering a constructed narrative. She speaks the phrase quickly and laughs lightly afterward. She does not describe the smell, and she does not provide any details.[45] This type of error can be characterized as a *composite image*. In fact, research on personal event memory shows that the composite image—the combining of two separate and accurate core images into one—is the most frequently occurring type of memory error.[46]

Accurately remembering locations and people but placing people in the incorrect location is a mistake of memory that older survivors also commit. With very young survivors, however, the connections between episodes are either faint or nonexistent, so the episodes seem suspended in isolation—and less real. In fact, very young survivors can sincerely doubt the reality of events they lived through. Witnesses who were teenagers or adults during the Holocaust often state that listeners will not believe the events described in Holocaust testimony and that they themselves have difficulty believing what they lived through. But these witnesses do not refute the reality of the remembered events because they construct their own narrative memories from their core sensory memories. Very young children, however, often have others construct narratives for them. For these very young children, placing their own foundling memories within a web of narrative imparted by others can create confusion, which can lead these children to doubt their own memories.

Witnesses who were young children may simultaneously remember the events *and* become convinced that they never actually occurred. Their core memories are vivid and accurate—and child survivors are often surprised at the accuracy of their memories, but these young survivors are uncertain about the veracity of these memories. Moreover, when some of these children initially tried to describe what happened just after the war, they were routinely told that their stories were untrue or that they were too young to remember. Later in life, they may believe the events never occurred at all.

Clemens L. describes a memory that he thinks is simply wrong. At the end of his testimony, a rare dialogue ensues among the two interviewers and Clemens. Interestingly, the interviewers had recently taped the testimony of Clemens's mother.

CLEMENS: Some of the memories I have, didn't happen. Like I have a memory of being in a———, under a sewer system, during the war, when the Germans invaded Poland in 1941. I have a memory of being in the sewer system hiding out, hiding out. My father and my grandfather stayed on top, because they felt secure. They were misguided, obviously. My father bravely got us Catholic papers [for] my mother, my grandmother, and myself to leave the ghetto. So I remember hiding there, and I remember climbing—being taken out—and my father and grandfather refusing to hide and staying on top. And getting killed for that. . . . This image I have is my father putting us down into the sewer, under the sewer, somehow. I remember him putting us there. But, I checked with my mother, and I don't think that that's accurate.

FIRST INTERVIEWER: It *is* accurate.

SECOND INTERVIEWER: It is.

CLEMENS: It is accurate?

FIRST INTERVIEWER: Listen to her tape. It may not have been a sewer, but it was an underground bunker . . . It was a bunker. It was dug out under the ground. They were on top and that's when they never came back. It's accurate. Listen to her tape. What strikes me is that you came to believe it's not accurate.

CLEMENS: I thought it was accurate once, and then I was told it's not accurate. So, you know, it's a little puzzling . . . but I have memories of that.[47]

Young children are aware only of their immediate surroundings, and individual memories remain isolated from meaningful context. These isolated memories are clear, but because they are unsupported by knowledge of the larger context, they are less stable, more prone to later contradiction, and sometimes thought to be unbelievable. Frieda J. describes one early memory, a memory she is unsure of. "We began to hide. I remember my family, everyone going into a false closet. I can't really describe it. Because I———. In fact, I had to ask my uncle who still lives in Belgium if I remember this: if it was a dream or if was really so." She maintains an image of the closet, but is unsure of the memory because as a young child she was unaware of the immediate reason for going into the closet. She explains: "I didn't know that there were calls for a meeting on the town square—the selection at that time—because they began very quickly. Jews began to be deported. I didn't know that at the time."[48] There is no remembered motivation for the event and no causal connection to other events in the world, so the memory for this unlikely event remains unvalidated by other remembered events.

Young survivors can remember some experiences in clear glimpses that are not integrated with other memories and have not been connected by strings of narrative. The very isolation of these memories— not uncertainty about the core images—can lead the young survivor to doubt. Chana B. was eight years old when the war began. She remembers an isolated but extended episode in Auschwitz, in Block 12, which she describes as housing children and women who were early in their pregnancy:

> I remember noises at night, children being born. And they had a long furnace, the length of the block, and that was the delivery table. All I remember was that in the morning they had sometimes little boxes, moving boxes. They put the babies into box, like you carry a large doughnut box or something, that's what they put—collected the boxes in one place. I don't know, I think—I'm sure it's true. But I don't believe it's true. I remember the boxes, the moving boxes. . . . I know what I'm saying is true, but I don't believe it. Does this make sense? I don't believe I saw it. Many times I have great difficulty believing.

Clear, external validation can place these unbelievable images into the category of the believable. In fact, Chana later tells how she indirectly verified her memories of the murdered infants:

> I'm talking and I think, Chana you must have read that. But it is true. Like for example, I was freed in Salzwedel. And I have some memories about it, and I said, oh, it's not true. It can't be. Didn't happen. But then, last year, I received a book of essays from Israel, poetry and essays, from a woman who was from Budapest, and she was freed in Salzwedel. And she writes. She writes out the name "Salzwedel" and all the experiences that I think were just fruit of my imagination.[49]

For Nadia R., the memory of Terezin underwent the same transformation from unbelievable to validated.

> I always went for the lunch with this wooden tray. And an SS man on a *horse* whipped me with his whip. Around my ankles. And that stayed for the longest time. All these things were *in* me. I never talked about them. Only in the nightmares this

would come out. And then when I started to read, I said this must be something I must have dreamt. Or why would I say I never saw any SS men—from any of the pictures in the books—I never saw them on a *horse*? And three years ago we went to the Washington Museum, and we picked up a book called *Theresienstadt: Hitler's Gift to the Jews*. And there it is written that Commander SS never went out without his horse. And when I spoke to people, I never mentioned that because I always didn't know if this was *real* or wasn't. Because it was so strong in my memory. But, after all these years, I thought, well how come nowhere, nowhere I see like any scenes from Auschwitz—or you never see anybody on a horse? And *here* I found out.[50]

Child survivors can also remember emotion from specific events without confident memory of the events themselves. During his testimony, Clemens L. states directly, "My emotions are so powerful. I'm surprised I'm feeling them as much as I am here. So that's there. But the *placement* of it, the specific memory of it, that's difficult."[51] From her early childhood, Hilda S. describes her memory of Kristallnacht.

I seem to recall seeing smoke and fire. Whether it's my imagination I really don't know. Our synagogue. But there were fires all over the city and obviously we all *knew* about that and there was talk in the family about these events. Whether I saw it or whether I heard it, I really can't remember. But I do clearly recall being very frightened—being "terrified" is more the word for it—by what was happening.[52]

The memory of strong emotion *unconnected to specific events* creates further confusion in child survivors.

When young survivors doubt their own personal memories, one solution is to revisit the site of their torment. Most survivors are insistent; they refuse to return. Some young survivors, however, decide resolutely that they *do* want to return. One reason for the marked difference between younger and older survivors is that for survivors who were young children, a visit may be necessary to validate memory. Renee G. insisted on returning to her childhood home in Poland and to the barn where she hid during the war. Renee was old enough to remember her childhood trauma, but she kept it separated from her postwar self and consequently had difficulty believing that this young person was her. For twenty-five years following the war, Renee maintained a parallel self, even while she narrated her life during the Holocaust:

> I felt as if I were talking about this little girl, somewhere in the background, whose name was Rifka, had gone through all these things. And I would talk about it completely dispassionately as if it weren't me at all. I naturally knew it was me, but I could not believe that this really happened, that such a thing is even possible to happen.[53]

She says she described her own experiences, "in the third person, 'she' . . . as if . . . it wasn't really me. . . . It was that little girl."[54] Renee describes the visit to her childhood home to validate her memories as her own:

> Sure, it was painful, but it was real . . . and of course, this was like a ghost house. But still, there it was. It was real. It stood there. And it all began to have meaning, a beginning and an end. Sure, they're not there anymore, but this was a reality. I *did* have grandparents. I *did* have uncles and aunts and cousins. It was true that I was running up and down and played with them. And my grandfather at Hanukkah gave me five cents. And all the grandchildren had to line up and get it. So it was a bittersweet experience, that was just great. It was terrific. I felt so much better than I had before when I was sort of shoving everything into a corner, like a dirty corner.

Renee then summarizes her response to the visit: "I felt good. I saw what I came for. The house was there . . . I touched reality."[55]

In contrast, Sabina S. is typical of survivors who were older children and teenagers during the Holocaust. She *has* maintained clear and continuous memories that anchor her tormented childhood and do not demand validation. These memories provide no reason for returning to the site of profound trauma:

> If they would pay me a million dollars, literally, I wouldn't want to go back to the place where I was born because all I remember is hatred, murderers, people trying to kill me. They were like

people turned into animals. And I do not want to step on that ground where I was born. And I really would never want to go back there. Because all I remember is horror, killings, and bloodshed.[56]

LEARNED SILENCE

Most Holocaust children were instructed to remain quiet while in hiding, a constraint that reinforced the segregation of their early memories of trauma. Prohibited from speaking, these children could not use language to interpret and assimilate events. Frieda J. was still a young child even when she was transported to Bergen-Belsen near the end of the war. She says, "[We learned] very quickly to be as invisible as one could be. And as a child, you are fairly close to the ground so you learn to hide very quickly and not to make too many obvious remarks, to be quiet for hours on end. You learn not to speak."[57]

Verbal summarizing of one's personal events is important in the construction of a continuous stream of remembered events, and without such practice, memories can remain disjointed. In their study of the development of autobiographical memory, Robin Fivush, Catherine Haden, and Elaine Reese document the complex linguistic interactions between mothers and children that draw out the children's memories for personal events. They emphasize the importance of having children speak about their past, and they describe the two functions that this memory talk serves: Children develop skills in recounting memories in language and they learn the value of reminiscing.[58] In stark contrast, Holocaust children do not practice recounting their childhood memories in language. They do not use language to shape their memories and they learn the value of not talking about the past.

At age eight, Karl S. hid in the barracks of a slave labor camp. He explains:

When everyone went to work, including my parents, they took two pieces of furniture . . . they put in the corner of the room, and I was in that corner. They left some food with me and a pail for, in case I had to go, and that's where I was from about seven, eight o'clock in the morning until whatever time they came home. Occasionally someone entered such a barrack with a dog. The dog barked, and I just kept quiet, and that's how I lived arbeitslager, with my parents, for about three quarters of a year or so. . . . The rule was, don't talk. Now that you mention it, virtually, I did no talking for about three years.

The result: After the war, Karl S. never spoke with friends or his parents about the Holocaust, and his past came up only indirectly. At the time of his testimony, Karl admits that he only began talking a little with family in the past year: "So, for thirty years, nothing, complete blank." Though his parents talked with each other, Karl avoided all opportunities to talk, and as he grew up, he did not want to hear. Many years later, Karl discussed his wartime childhood with his wife, but he never gave a detailed account of his experiences.[59]

Zezette L. was transported to Auschwitz in April 1943, where she spent the next two years in daily torment: "*Appell*. Peeling potatoes. Working. Shoving stones, and going to the munition factory." She rarely spoke at Auschwitz, choosing to remain silent. Consequently, she had difficulty speaking afterward. After liberation, she traveled back to Belgium in open cattle cars, eventually reuniting with her great uncle and great aunt. She describes the silent reunion: "And the next thing I knew I was sitting in the living room of this great uncle and great aunt, sitting in a corner, in a chair very much like this, with all these people coming and looking at this strange animal that just had come back and who really didn't want to talk." Zezette's older brother also survived in hiding. She says he is the most important person in her life, and they see each other often. Even so, they both continue their learned silence. "He and I have as yet to speak about the experience," Zezette says. "We never, never, never have spoken."[60]

Menachem S. survived mostly on his own as a young child, while his parents eluded death by performing slave labor at the munitions factory owned by Oskar Schindler. As Menachem grew up in Israel after the war, his parents discouraged talking about the Holocaust. He was told to forget: "You shouldn't be talking about it. Father will get upset. I'll get my nightmares. Mother will cry. So let's pretend it's never been. It's never happened." Until the late 1970s, he did not read "one word" about the Holocaust. He went to no movies. He says, "I was pretending very hard that it never happened to me." After Menachem married and had a family, he continued to avoid talking about the Holocaust with his wife and children, though he never realized that he was doing so. He says his wife knew about his past but, "going into the feelings, and what happened. Never." Menachem suppressed his memories of the war until the 1978 television movie *Holocaust*, which he watched with his family. According to Menachem, the artistic weaknesses and historical inaccuracies of the movie did not diminish its insistence on revealing his memories. He says, "It was a moving experience. Okay? So at one point, by the end of it, we were all crying. (He pauses.) And my nine-year-old daughter said to me, 'Hey Daddy, you're crying.'" More than thirty years after the war, with his daughter's simple observation, Menachem began to talk about his memories of the Holocaust for the first time.[61]

The necessity of remaining silent stays with many child survivors well into adulthood, with some expressing their memory much later in their lives and others remaining quiet all their lives. Some child survivors, released from their learned and imposed silence, believe the responsibility of remembering now falls most heavily on them. Frieda J. explains her slow metamorphosis from learned silence to speaking her memories, from the denial of reminiscing to the giving of testimony:

> What you're looking at, of course, is a transition. . . . It's really not a question of remembering, it's a question of *talking*. . . . I would not for a long time discuss it. . . . My aunt and uncle and I were reunited. We lived in Belgium, in Brussels, for a number of years, and I remember that any time the adults began to reminisce and try to compare notes and try to find out who might have done what, I would leave the room. And this carried me and followed me to America. And it was a very long time before I really came to grips with the fact that it did happen. And it happened to me, and I had to face it. But it really was not until I was an adult . . . that it began to dawn on me that if people, the few of us in my age bracket who had memories, who knew, who could remember, who could reconstruct, that if we didn't openly and avowedly discuss what our life was like and what it——, what took place, that it would too soon be forgotten. And it was sort of a dawning, a realization, that it was a duty to bring it up, to talk about it, to try to remember, to try to reconstruct and pass it on. Because after us, there is no more.[62]

CHANGING FOCUS

Clearly, witnesses who were children during the Holocaust were younger on average than other witnesses when they came to give testimony at the Fortunoff Archive. Their relative youth should be noted, but so should the influential characteristics associated with it. Most of the witnesses who are child survivors have spent most of their lives in the United States. They speak English with more fluidity than older witnesses and are more familiar and comfortable with popular culture in this country—including an increased awareness of the theories and findings of clinical psychology. Witnesses who are child survivors are adept at self-analysis and receptive to insights from contemporary psychology. They are also intensely interested in the influence of early traumatic memories, in part because their memories possess intriguing incompleteness and in part because memory's effects remained hidden from their view for many years—only to emerge unexpectedly later in life.

One focus of these witnesses is on the initial formation of their early memories of trauma and on the changes they experienced in interpreting the horrors of their early childhood. This focus parallels the recurring observations of older survivors about the early shock of trying to understand atrocity. All of these observations—from child survivors and older survivors—fit together within the superordinate theme of *apprehending atrocity*. Retrospectively, these witnesses depict what it was like to encounter unprecedented atrocity and to live through an extended series of horrors. They analyze their own memories, working back in time to capture their initial impressions and their later adaptation. Their observations coalesced into identifiable categories, which I present in the following chapter. This chapter analyzes the encoding of atrocity—the witnesses' attempts to understand the experience of a prolonged trauma.

NOTES

1. This chapter is based on the testimony of thirty-two witnesses who were between infancy and eight years old at the beginning of World War II. In addition, twenty-four witnesses who were older children (between the ages of nine and fifteen) were studied for comparison.

2. Tape HVT-115, testimony of Frania R., 1979.

3. Tape HVT-2741, testimony of David K., 1994; Tape HVT-3380, Henry S., 1996; Tape HVT-1892, Meir V., 1994; Tape HVT-2609, Esther W., 1994.

4. Tape HVT-1315, testimony of Clemens L., 1990.

5. Tape HVT-191, testimony of Frieda J., 1980.

6. Tape HVT-3132, testimony of Nadia R., 1995.

7. Tape HVT-152, testimony of Menachem S., 1979.

8. Tape HVT-641 and Tape HVT-1091, testimony of Martin S., 1986, 1988. The testimony of Martin S. and other child survivors presents a dilemma for clinical psychologists: Should therapists adopt conventional strategies to promote fuller integration of the Holocaust survivor or should they encourage the different selves to remain separate?

9. Tape HVT-1091, testimony of Martin S., 1988.

10. Tape HVT-1637, testimony of Nat G., 1991.

11. Tape HVT-869, testimony of Josephine B., 1992.

12. Tape HVT-1091, testimony of Martin S., 1988; Tape HVT-173, Karl S., 1980.

13. Tape HVT-623, testimony of Sabina S., 1985; Tape HVT-869, Josephine B., 1992; Tape HVT-1315, Clemens L., 1990; Tape HVT-173, Karl S., 1980.

14. Tape HVT-641, testimony of Martin S., 1986.

15. Tape HVT-318, testimony of Robert K., 1984; Tape HVT-173, testimony of Karl S., 1980.

16. Tape HVT-152, testimony of Menachem S., 1979.

17. Tape HVT-2148, testimony of Hilda S., 1993.

18. Tape HVT-976, testimony of Renee G., 1988.

19. Tape HVT-48, testimony of Paul D., 1980; Tape HVT-1315, Clemens L., 1990.

20. Tape HVT-2148, testimony of Hilda S., 1993.

21. Tape HVT-1537, testimony of Jacqueline R., 1991.

22. Tape HVT-173, testimony of Karl S., 1980; Tape HVT-318, Robert K., 1984.

23. Tape HVT-2148, testimony of Hilda S., 1993; Tape HVT-318, Robert K., 1984.

24. David P. Boder, *I Did Not Interview the Dead* (Urbana, Ill.: University of Illinois Press, 1949).

25. Nechama Tec, "A Historical Perspective: Tracing the History of the Hidden-Child Experience," in *The Hidden Children*, by Jane Marks (New York: Fawcett Columbine, 1993), 273–291. It should be noted that there is not a definitive finding on the exact number of children killed. Research conducted by a number of scholars places the figure between one million and one and a half million.

26. Tape HVT-136, testimony of Hanna G., 1982.

27. Sarah Boxer, "Giving Memory Its Due in an Age of License," *New York Times*, 28 October 1998, B1. Shlomo Breznitz is quoted in this article.

28. Tape HVT-933, testimony of Annette G., 1987.

29. For portions of her testimony, Annette presents the perspective of a child. She portrays her father as a bad man, repeatedly blaming him for not saving her twin brother. She does not recognize his victimization, which included internment in several concentration camps and slave-labor camps, followed by a death march to Stutthof. Annette's appearance also suggests a younger self. For the videotaped testimony, Annette has her hair fashioned in a pony tail and she wears a young person's Navy midi blouse.

30. Tape HVT-201, Donald W. in the testimony of Klara A. and Donald W., 1980.

31. Tape HVT-623, testimony of Sabina S., 1985.

32. Tape HVT-48, testimony of Paul D., 1980.

33. Tape HVT-46, testimony of Dori L., 1980.

34. Tape HVT-173, testimony of Karl S., 1980.

35. Hana Hoffman-Fischel describes these games in Inge Deutschkron's book *Kinder in Ghettos und Lagern: Ihrer war die Hölle* (Cologne: Mohn, 1965), 54–55. This excerpt was translated from the original German. Note that the initial reference in English to this information is in the 1983 book by Sarah Moskovitz, *Love Despite Hate* (New York: Schocken Books).

36. Tape HVT-139, testimony of Rachel G., 1980.

37. Tape HVT-1537, testimony of Jacqueline R., 1991.

38. Tape HVT-1315, testimony of Clemens L., 1990.

39. David B. Pillemer, *Momentous Events, Vivid Memories* (Cambridge, Mass.: Harvard University Press, 1998), 63–98.

40. Tape HVT-107, testimony of Edith P., 1980; Tape HVT-974, Edith P., 1988.

41. Tape HVT-59, testimony of Dori K., 1979.

42. Tape HVT-969, testimony of Dori K. 1988.

43. The accuracy of Holocaust testimony from child survivors can be assessed by comparing their testimony with that of older witnesses who were present, such as the testimony of surviving parents.

44. Tape HVT-1315, testimony of Clemens L., 1990.

45. Tape HVT-59 and Tape HVT-969, testimony of Dori K., 1979, 1988.

46. Robert Kraft, "Revealing Mistakes in Personal Memory" (paper presented at the annual meeting of the Psychonomic Society, New Orleans, November 2000).

47. Tape HVT-1315, testimony of Clemens L., 1990.

48. Tape HVT-191, testimony of Frieda J., 1980.

49. Tape HVT-92, testimony of Chana B., 1980.

50. Tape HVT-3132, testimony of Nadia R., 1995.

51. Tape HVT-1315, testimony of Clemens L., 1990.

52. Tape HVT-2148, testimony of Hilda S., 1993.

53. Tape HVT-5, testimony of Renee G., 1980.

54. Tape HVT-976, testimony of Renee G., 1988.

55. Tape HVT-5, testimony of Renee G., 1980.

56. Tape HVT-623, testimony of Sabina S., 1985.

57. Tape HVT-191, testimony of Frieda J., 1980.

58. Robyn Fivush, Catherine Haden, and Elaine Reese, "Remembering, Recounting, and Reminiscing: The Development of Autobiographical Memory in Social Context," *Remembering Our Past: Studies in Autobiographical Memory*, edited by David C. Rubin (New York: Cambridge University Press, 1995), 341–359.

59. Tape HVT-173, testimony of Karl S., 1980.

60. Tape HVT-100, testimony of Zezette L., 1980. *Appell* refers to the prisoners lining up at attention to be counted every day, an excruciating procedure that could take hours to complete.

61. Tape HVT-152, testimony of Menachem S., 1979.

62. Tape HVT-191, testimony of Frieda J., 1980.

CHAPTER 4

APPREHENDING ATROCITY: LEVELS OF AWARENESS DURING PROLONGED TRAUMA

In his testimony, Claude Lanzmann states that during the eleven years of filming *Shoah*, he was motivated not by concepts, but by "obsessions," and that a central motivating obsession was with the victim's *first encounter* with the specific horrors of the Holocaust: "The first shock. The first hour of the Jews in the camp, in Treblinka, the first minutes."[1] In videotaped testimony at the Fortunoff Archive, many witnesses speak of such encounters with horror. They recall in detail their thought processes during particular acts of cruelty and violence. They record vivid accounts of their torment, exposing an anguished composite of perceptions, thoughts, and emotions. The testimony of these witnesses makes it possible to characterize the distinctive psychological responses to atrocity—the initial apprehension of the horrors as well as later adaptation to extended atrocity. Analysis of this testimony retrospectively reveals the process of *encoding* and provides a way of knowing how the assimilation of traumatic events translates into the indelible characteristics of traumatic memory.[2]

Holocaust testimony reveals that adaptation to extended atrocity moves through four stages. In the first stage, the initial exposure to unprecedented cruelty leaves people bereft of understanding, unable to apply prior learning and unable to comprehend. Reflective thought disappears; emotion and response disconnect. Contact between on-going events and existing knowledge breaks apart, resulting in un-guided perception of the events. Those who are victimized come to know the specific horrors through isolated glimpses, with fragmented perception of an unbelievable reality proceeding through a subversion of Martin Buber's epistemology—in fleeting moments of painful clar-ity—ultimately creating memories that are sensory and relivable in the form of smells, sounds, scenes, emotions, and physiological sen-sations.

When describing her arrival at Auschwitz, Jolly Z. tries to instruct the listener:

> I think that people who do these interviews or people who deal with the Holocaust often don't realize that when these things actually happen, you don't think, you just act. Your feelings, the reactions, come later. When the selection took place, you prob-ably just think, which way did he say to go, so I'll go right or left. There are no emotions. There is no observing reaction. There's just action. The rest comes later.[3]

During the onset of severe trauma, numbness sets in—a numbness so pervasive that victims often feel drugged or in a trance. Attention immediately constricts, becoming myopic and desultory, confining it-self to one or two details, sometimes narrowing so much that there is little memory at all of the initial events. During the early stage of trauma, people are unable to gather general, orienting information. The focused glimpses of atrocity do not fit together into a larger understanding of events. In the altered reality of trauma, people ex-perience a radically distorted sense of time—usually slowed, but sometimes accelerated. Within this temporal distortion, people can experience a separation of the self from the ongoing events, with some experiencing *dissociation*.

After living through the early events of atrocity, those who have been victimized move into a second stage of adaptation. In this stage, people may use prior knowledge in an effort to assimilate the horrible events, in some cases overriding their perceptions, with a resulting *denial of perception* or the holding of conflicting interpretations of re-ality. Through a process of momentary glimpses, new schemas of atrocity are pieced together, and there are attempts to organize the unrecognizable. If people manage to survive for a time, they move into a third stage of adaptation to atrocity, accepting the malignant conditions that engulf them and applying primitive schemas for survival. In this third stage, when people rely on primitive survival schemas, they report a strong sense of being nonhuman, animal-like. Eventually, toward the end of this stage, in order to cope with unrelenting mortal threat and routine atrocity, people partially adapt, leading to an exclusive focus on survival that results in long-term emotional numbing. With continued exposure to horror, those who manage to elude death can move into a fourth stage of adaptation. After the destruction of fundamental assumptions of normal life, after numbed acceptance of chronic atrocity, people form new schemas that allow them to apprehend their alien world. The struggle to cope with extreme deprivations and daily terror ultimately leads to a fuller awareness of the unprecedented horrors and to the reemergence of cognitive initiative.

Before presenting the analysis of oral testimony, it would be useful to outline the physiology of extreme trauma and memory. During the past decade, neuropsychological research has identified palpable physiological responses that are associated with the formation of memories during the onset of extreme trauma. In particular, the research of Paul E. Gold, Bessel A. van der Kolk, James L. McGaugh, Sven-Åke Christianson, and Joseph E. LeDoux and his colleagues has elucidated the physiology of trauma and memory, documenting dramatic increases in the level of stress hormones that may fundamentally alter the psychobiology of memory.[4] Specifically, the brain responds to increased physical and psychological stress by releasing norepinephrine from the locus ceruleus and adrenocorticotropin hormone (ACTH) from the anterior pituitary gland, activating a complex of reactions. Peripherally, the sympathetic nerves secrete norepinephrine, the adrenal medulla secretes epinephrine (adrenaline), and the adrenal cortex releases glucocorticoids. These reactions help human beings concentrate energy during intense short-term stress.

The influence of norepinephrine on integration of memory may follow an inverted-U function: Low levels do not enhance memory, moderately high levels strengthen the integration of memory, and excessively high levels create fragmentation. The focus of this process is on the relationship between two critical structures in the limbic system: the hippocampus and the amygdala. Hippocampal functioning is necessary to coordinate the formation of explicit, coherent memories, and the amygdala mediates the evaluation of emotion in incoming information. Excessive stimulation of the amygdala interferes with this integrative function of the hippocampus and leads to perceptual and emotional memories that are not assimilated into the overall memory system, creating vivid and fragmented emotional memories that can be indelible. These neurophysiological findings can be summarized in general cognitive terms: Traumatic stress *impairs* the formation of integrated narrative memory and *strengthens* the vividness and endurance of fragmented perceptual and emotional memories.[5]

By analyzing firsthand accounts of the experience of atrocity and by placing these descriptions in the context of physiological findings, we can more fully understand the nature of traumatic memory itself, ultimately resolving stubborn contradictions that currently exist in the relationship between trauma and memory. One such contradiction is that terrifying events can be remembered with exquisite and painful vividness—and usually are—or these events may not be remembered at all. Why this difference? Moreover, a person subjected to atrocity can experience extreme emotion—or the absence of emotion, and it is difficult to predict which response will occur. Both meanings of the word "petrify" accurately convey the victim's emotional state during extreme trauma: to paralyze with terror and to convert organic matter into a stony replica.

More broadly, as we improve our understanding of the experience of extended atrocity, we can educate people more effectively about the Holocaust. By learning how survivors of the Holocaust perceived the horrors, we can teach more than the impossible facts and the historical summaries. Equipped with the revelations of Holocaust testimony, we can transform the naiveté that often generates unintentionally cruel questions—questions about the accuracy of memories, about the lack of resistance, about the failure to anticipate the impending disaster. (How could such things happen? Why did you not fight back? Why did so many people willingly walk to the gas chamber? How could you *not* know what was going on? Why not do *something*?) Though such questions are less frequent today than a decade ago, those who first learn about the Holocaust will invariably ask.[6]

For people first learning about the Holocaust, the profound cruelty and suffering described by the witnesses can seem more farfetched than claims of being abducted by aliens from outer space. Students of the Holocaust find it difficult to understand the concentric circles of absolute betrayal, from neighbors, to friends, to teachers, moving inexorably to local leaders, governments, and the international community. People hear the word, "hunger," but cannot fully understand the relentless gnawing pain from early morning until late at night, cannot assimilate the violation of unquestioned societal rules or the disintegration of family bonds, cannot anticipate the bodily state that led hundreds of starving people to die from eating too much too soon after liberation. In a later section of this chapter, witnesses discuss their experience of hunger within the context of the engulfing trauma. In general, a more detailed understanding of the thoughts of the people who lived through the horrors—first thoughts and later thoughts—will intensify and particularize our strategies for teaching others about the Holocaust.

In fact, the witnesses themselves state that before directly experiencing the unprecedented horrors, they were not able to assimilate circumstantial evidence or secondhand information. Lorna B. tells how the clothing from those who were murdered at Auschwitz or Chelmno was sent back to her ghetto, with notes in the pockets, describing the camps. But, she says, no one believed that they were "chlorinating people." Parents recognized the clothes of their own children, but still could not believe that their children were dead.[7]

Just before describing his transport to Auschwitz, Walter S. explains that he had heard stories about the Nazis gassing people, yet he did not connect the description of Auschwitz with his own experiences of cruelty and deprivation.[8] Like Cassandra, those who passed on their predictions of destruction were not believed. People chose more likely explanations for the unreal facts, explanations that conformed to schemas constructed from familiar events that occurred before the war. David K. recounts such an incident:

Once we were walking through the woods, and we met a ranger, a uniformed ranger that was probably watching for fires. And he told us that he used to be a ranger in the woods in Sobibor. And he said transports of Jews are brought into Sobibor and they are being killed. And he told this to us. And *we* said, "Ah, anti-Semite, he wants to frighten us." Didn't believe it. We didn't believe it.

Later, during the transport to Auschwitz, when the train stopped, David asked a Polish railroad man where they were going. The man answered: "To the chimney." And when David asked what he meant when he said "to the chimney," the man answered, "Many trains coming here. All go in, and that's it. To the chimney." David explains how he reacted to these comments:

> We tried not to understand. We tried to use the same explanation as with that guy who was in Sobibor. We didn't really believe him. We figured, we bunch of Jews, he wants to frighten them. That's all. I can tell now, fifty years later, as far as I remember this was the total attitude. Nobody knew what was going on in Auschwitz. Absolutely nobody. Even if we knew, we wouldn't want to believe it.[9]

David's prior knowledge of anti-Semitism, gained through past experience, overruled the truth of the man's statements.

Holocaust testimony provides a unique retrospective view of the direct perceptions of those who have undergone extreme trauma. Though the testimony presents spontaneous recall of personally experienced events, witnesses describe the experience of atrocity in strikingly similar ways, with the exact wording repeated from one witness to another. This chapter characterizes the testimony of these witnesses.

STAGE 1: NUMBNESS AND DISTORTION

Most Holocaust survivors who discuss their understanding of the horrors state clearly that they were "numb."[10] They also use a variety of phrases to illustrate this state of numbness: "in a trance," "like a piece of wood," "frosted over," "frozen," "like a stone," "hibernating," "like a vegetable," "like robots," "in a catatonic state."

After leaving the transport at Auschwitz, Eva L. was immediately separated from her mother. At first Eva really believed she would see her mother again. Then she witnessed the chimneys and "the burning," and the guards told her that her mother had been killed. Eva depicts the events:

> We just couldn't believe that such things—it was like a nightmare, like a dream, like a nightmare. We couldn't believe that everything was happening so fast. And then, we just didn't feel anything, didn't feel anything. Was just like in a trance. I just

didn't feel anything. They pushed me into a bath, they stripped me, they shaved my hair. They took—stripped me of my clothes. They just gave me a little rag, just a little blouse that covered my front. The back was ripped. The rest was naked. And I was just pushed, like in a trance, I didn't care.[11]

Survival demanded the shutting down of emotional response. Sabina S. describes being surrounded by German soldiers, then walking with other Jews to a field that held a large mass grave. While walking, Sabina managed to maneuver her way to the back of the group, then ran into the woods and escaped. In her testimony, she describes her state of mind during the ordeal: "I felt numb. It was unbelievable. . . . At that moment all you think is how . . . to survive. How to escape. All you want is to try to remain alive." Irene W. wonders out loud about her sanity at Auschwitz: "Why weren't we screaming maniacs at that point, those of us who saw it daily?" She says, the "enormous roar of screams" became "the routine of the day," with the flames from the chimneys lighting the forest, exposing the horrors even at night. After reflecting on how she could have existed so unemotionally for six long months, Irene says simply, "The imperative was to survive."[12]

Meir V. subsisted in the Vilna Ghetto until it was liquidated in September 1943. He then went to Kaiserwald, followed by a succession of camps, including Stutthof, Buchenwald, and Terezin. He describes his emotional state throughout:

There was one thing I have to say, that throughout my experience then, I don't remember feeling fear, but————. And this is perhaps true for others, too. What I remember feeling is *numbness*. You feel numb. You don't know what goes on. You just try to beat the odds every single moment to see how you can get out of this mess. But you actually become numb.

Meir offers a theory: "Some animals when they are attacked by a predator, they freeze up, they don't offer resistance. And I have a feeling that that's exactly what happened with people at that time. You just deal with what *is*. You cannot change anymore what is imposed on you."[13]

The numbness was so alien and so pervasive that some survivors say they were given drugs. Adele W. describes her arrival at Auschwitz:

We were so doped up. We saw————. You know what we saw
and smelled, the way that the smoke—the smell from it—I can't
explain it to you. And we saw the flame. They gave us dope, I
mean, there is nothing, no question about it. But, to make us
blind, they couldn't make us blind. We saw it, and yet it didn't
bother us.[14]

Along with other older teenagers, Nina S. was sent to Birkenau
after losing her mother during the initial selection at Auschwitz. Nina
asserts, "They gave us tranquilizers because the next day nobody was
crying." She explains: "Suddenly we became all calm at the same time.
They gave us some soup. And everybody said there was something
in it because we became like different people. The next day nobody
missed their parents. Nobody was crying."[15]

The persistent numbness caused by constant horror showed itself
clearly at liberation. After struggling to live through the camps, some
survivors expected to feel joy or elation when liberated, but that expectation often could not override their adaptive numbness. In fact,
liberation only highlighted the survivors' blunted emotional state.
Emina N. specifically refers to feeling drugged at liberation:

It was a day before the liberation. . . . I was walking through the
dead [bodies]. I wanted to go to the toilet. I have to walk
through all the piles of dead people and I don't believe that I
had any feelings. It didn't bother me at all. I didn't————. Either way, like it would be some dirt or something, I walked away.
I think it was either something wrong with me, with us, with
everybody, or maybe they gave us something, like medication,
or something that you were just numb. And, in fact, when I was
liberated, I didn't even want to go out. I was there. I still didn't
believe it.[16]

Daniel F. managed to elude death at Auschwitz, while his entire
family perished. He describes liberation: "It really didn't make any
difference. So we are liberated, so what? I didn't have the strength. I
didn't have the will at that point really, to want to live. . . . I didn't
feel anything. I didn't even feel the elation that I thought I was going
to feel." Leon W. agrees: "I don't think I was happy. . . . I don't think
we had any feelings for dancing or joy or smiling." Celia K. sum-

marizes her emotional state just after liberation: "There weren't any emotions at all. You couldn't hate. You couldn't feel."[17]

Chana F. describes the quick steps to long-term numbness:

> If you ask people about feelings, I ask myself in the beginning the same thing. The first ordinance was tragic: we cried, we pulled our hair, what's going to be. The second was bad. The third you take already, and then it just comes to you. . . . We were numb. We were already numb. We were numb the five years. There were no feelings.[18]

Survivors can remain numb long after the horrors end, experiencing strong emotion only after many years have passed. Clemens L. describes an image from early childhood, just before he went into hiding. While playing with other children in a courtyard near his apartment, the owner of the apartment building came over to him and demanded that he pull down his pants. Clemens complied, and the owner saw he was circumcised. Clemens then told his mother about the incident, and they quickly escaped. Clemens goes on to describe his emotions then and now. Blunted by adaptive numbness, emotions emerged much later in life:

> It seems like I don't remember the feelings at the time. I think when I speak about those images, I have———. I'm speaking from the point of view of a stunned person. I have feelings *now* of course. . . . I do have very strong feelings about it. And I think I guess I have more feelings about it than I *thought* I did.[19]

Learned numbness can follow survivors throughout their lives. Alina Z. lived through the Warsaw Ghetto, survived the ghetto uprising, then suffered through two months in Birkenau, where she was five months pregnant, and three months of hard labor and beatings at Majdanek. It was in a concentration camp, under horrible conditions, that Alina gave birth to a son. The midwife who helped deliver the boy then disposed of him. In testimony given nearly fifty years after the war, she then describes her present emotional state: "I'm like a *stone*. Sometimes I feel I am a stone inside me."[20]

Within the containment of horror, pervasive numbness can create a distorted sense of time. Edith P. is asked how long her transport to Auschwitz lasted, and she replies, "I don't know. Maybe an eternity. Maybe only two days. Maybe only twenty-four hours. Maybe just six hours. I do not know. But it seemed an eternity."[21] In strikingly similar words, Zezette L. describes the duration of her train transport to Auschwitz: "If I told you days, I don't know. I really don't remember . . . but I do remember that if I would tell you an eternity, that would probably be the truest answer." Zezette explains:

> I believe very much that one's mind can become so immobilized by terror that you become like robots. I think that we were robots and not much more than that. That we were so terrorized that we couldn't think, or didn't want to think. . . . There is an element of fear that can absolutely immobilize you. And I think that's what happened to all of us.[22]

The numbness during atrocity and the resulting temporal distortion can be accompanied by a distinct splitting of the self or *dissociation*—a dual perception of self as both subject and object. Sally H. describes the experience of detaching from her tormented self within the train transport to Skarzysko: "I always thought, after a while I don't know if I was getting lightheaded or something, I always thought I'm sitting on the fence, looking in. It just couldn't be *me* in there." In a second interview nine years later, Sally again talks about perceiving as if she were outside herself on the train transport: "It wasn't *me* there. I was just out there watching, looking. . . . It wasn't me who goes through all that—because it's impossible. I was sitting out there—looking in."[23]

Bessie K. describes the disintegration of self during the horror of losing her young child. As Bessie was transported from the ghetto in Kovno to a concentration camp in Estonia, her baby was taken from her. She details the shock and dissociation:

> As I look back, I think that for a while I was in a daze. I didn't know what was happening, actually. I saw they [were] taking away the men separate, the children separate, and the women separate. So, I had the baby, and I took the coats what I had with the bundles, and I wrapped around the baby and I put it on my left side because I saw the Germans were saying "left and right." And I went through with the baby. But the baby was short of breath, started to choke, to choke, it started to cry. So the German called me back. He says "What do you have there?"

in German. Now, I didn't know what to do because everything was so fast. Everything happened so suddenly. I wasn't prepared for it. To look back, the experience, was I think I was numb. Or something happened to me, I don't know. But I wasn't *there* even. And he stretched out his arms I should hand him over the bundle. And I hand him over the bundle. And this was the last time I had the bundle with me.

Bessie then describes the train transport:

I don't know how long we were going in the trains, but to me it was a lifetime. I think, the way I felt is: I was born on the train and I died on the train, because everything was such a mix-up. Everything was so————. It was hard to take it. (She pauses.) And I actually didn't know why I was there, on the train and what was happening to us. (She becomes animated.) I wasn't even alive! I wasn't even alive. I don't know if it was by my own doing, or it was done—or how, but I wasn't there.

As a result of this dissociative horror, Bessie K. repressed the memory of losing her child.[24] She was taken from the camp in Estonia, detained in a field for two weeks with other inmates, then placed on a ship to Stutthof in Danzig. In Stutthof, Bessie happened to see the doctor who operated on her in the ghetto following the birth of her baby. She describes their meeting:

And when she saw me there, she was so happy to see me. Right away she said, "What happened—where's the baby? What happened to the baby?" And right there I said, "What baby?" (Bessie pauses.) I said to the doctor, "What baby? I didn't have a baby. I don't know of any baby." *That's* what it did to me. (She points to her head with her index finger.)[25]

In describing her arrival at Auschwitz, Chana B. exemplifies the different *distortions of attention* that can occur during the onset of severe trauma, distortions that ultimately direct one's memory of the events. Initially, attention narrowed, sometimes focusing tightly on one central detail, ignoring all other information. Chana says, "I remember we were in a line, my mother, my two brothers, my grandmother. And there was an officer, a German officer, extremely handsome, extremely well-dressed, and he just pointed at me, and (she gestures, waving her finger) I don't remember. I just remember I went in the direction of the pointing." Attention can also be drawn uncontrollably to a peripheral detail. After being selected not to die immediately at Auschwitz, Chana and others were ordered to undress completely. They were shaved, sprayed with harsh chemicals, then ordered to dip their shoes in disinfectant. As Chana relates this sequence of events, she appears to be reading from a visual image: "I remember the dark blue shoes. And I remember standing there with pins in my hand. Hair pins, and no hair, and the shoes dripping the blue color."

The shock of atrocity can pinch attention and constrict encoding to such an extent that very little memory may result. Chana waited in a local concentration camp before being deported to Auschwitz. She describes how little she remembers of the deportation:

> And then names were called out. We just———. I remember marching to the train station. I don't remember the box car. I just read about it later. I know I was in a box car to go to Auschwitz . . . [but] I only remember looking at the countryside. . . . I don't remember what I ate. I don't remember what I did. All I remember, looking out through the—(She draws a narrow rectangle in the air with both hands) barbed windows and looking at the beautiful countryside.

Many years after the war, Chana read a published account describing this transport and determined it took a full week—though she remembers little of that week.

Chana's memory of arriving at Auschwitz reveals glimpses of horror that are clear but isolated, and not integrated into a coherent understanding: "First we just noticed like different things. Like the tall barbed wire, with the outlook, with the posts. The people, the shaved people with all kind of funny clothes. . . . I just noticed different things. I didn't put them together."[26] The testimony of Daniel F. describes a similar experience. Daniel details his perceptions at the railroad siding entering Auschwitz, his testimony revealing vivid and disjointed odors, sounds, and visual images:

> Unbelievable smell of burning something or other, feathers, that later, realized was something else. . . . The closing of the door,

that metallic click of the door being locked . . . Move! Get out! Form lines of five, in columns . . . German soldiers and their submachine guns on the perimeter. The tremendous smell. The fences . . . then somewhere along the line, I saw chimneys. But all this came in fleeting moments.[27]

STAGE 2: DENYING PERCEPTION

In the second stage of adapting to atrocity, knowledge may actually override perception of worldly events—to the extent that the senses themselves are not believed. Cognitive psychologists speak of "the curse of perception" when describing our tendency to disregard institutional knowledge that conflicts with direct perception of the world. (For instance, young children insist the Earth is flat because it looks flat.) Within the unearthly world of the Nazi camps, the curse of perception took on an inverted meaning: a lifetime of learning overruled the perception of an unbelievable reality. In describing the deadly torture of living through Bergen-Belsen, Renee H. elaborates on her confusion: "I think that one of the things that . . . I have suffered from is that I did not know what was going on, so that I was able to imagine things which may not have been true, so that often my sense of what *really* was going on got lost in what I *thought* was going on." Chaim E. summarizes: "You were like in a dream really. It's hard to believe. You have to force yourself to believe what you see."[28]

Aaron S. provides a specific example:

When we arrived [at Auschwitz], there were Russian prisoners. And I'll never forget the first scene I saw. This truckload of bread came in and the Russian prisoners saw the bread. They were so hungry. They were wild. . . . And two SS were sitting on the edge of the truck and machine gunned them down as they ran for the bread. I saw this. . . . They kept coming and they kept machine gunning them down. We looked at it, we couldn't *believe this*. We were young. I mean, we cannot believe what we *saw*.[29]

Violet S. tells of Bergen-Belsen, of starving people pulling carts overloaded with corpses to be taken to mass graves, "poor miserable skel-

etons" trying to pick up the dead bodies piled so high on the carts
that they kept falling to the ground:

> Those who pulled the carts looked like they [were] going to be
> next. And what I have seen there, I don't want to—I didn't want
> to believe. But I actually saw cannibalism. I have, with my eyes.
> There was a male camp. The women and men were separately
> there. We passed by a male camp and . . . when I saw it, I wasn't
> sure. I———. You see it and you don't want to believe. And
> you don't want to accept it. But I know that's what was taking
> place.[30]

It is not the case that the perception was merely denied or set aside
as something too unbearable to think about. The horrors were perceived, and there was a distant awareness of them, but even in the
alien world of the concentration camp, some events were so far re-
moved from expectation and prior perceptions that their existence
was not perceived as real. This perceptual doubt can ultimately lead
to memories that are now experienced as the ugly residue of haunting
nightmares and not as images of real events.

In a perversely similar way, the perceptions of Frieda J. denied the
reality of liberation. For Frieda, the dominant schemas for understanding the world were those she learned as a young child trying to
survive the horrors of Bergen-Belsen. Her belief system only accom-
modated the experience of deprivation, terror, and captivity, which
then blocked her comprehension of the unprecedented events at liberation:

> I remember not believing. I remember that we ran when peo-
> ple———, when we were told that the British were in the camp
> and that we were free. I remember thinking, Oh, it's just another
> trick. They've just found other uniforms. This is not, this is not
> real. Because freedom was no longer anything I could under-
> stand.[31]

When the results of specific atrocities *were* perceived and registered, survivors did not assemble their observations into a larger interpretation of the horrors. After one night in Auschwitz, Eva B.
discovered that most of the women on her transport were dead. She
says, "In the morning we were told . . . that everybody who was not

in that one room with us was dead. Gassed, they told us. . . . I mean, it was just too big and too shocking to absorb. . . . It was too monstrous, too big." Frieda J. describes events at Bergen-Belsen just after liberation. "The true horror . . . we *knew* about, and of course we *saw*. But the *enormity* of it was not really registered in our conscious minds until the British began to open up a lot of the barracks that had been closed. And . . . we saw the piles of bodies and arms and legs and skulls."[32]

Profound confusion characterized this transitional stage of adaptation to atrocity: Old schemas coexisted with partially formed schemas of the alien world of the ghettos and camps. Many people held dual beliefs, simultaneously believing and not believing.[33] Eva V. lived in Oradea Mare, Romania, before the war. As a young person, she observed as her parents helped refugees find safer areas to hide. Though her family was in the midst of helping people escape the horrors of Nazi deportations, she explains their inability to comprehend:

We didn't believe. Between '40 and '44, all the Polish Jews who were coming. And the Czech Jews who were coming. And from all [over]. We saw the Italian Jews in the wagons, taking them, and we didn't believe that *we* will be taken. It was already '43, '44, and we heard all the time the "Voice of America," and we didn't believe . . . We *heard* but we didn't *heard exactly*.[34]

STAGE 3: FOCUSING ON SURVIVAL

In the third stage of adaptation, people applied primitive survival schemas in order to stay alive in their progressively deprived world. As they began to adapt to the horrendous conditions, the inexorable struggle to survive violated fundamental schemas about human beings. Witnesses speak in particular about the disintegration of basic concepts of humanity brought about by profound humiliation, moral degradation, and persistent hunger. Witnesses describe the physical disorientation produced by the cruelty of humiliation, especially during selections. Stripped of their clothing, the victimized became bodies to be examined, selected for existence or extermination on the basis of physique. Humiliation consumed the core of one's self, which Edith P. characterizes as, "Such despair, it's so infinite, it pains so. I think that it is a separation, the soul and body."[35]

Violation of fundamental moral principles eroded basic concepts of humanity, further disorienting the victims, a condition described by Renee H. as she witnessed people being loaded onto transports:

In the process, also, there would be a lot of hitting, especially of old people, and of sick people, and children. And shoving, pushing. And these gatherings of people just terrified me. I really————. It was a way of behaving which I could never experience except in—not even in nightmares. I even remember my nightmares as being mild compared to this. But what was terrible is that it was the behavior towards the very people that the Jewish religion says you must have a great deal of kindness— their sick, their old, and their children. And I saw everything being done which was opposed to what I believed in and what I had grown up with.[36]

Persistent hunger relentlessly desecrated fundamental concepts of humanity—a hunger Martin S. describes as, "That wrenching, twisting pain that lived with you on a daily basis. All you could ever think of is to get something to eat." Leon W. says of the Lodz Ghetto, "The only thought in them days was hunger. You wake up in the morning hungry, and you went to sleep hungry. I was hungry for four years." He continues: "I don't know if too many people realize, that when you are hungry, there is nothing else in the world which matters. . . . There was just nothing else in your mind, but hungry."[37]

For those who eluded death in the ghetto and the camps, the primitive survival strategy of searching for and finding food consumed their waking hours. Chana F. elaborates: "This was their scheme, to make animals of us. Our only dream was a piece of bread. Went to bed at night dreaming about a piece of bread. You got up in the morning dreaming of bread. You would do anything for a piece of bread. A piece of bread was your whole life." Edith P. summarizes Auschwitz: "The only thing you can think of is you are hungry." She concludes, "Hunger pains like nothing on Earth."[38]

Witnesses repeatedly convey the message of Elie Weisel, that a human being at Auschwitz was "a starved stomach," and then they tell of the moral implications. Profound hunger went beyond physical suffering to violate basic relations within the family. Continued deprivation not only destroyed existing schemas of daily events but fundamental moral principles as well. Leon W. describes how hunger broke families apart, despoiling basic rules of family life, that in a few short months, highly intelligent, well-educated people changed in ways unimaginable prior to the hunger. He cites his uncle's family as an example. They would sit in their cramped apartment in the Lodz Ghetto, each one with a separate dish of food that no one else touched, and each one conscientiously concealing the dish from the rest of the family. Leon says, "It gets to the point where you don't mind stealing from your own sister, your own father." He admits that he would slice a piece of his sister's ration in the middle of the night and eat it himself, concluding, "And I can't even imagine myself doing that now."[39]

With numbness to the surrounding horror, with constricted attention, with an exclusive focus on survival and disintegration of basic moral principles, human qualities disappeared and witnesses speak of turning into animals. Eva L. describes the Lodz Ghetto: "Everything was eaten. Not a speck of grass, you could find in the ghetto. Not a bird. Not a cat. Not a dog. Because everything in sight was eaten. People wanted to survive." She explains, "A human being changes into an animal. And an animal lives for survival. And that's what a human being is." Walter S. says, "As time goes on, you get to a point that you don't have the real feeling anymore of a human being. You feel somehow completely different."[40]

In this stage of living through extended atrocity, people accepted the alien world of starvation, betrayal, and inevitable death. Many of those who outlasted the murderous conditions and who escaped execution by gas or bullets, learned to adapt to the unprecedented deprivations. Adaptation to the normality of starvation began in the ghettos, where conditions inexorably worsened over time, and death became routine. In 1940, the Nazis started eliminating sections of the Lodz Ghetto, seizing and deporting people until the ghetto became a kind of concentration camp, which Eva L. describes:

It was like a nightmare. Friends, relatives, just swelling up from hunger. First there was swelling, then they were dying . . . my father, too. He also died from hunger. He swell up like a balloon. (She cries.) And then they dry up, and then they lay like a vegetable. And people just step over them. It comes to a point that people just step over them and they don't care anymore because everybody just cares for themselves.[41]

The description of ghetto life provided by Eva B. is similar: "Old people were dying very rapidly. . . . I watched a woman die while we were having lunch and we kept having lunch . . . because death was such an ordinary occurrence."[42]

One pervasive form of adaptation was to focus on the immediate, shortening one's view to the present moment. In his description of Sobibor, Chaim E. reveals this immediacy:

> It was horrified and horrible. And when you live once with this tension and horrification, if that's the right word, then you live differently. *Your thoughts don't go too far.* In normal life, you think about tomorrow and after tomorrow, another year, next year, a vacation there. And things like that. Here you think on the moment, what it is. What happened now, on the moment. Now is it horrible? You don't think later.[43]

Aladar M. summarizes his perceptions in Birkenau: "I let everything go as it will go. I felt I had no power over anything. If they fed me I was eating. If they didn't feed me, I was dying." Frieda J. describes survival in Bergen-Belsen: "All I can remember is just everyone being mindful of their own existence that day. And would they see the light of another day." Alfred F. depicts a similar view of Bergen-Belsen: "You are concerned about food and resting and making it to the next day. You don't think about many other things."[44]

Survivors of concentration camps describe the unrelenting mortal threat that characterized daily life. Chaim E. summarizes Sobibor: "It was so often a routine, to torture us . . . so, if a day went by through, we were lucky that this day didn't happen anything special." Jolly Z. tries to relate a typical day in Auschwitz: "Actually, it was very routine. And yet how can one use the word 'routine' for a series of tragedies that took place every day?" She reduces the routine to a single sentence: "We were there, waiting to die, hoping to live."[45]

With adaptation to prolonged trauma, numbness remains, giving rise to *detachment*—from others and from oneself. Hanna G. tells of the first three days of Auschwitz when inmates were required to kneel, holding their arms up for long periods of time, beaten with clubs when they faltered. "We had no feelings whatsoever. It didn't matter one way or the other. Just praying for death. Because we saw what's going on in Auschwitz."[46]

In this third stage of adaptation to extended atrocity, people perceived and then accepted the daily horrors. Wolf Z. describes how Amon Goeth and others murdered people daily at Plaszow. Wolf says, "I had the honor [to] bury them. So, as I just mentioned, you get used to it . . . and now I bury them. The next day, it was like nothing." In the slave labor camp of Landsberg, with five hundred people living underground, Pincus S. witnessed evidence of cannibalism. He conveys the detachment and the singular focus on survival in these conditions: "You didn't have any mind at all. You live like— like an animal. You see something, and you don't care about it. Because that was life. You think *one* thing: You want to go out alive if you can. That's all." In describing Bergen-Belsen, Nina S. says, "People were dying right next to another. And it *didn't* bother us. We became so immune to it. That all we wanted was a little potato. When a person is dying, you see a skeleton next to you, but it doesn't bother you anymore because that's what life is all about. People should die from starvation."[47]

Acceptance of the increasingly deprived conditions in the ghettos and the camps was far from a passive state and should not connote resignation. Acceptance in this context was an exhausting daily struggle to cope with the realistic awareness of the unprecedented horror. It was a form of adaptation that required numbing and primitive survival schemas in order to live.

The testimony of Frieda J. shows a witness struggling to make sense of the horrors visited upon her as a child in the ghetto and later in Bergen-Belsen. Her tenacious sincerity and fierce thoughtfulness cannot satisfactorily explain the results of adapting to daily living with depravity. After two hours of revealing testimony, after Frieda J. describes the shock of seeing a shack overflowing with rotting corpses, an interviewer asks a question: What is the effect of that horror on a young mind? Frieda pauses and then answers:

For many years, even after I came to America, it was a long time before I could eat anything that was charcoal broiled. Anything that was cooked outdoors. The idea, visual, of a barbecue, of meat roasted outdoors was—it just took a very long time to get out of the connective devices that came through a young mind. But I don't———. It's very difficult. I find myself stumbling when I explain it because I don't think that any of it can be explained.[48]

Instead of providing a general revelation of how the horrors of Bergen-Belsen affected her as a child, Frieda begins speaking specifically of her aversion to burning meat, revealing a separation between the question and the answer. She quickly recognizes the answer as insufficient, as she recognizes the inadequacy of her words. What remains after such questions is a descriptive lacquer—one that covers the underlying disturbance while also suggesting its shape.

STAGE 4: COEXISTING WITH ATROCITY

In the final stage of adaptation, people learned to cope with chronic atrocity, forming new strategies and resorting to limited tactics for survival. Those prisoners selected for slave labor were able to develop strategies for living through each day. (These were prisoners selected to die slowly, outside the gas chamber, from hard labor, starvation, beatings, and persistent diarrhea.) Many of these prisoners employed local rules of conduct, without needing to assimilate knowledge of larger truths into their belief systems. Alan Z. followed such a rule: "Never go to Chelmno," which he managed to do. He believed quite accurately that the Jews were being murdered at Chelmno but did not consider a widespread, systematic extermination of the Jewish people. While Meir V. stood *appell* at Kaiserwald, he had one rule: Avoid the line of sight of the guards. He recalls specific incidents when violation of this rule led to beatings and death. In one incident he reports, the guards pulled a man out of line and threw him to his death into the feces pit. Many strategies focused on staying out of sight, which Frieda J. summarizes through analogy: "The only parallel I could draw is a very frightened small animal. Because you know that you *don't* know what's going to happen next, but you know *enough* to know that you don't want to be noticed."[49]

As time went on, feeling returned to some camp inmates who survived the beatings, and each survivor struggled to cope. Alina Z. describes her brutal beatings at Majdanek. "You became cripple from the beating. I remember I couldn't walk. Because when they beat me so much I got blue marks and I walk and you move and you *feel* the beating. Couldn't walk. But you manage, you have to manage."[50]

The restoration of initiative was accompanied by internal conflict, and the testimony reflects this conflict. Daily deprivations inexorably leading to painful death can create confusion about the reasons for survival. To this day, survivors continue to struggle with the respective roles played by chance and decision. Alan Z. says, "Looking back I believe strongly, maybe it was fate or luck, that you survive. Not because of special efforts on my part. I did my best. I run away a couple of times. I escaped a few times." The words of Alan Z. show his underlying conflict: "maybe" immediately follows "I believe strongly." Later in his testimony, he describes his survival as "sheer luck," but also says, "I had the will to survive."[51]

Many witnesses discuss actions they took that resulted in their lives being saved, while at the same time emphasizing the necessity of luck.[52] Walter S. makes this clear:

> People have asked me, "How did you actually survive? How did *anyone* survive?" And I can tell you one thing: You could be the strongest man. You could have the strongest ever will to live. You could be very religious and have prayed all your life. It really didn't help. . . . Because the malnutrition and the sufferings you had to go through, somehow, wouldn't help you to survive. You had to have *luck*.[53]

Though most witnesses refer to the fundamental role of chance, within the horror of the camps, they also remember decisions and initiatives—in the form of small acts of disobedience and sabotage. With continued survival in an increasingly depraved world, people took the initiative to disobey. Herbert L., for example, remembers that at Auschwitz inmates were ordered to turn in their boots—but not their shoes. One inmate risked his life by carefully pulling the cuffs of his pants out of his boots and disguising them as shoes, which he did not give up. That was his rebellion.[54]

Though people realized that arbitrariness was the rule, survival demanded that they separate that realization from their efforts to survive. Consequently, they did not fully accept the arbitrariness of life and death. As Walter S. describes, even though there was adaptation to unprecedented daily suffering, this adaptation did not apply to the uncertainty arising from the unpredictable bestowal of life and death. Walter says, "Somehow you get used to hunger and you also get used to pain. The one thing you don't get used to is what's going to happen the next day. You just don't know how the next day goes on."[55] But even within that grim world, many of those who managed to survive were able to initiate. Though there was no certainty about the consequences of their actions, no assurance of guessing correctly, those who were experienced with victimization acted nonetheless. And as initiative returned, some of the adaptive numbness left, accompanied by the reemergence of emotional and physical pain.

Performing slave labor at Skarzysko as a young boy, Martin S. proved his worth by operating four machines by himself, tooling bullets. As he excelled at his labor, he felt guilty because others were doing what they could to hurt the German war effort. So Martin began making defective bullets, cutting them so they would jam in the rifles. One day, after making boxes and boxes of defective bullets, Martin suddenly noticed the camp inspector approaching, and he quickly adjusted the machines, turning out several dozen good bullets. By chance, when the inspector examined Martin's work, he chose one of the properly engineered bullets. Martin describes how he felt: "Oh, the *fear* was unbelievable. I thought I had had it." He continues: "We all went through many terrifying moments." Even within the severe constraints of Skarzysko, many inmates engaged in small acts of sabotage, and not getting caught depended on luck and on the reacquired ability to think quickly.[56]

Toward the end of this final stage, with continued adaptation to prolonged trauma, a more complete comprehension of the malignant world began. Clara L. tells of standing *appell* at Auschwitz, until the guards completed the counting. On the first day, she was not aware of the industrial murder of Jews; on the second, she began to suspect. The next day, she remembers telling her sister about the strong smell of broiled liver and her suspicions about the source of the odor. Slowly, gradually, after suffering through the daily torments of Auschwitz, Clara pieced together the horrors:

> And apparently that was the first sign that we knew that there must be some place away that there are bodies burned. Also there would be in the morning, in the distance, I could clearly see in the distance, that there were chimneys, but we always thought that these are—these belonged to the neighboring cities, manufacturing plants. We never knew that would happen. Then, we slowly found out.[57]

After two years in Auschwitz, Hubert W. had learned: "We knew what's going on. I mean we saw the chimney working. We knew what's behind those fences."[58]

For those in the concentration camps, adaptation to the daily tortures was accompanied by a fuller awareness of the horrors and un-bearable psychic pain. Daniel F. adapted to the conditions at Auschwitz the best he could, struggling each day to stay alive, actively trying to avoid death. He describes the notorious selection at Ausch-witz during Rosh Hashana when 1,400 boys were selected for death. For this selection, a board was nailed to a soccer goal post; those who hit it with their heads passed; those who walked underneath were too short and were selected for death. Daniel F. walked under the board and was sent to the special barracks to await his murder, along with the other inmates selected for death. He describes the waiting: "Hor-rendous. Waiting to be gassed. The most horrible of times. The fear of being selected. Being terrified during the selection is horrible. But once I was selected, there was just nowhere to turn. Your life is going to come to an end."

According to Daniel, after a selection the guards played a cruel game. They would pick people at random from outside and bring those people into the doomed barracks, intending to trade the un-fortunate souls back to family members or friends for alcohol, food, or gold. During Daniel's selection, the guard in his barracks failed to trade away the two people he chose at random and ended up with two extra selectees. Just before they were to be gassed, this guard motioned to Daniel, ordering him out of the barracks. Daniel ran out and escaped the gas chamber.[59]

With considerable exposure to horror, those who managed to elude death adapted to the extreme deprivations and routine terror and developed an understanding of the absolute and unprecedented hor-ror. Three years at Terezin followed by eighteen months of slave labor at Lipa prepared Herbert L. to understand the atrocities that awaited him on his arrival at Auschwitz:

We had seen all these striped uniforms and all these horrible looking creatures in it. And we didn't really understand exactly what the smoking chimneys were. And what these characters were. And what it was all about. But reality suddenly dawned on me . . . I knew exactly where I was. We were marched from the ramp to the barracks. And we had food in our pockets and we had all kind of things. And these striped creatures. We walked by the . . . woman's camp, in the rags, begging us. And we throw things over the fence because we knew we don't need that. When suddenly an SS guy, he was about five feet behind me, shot his gun straight over my head, through the girl's throat. *And, it already suddenly dawned on me*————. (He stops for five seconds, looks down, and quietly cries for the first time.) Well we were taken————. There she was lying, clutching her throat. Her legs were spread. Mud. Terrible. Because I don't know, she wasn't supposed to take anything you throw over the fence.[60]

At the end of the final stage of adaptation, initiative and reflective thought reemerged. Renee H. eluded deportation, repeatedly running from authorities and hiding in order to save herself and to care for her younger sister. After a time, desperate and alone except for her sister, Renee finally turned herself in, hoping to find her parents who had been transported to Auschwitz. Instead, she and her sister were transported to Bergen-Belsen, where they managed to survive for more than a year. After adapting to the alien world of hunger, sickness, beatings, and death, thoughtful strategies for survival emerged. Renee describes what went through her mind as she navigated the horrors of Bergen-Belsen: "There were corpses all over. I lived, walked, beside dead people, and after a while, it just got to be so that one noticed and one had to say to oneself, I'm *not* going to see who it is. I'm not going to recognize anyone in this person who is lying there. . . . Otherwise I would not have survived."[61]

Eva L. actively managed to maintain cooperation within her group of five women at Auschwitz, even when people in her group were killed and replaced with people she did not know. Eva shows more complete adaptation to the dreadful conditions engulfing her, accepting these conditions, but also recovering the ability to initiate small acts and to think in ways that maintained her. For Eva, nurturing hatred and creative thoughts of revenge motivated survival within her group of five at Auschwitz.

We started encouraging each other. We said, we are going to live this through. It's going to be one for all, and all for one. We going to live this through and we going to help one another, and we encouraged. And we said . . . we are going to live. And we started building hatred. Hatred, and all kinds of ideas what we going to do to the Germans when we live through this. And that hatred made us survive and made us live. The thoughts that we had . . . were sickening. . . . We said we going to cut them into pieces. We going to put salt on them. We going to tie them to two horses and let the two horses run. The most horrible, horrible things that could come to mind. We fed ourselves with that hatred, and that made us go.[62]

FROM PAST TO PRESENT

As my analysis of memory proceeded, it became clear that the long-term effects of memory on the present lives of the witnesses are profoundly important to the witnesses—and linked to the analysis of memory itself. In their testimonies, witnesses are clear that the consequences of Holocaust memory today should be studied as part of the experience of memory itself. The following chapter resulted from listening to the witnesses describe memory's persisting effects on their daily lives.

NOTES

1. Tape HVT-700, testimony of Claude L., 1986.
2. Through analysis of oral testimony, this chapter describes and categorizes witnesses' accounts of experiencing atrocity. Although this analysis takes place in the past tense, based on retrospective accounts of the victim's phenomenal experience, it may be the most direct, feasible way to study systematically the experience of trauma in human beings. In Volume Four of the *Diagnostic and Statistical Manual* of the American Psychiatric Association (DSM-IV), the first diagnostic criterion for Posttraumatic Stress Disorder (PTSD) is in the past tense: "The person *has been exposed* to a traumatic event" ([New York: American Psychiatric Association, 1994], 428.) (The emphasis is the author's.) In the book *Unchained Memories*, Lenore Terr states succinctly, "You can't replicate trauma in an experimental lab. You can't simulate murders without terrorizing your research subjects." ([New York: Basic Books, 1994], 52.) One fact is clear: Laboratory simulations of traumatic events with human beings fortunately lack many of the essential characteristics of trauma: the suddenness, the overwhelming emotion—including shock, helplessness, and terror, the violation of one's body and psyche, very real physical pain, confusion, the complete experience of betrayal and humiliation, a flood of information that has not been perceived before and that is not attended to effectively, an inability of existing schemas to predict outcomes, a flight response that is not possible, a hyperaroused state of mind, and a complex of neurophysiological responses.
3. Tape HVT-972, testimony of Jolly Z., 1988.
4. This research area is active and growing, with a substantial knowledge

base and with critical questions yet to be answered. The following four studies are illustrative: Paul E. Gold, "A Proposed Neurobiological Basis for Regulating Memory Storage for Significant Events," in *Affect and Accuracy in Recall*, edited by Eugene Winograd and Ulric Neisser (New York: Cambridge University Press, 1992), 141–161. Bessel A. van der Kolk, "The Body Keeps the Score: Memory and the Evolving Psychobiology of Posttraumatic Stress," *Harvard Review of Psychiatry* 1 (1994): 253–265; James L. McGaugh, "Involvement of Hormonal and Neuromodulatory Systems in the Regulation of Memory Storage," *Annual Review of Neuroscience* 12 (1989): 255–287; Joseph E. LeDoux, "Emotion as Memory: Anatomical Systems Underlying Indelible Neural Traces," in *The Handbook of Emotion and Memory*, edited by Sven-Åke Christianson (Hillsdale, N.J.: Erlbaum, 1992), 269–288. Also factored into a neurobiological analysis of stress and memory should be basic physiological facts of prolonged trauma: hunger, thirst, exposure, fever, exhaustion, and pain.

5. The articles cited in Note 4 describe the proposed relationships between memory formation and the physiological effects of stress.

6. There was justifiable naiveté among early researchers and rescuers. For example, in the seminal 1949 book *I Did Not Interview the Dead*, David Boder questions one of the survivors about the slave labor camp, "Lager Furstengrube," near Katowice. He asks, "Were you personally mistreated?" ([Urbana, Ill.: University of Illinois Press], 208.) Millie W. describes a visit from the Red Cross shortly after liberation. The Red Cross workers observed her distended stomach, bloated from starvation. She says they then went off looking for big pots to heat water because they thought she was going to have a baby. "That's how ignorant they were," Millie says. (Tape HVT-134, testimony of Millie W., 1981.)

7. Tape HVT-1126, testimony of Lorna B., 1988.

8. Tape HVT-146, testimony of Walter S., 1979.

9. Tape HVT-2741, testimony of David K., 1994.

10. Approximately seventy-five percent of those Holocaust witnesses who described their emotional state referred directly to numbness.

11. Tape HVT-71, testimony of Eva L., 1982.

12. Tape HVT-623, testimony of Sabina S., 1985; Tape HVT-65, Irene W., 1982.

13. Tape HVT-1892, testimony of Meir V., 1992.

14. Tape HVT-213, testimony of Adele W., 1982.

15. Tape HVT-3260, testimony of Nina S., 1996.

16. Tape HVT-144, testimony of Emina N., 1979.

17. Tape HVT-153, testimony of Daniel F., 1980; Tape HVT-628, Leon W., 1979; Tape HVT-36, Celia K., 1980.

18. Tape HVT-81, Chana F. in the testimony of Henry F. and Chana F., 1980.

19. Tape HVT-1315, testimony of Clemens L., 1990.

20. Tape HVT-2045, testimony of Alina Z., 1993.

21. Tape HVT-974, testimony of Edith P., 1980.

22. Tape HVT-100, testimony of Zezette L., 1980.

23. Tape HVT-3, testimony of Sally H., 1979; Tape HVT-1154, Sally H., 1989.

24. The distinct experience of *dissociation* appears to be a necessary factor for producing repression. In this context, several points about the concept of repression should be noted. First, the vast clinical literature, though informative, does not reach a clear consensus on the definition of repression. The particular definition applied in this analysis is a conservative one: Repression is the inability to recall a distinctive personal event that is generally agreed upon to be consequential in one's life. After active attempts to recall such an event, the resulting memory failure can justifiably be labeled repression. Applying this definition to 125 witnesses and thousands of specific memories, I was able to identify four cases of repression. The main generalization about retrieval of Holocaust memories is that they are vivid, enduring, and readily available. It should be noted, however, that analysis of oral testimony may underestimate the likelihood of repression because if witnesses are unable to recall a particular event at the time they are providing testimony, then that event will stay hidden and the repression will remain undetected. (William Banks provided this critique following a presentation at the annual meeting of the Psychonomic Society in St. Louis, November 1994.) Identification of repression occurred when the repressed event was remembered before testimony was provided or when historical documents or other witnesses independently identified the event in question. For a more direct approach to the study of repression, refer to the debated methodology of Linda Meyer Williams. ("Recall of Childhood Trauma: A Prospective Study of Women's Memories of Child Sexual Abuse," *The Journal of Consulting and Clinical Psychology* 62 [1994]: 1167–1176.)

25. Tape HVT-206, Bessie K. in testimony of Jacob and Bessie K., 1983.

26. Tape HVT-92, testimony of Chana B., 1980.

27. Tape HVT-153, testimony of Daniel F., 1980.

28. Tape HVT-50, testimony of Renee H., 1979; Tape HVT-756, Chaim E., 1986.

29. Tape HVT-1533, testimony of Aaron S., 1991.

30. Tape HVT-1650, testimony of Violet S., 1991.

31. Tape HVT-191, testimony of Frieda J., 1980.

32. Tape HVT-1, testimony of Eva B., 1979; Tape HVT-191, Frieda J., 1980.

33. In *The Genocidal Mentality* (New York: Basic Books, 1990) Robert J.

Lifton and Eric Markusen introduce the concepts of "dual belief" or "middle knowledge," to account for those who have been victimized by great tragedy who do not integrate contradictory ideas of believable tragedy and unprecedented horror.

34. Tape HVT-2254, testimony of Eva V., 1993.

35. Tape HVT-974, testimony of Edith P., 1987.

36. Tape HVT-50, testimony of Renee H., 1979.

37. Tape HVT-641, testimony of Martin S., 1986; Tape HVT-2, Leon W., 1979.

38. Tape HVT-81, testimony of Henry F. and Chana F., 1980; Tape HVT-107, Edith P., 1980.

39. Tape HVT-2, testimony of Leon W., 1979.

40. Tape HVT-71, testimony of Eva L., 1982; Tape HVT-146, Walter S., 1979.

41. Tape HVT-71, testimony of Eva L., 1982.

42. Tape HVT-1, testimony of Eva B., 1983.

43. Tape HVT-756, testimony of Chaim E., 1986.

44. Tape HVT-2854, testimony of Aladar M., 1995; Tape HVT-191, Frieda J., 1980; Tape HVT-2762, Alfred F., 1995.

45. Tape HVT-756, testimony of Chaim E., 1986; Tape HVT-220, Jolly Z., 1983.

46. Tape HVT-136, testimony of Hanna G., 1982.

47. Tape HVT-2188, testimony of Samuel and Wolf Z., 1993; Tape HVT-163, Pincus S. in testimony of Pincus S. and Sylvia S., 1980; Tape HVT-3260, Nina S., 1996.

48. Tape HVT-191, testimony of Frieda J., 1980.

49. Tape HVT-284, testimony of Alan Z., 1984; Tape HVT-1892, Meir V., 1992; Tape HVT-191, Frieda J., 1980.

50. Tape HVT-2045, testimony of Alina Z., 1993.

51. Tape HVT-284, testimony of Alan Z., 1984.

52. Death could come suddenly and painfully in the ghettos and the camps: through illness, beatings, selections, or the whim of a guard. Leo G. says that survival demanded luck and that "luck took place in many forms." He cites examples. An extra piece of food was lucky. If inmates received a small piece of potato in their soup, that was lucky. Even the size of a tiny piece of bread mattered: A slightly larger piece provided extra nutrition *and* increased morale. If a guard beat a person with a stick and there were no broken bones, that was lucky. Broken bones meant death. If a person passed out from pain while being whipped by a guard, "given twenty-five," that was lucky. If the victim cried out, that meant unlimited whipping and death. (Tape HVT-158, testimony of Leo G., 1980.)

53. Tape HVT-146, testimony of Walter S., 1979.

54. Tape HVT-2830, testimony of Herbert L., 1995.

55. Tape HVT-146, testimony of Walter S., 1979.

56. Tape HVT-641, testimony of Martin S., 1986.
57. Tape HVT-1850, testimony of Clara L., 1993.
58. Tape HVT-2809, testimony of Hubert W., 1995.
59. Tape HVT-153, testimony of Daniel F., 1980.
60. Tape HVT-2830, testimony of Herbert L., 1995.
61. Tape HVT-50, testimony of Renee H., 1979.
62. Tape HVT-71, testimony of Eva L., 1982.

CHAPTER 5

AFTERSHOCKS OF TRAUMATIC MEMORY: DISTURBING BEHAVIOR AND BELIEFS

While recalling events from the Holocaust, witnesses invariably describe memory's influence on their present lives. Though the traumatic past is clearly separate from present life, witnesses speak of Holocaust memories and the direct consequences of these memories as interconnected—and not as two separate topics. In their testimony, these witnesses particularize the aftershocks of traumatic memory. They detail the ways in which core memories guide their current actions and thoughts, evoking specific fears, invading their sleep, altering interactions with family and friends, influencing religious beliefs, and ultimately shaping concepts of the self.

Although witnesses know that the dreadful losses of the Holocaust were beyond their control, at the same time, they describe how their traumatic memories generate guilt. Analysis of the testimony reveals that this guilt assumes several forms with multiple causes and is not the canonical concept from normal life. In fact, Holocaust memory can engender the experience of feeling guilty and not guilty simultaneously. Witnesses also reveal the reasons they avoided speaking about the Holocaust for decades, reflecting on the long-term effects of this active silence on themselves and their families.

This chapter broadly describes the behavioral and ideational consequences of traumatic memory from the perspective of those who lived through prolonged atrocity. The witnesses provided testimony in the fourth and fifth decades after the war, so they were able to look back over many years and assess the diverse influences of Holocaust memory as well as the changes that occurred in their awareness of these influences.

Nearly all the witnesses in this study allude to the general, underlying influence of Holocaust memories, though they speak in terms of particular examples.[1] Most behaviors that witnesses identify as being connected to Holocaust memory result from fears about losing what was lost in the traumatic past, with the most pervasive fear concerning the safety of their children. In her testimony, Nina S. evinces both the intensity of this fear and its source:

> I sometimes look out there and I say, "God All Mighty, it might happen again. What's going to happen to the babies?" I used to say when my children were born. I used to pray nothing should happen until they are six years old because in my mind, up to six years old, they going to take them, they going to kill them.

The source of Nina's fear resides in her specific memories of the Lodz Ghetto:

> They tore the children, the babies away from the mothers. And there were *screams*. Could you imagine? Babies. Up to six years old they tore them away from mothers' hands. Mothers were *crazy*. But they had no choice . . . they were going from one house to the next. And we sat there and we listened to it.[2]

For Nina, fears about the well-being of her children—and later her grandchildren—grow irradicably from specific memories of the Lodz Ghetto. Many years later when Nina became a mother, these memories evoked insuppressible anxiety.

Oral testimony reveals several specific fears that are nearly universal. Jolly Z. summarizes one such fear: "When I came over to this country, even on the railroads, even a conductor, I suspected. Because he had a *uniform*." Martin S. concurs, providing more detail: "A sharp, black, dark-blue, black type uniform still makes me freeze no matter where I see it." He adds, "Uniforms, to this day, especially when they're very sharply dressed, is something that changes my attitude immediately."[3] Other specific fears described in the testimony of many witnesses are the fear that food will no longer be available, fear of dogs, fear of being trapped, and fear of abduction, with each one linked to specific memories. About the persistence of such fears, Martin S. concludes, "Things like that, I just cannot seem to shake—and probably never will."[4]

Emotional and physical responses driven by specific memories of horror can seem automatic and immutable. Beatrice S. witnessed the absolute horror of family members being brutally murdered. She hid with her father in a small cellar, watching as a Gestapo officer shot her mother and crushed her younger brother to death beneath his boots. As she witnessed the murder, Beatrice's father clamped his hand over her mouth to prevent her from screaming. In her testimony, Beatrice describes the continuing physical effects of this horror: "To this day, I have trouble breathing, and I think it's because what happened." After surviving the war, Nadia R. discovered that she experienced powerful waves of panic in the company of other Jewish people. She says, "For the first time . . . after the concentration camp, I was surrounded with Jews. It brought me such an anxiety attack . . . I started to hyperventilate."[5]

When conditions in the world connect with core memory, the emotion of core memory floods into conscious awareness. At the same time, direct perceptions of the world obscure the images of memory. What the survivor is left with is a strong and automatic emotional response apparently connected to the particular set of worldly conditions. The activating event in the world acts as a tuning fork, vibrating at a precise frequency, causing a core memory that is in some way identical to resonate, releasing emotion. Survivors are initially surprised by the emotion, but after becoming aware of this connection, they construct intuitive theories to account for their overwhelming emotional responses. These theories provide an explanation for the emotional bursts, but they do not make contact with core memory and do not alleviate the emotional response. Awareness of this connection does not prevent the overwhelming emotions any more than awareness of the physics of pressure waves and resonant frequencies can prevent unwanted resonant vibration.

Many witnesses speak of automatic physiological responses when hearing the language of their tormentors. Eva B. says, "To this day, I cannot really hear German. I have not changed about that at all. When I hear the language . . . it does something to my insides. They turn over." Ernest R. agrees: "When I do travel in Europe and I hear Germans speaking, it does bother my ear . . . Even until this date, I cannot forget it . . . I will never forget it." Celia K. says, "Today, after so many years, if I hear Ukrainian spoken or Lithuanian, I cringe. I get very *sick*. I can't be in the same room with them. . . . Everything opens up all over again."[6] These responses are not the result of thoughtful resentment, and they are not the result of attitudes learned over a period of time. They arise from deep-rooted connections between survivors' specific memories of trauma and the language of their tormentors.

Activating events in the world can also be temporal. Isabella L. describes a recurring change in mood at the same time each year, the time of year she was deported from the ghetto in Kisvarda, Hungary, to Auschwitz:

For decades, the end of May, which is coming upon us soon, was an unbearable time for me. I never knew why suddenly I got terribly depressed and I couldn't cope with the days in May. And I never quite remembered why. And then it would dawn on me. . . . Then in June, I would have a different outlook on life. I would be more hopeful. *But it would hit me like a clock*. It reappeared every May.[7]

For Isabella, the time of year retrieves an underlying schema representation of the original event, which in turn connects to core memory, leading to a release of emotion and the resulting effects on her state of mind.[8]

For some survivors, unbidden memories of the Holocaust that become conscious can lead to active decisions. Living in Czechoslovakia in 1968 during "Prague spring," Nadia R. made such a decision. When Russian troops invaded, personal memories of the Holocaust rose into consciousness, "like oil on the water," she says. "Suddenly that was, I think, the *first* time that . . . nightmares and my own personal feelings and that *inside*—it *came out*. And I said I'm not waiting. I'm not waiting. One has to learn from history."[9] She took action and left Czechoslovakia. For Nadia, traumatic memory itself created a defining event, defining once again.

NIGHTMARES

One prevalent and terrifying result of reentering normal life after prolonged atrocity is the insistence of core memories during sleep. Nearly sixty percent of the witnesses in this study spontaneously discussed nightmares. One common pattern for survivors is to recover their physical health, establish a stable routine with family and work, and then begin experiencing nightmares, a pattern described by Menachem S. "Once I was safe again," he says, "this is when I disintegrated. I developed fears. I couldn't sleep. I started having nightmares."[10]

Though Menachem's nightmares eventually dissipated, other survivors continue to experience them until the present day. In testimony given in 1996, Solomon L. says, "I'm still suffering for it. I can't sleep nights. *Not at all.*" The continuing nightmares involve the intrusion of Holocaust memory into representations of daily life and are often about being abducted by the Nazis. Also in 1996, Nina S. says in her testimony, "Nightmares to this day. I'm always cornered. With the Germans coming. They used to come always with these big vans, and jumping off like the trucks and with all the people. Who did they grab? They used to grab people in the street and throw them in there." Forty-eight years after the end of World War II, the nightmares of Samuel Z. continue with a recurring scene: "I try to hide as a non-Jew—or hidden some place—and looking out at the crowd of non-Jews, looking why the Poles are so happy, laughing." He says, "The minute they discover me, I'm also Jew. The only [way to] save me—on panic, I wake up." He says, "Up until now, still have it. . . . Almost every night I have the same dream." In recent testimony, Sol F. states bluntly, "There's trouble in the night . . . every night I run away and every night I am in trouble. One night my wife wake me up. I was hollering. Because they took me away again."[11]

For some, nightmares go away with the distraction of work and family, a pattern described by Alan Z.:

After I came to the United States, and I started to work, everything disappeared. I mean, my life changed drastically when I was in the United States. My work. I was involved in my business and raising my family. And it just moved away from me. And I tried not to live with it all the time. Live a normal life with my wife. And this way we could build a family which was normal.[12]

In fact, the power of distraction is the one common palliative mentioned by all the witnesses who note improvement in their night terrors. Distraction does not ameliorate or suppress; rather, it blankets the traumatic memory. When distraction leaves, painful emotion re-emerges, and nightmares can intrude more frequently than in the past. Tenacious core memories of insuppressible horrors then emerge during the night, undeterred.

In testimony given in 1995, Aladar M. says he has nightmares, "even *more* lately than in the beginning." He explains, "And maybe that's why I felt *now* that I want to bring it out. Because in the beginning, it was more like I have to work, I have to make a living, I have to do things. I did not have the time to think about it." Aladar characterizes his nightmares ("I'm just angry, and I scream. Just anger.") and says, "My wife said I almost choke at night." The testimony of Clara L. concurs: "Very strange. I find that *now*, forty-nine years after all this experience, I have *more* nightmares than I even had in the immediate events, after."[13]

For some, the nightmares persist with the same intensity but not as frequently. More than fifty years after the war, Henry S. describes his torment at night:

And it's very hard, even *now*, to live with it. As most of my friends, we still get nightmares from time to time. . . . The first twenty years after the war, we get practically *nightly*. And then they became less frequent. But still, seldom week or two pass by without having in front of my eyes some part of the camp or some of the camps, with the barbed wires and———. Or see this one hanged or this one shot. And we cannot do anything about it.[14]

ALTERED CONCEPTS OF THE SELF

In testimony, witnesses frequently specify how Holocaust memory has altered forever what they perceive to be central characteristics of their personalities.[15] Years that were "congested," in the words of Henry S., with one atrocity "after the other after the other," filled with daily—even hourly—terrors, carve patterns of thought and behavior that show themselves as permanent characteristics in the self schemas of the survivors.[16] The most frequent characteristics discussed by witnesses in this study are an unwillingness to depend on others, wariness about trust, and an inability to show emotion.

Hilda S. hid in an orphanage outside of Brussels during the war, with adult caretakers responsible for her physical needs, but little else. She now prides herself on being self-sufficient, a trait she learned to value as a child in hiding:

> I used to think the best thing a person can do is to be responsible for herself. Not to depend on anybody. You don't need friends. You don't need parents. You don't need relatives. The highest level of achievement that an individual could reach would be to be his own person. And to be totally self-sufficient.

After immigrating to the United States, Hilda grew to despise American children for being dependent on their parents. As a mother, Hilda brought up her three children to be independent, supporting their physical needs, but leaving the rest to them, mirroring her own childhood. She cites as an example that when visiting Paris, she left her twelve-year-old daughter alone to navigate the complicated Parisian subway system on her own. "That was the only way I knew," she explains. Similarly, another child survivor, Jacqueline R. describes herself as "self-sufficient . . . to the extreme."[17]

Specific memories of betrayal during the Holocaust prevent the establishment of trust many years later, maintaining personal barriers that sequester survivors. Eva L. explains her attitudes about her current neighbors, attitudes that arise from specific memories of neighbors in Poland who betrayed Jewish families to the Nazis:

> I have neighbors, very nice neighbors, but I cannot trust them as friends. It is also from my experience because before the war we lived in a non-Jewish section. We had neighbors, Polish neighbors. My mother was most respected, they adored her. Even so, she was a Jew, but they adored her. The anti-Semitism in Poland was always great, but *we* never felt it because we lived with our neighbors, so close and so nice and so fine. But when the war broke out, when the Germans came in, they were the *first ones* to show: this is a Jew; here lived a Jew.[18]

Many witnesses speak of their difficulty in showing emotion later in life. The experience of Alina Z. is representative of these witnesses: "I was like stone. I couldn't believe. And something *stay* in me. I'm very happy, but I can't show a lot. I can't cry with tragedy." Now, she says her children cannot tell when she is happy: "I said I'm happy. I'm *very* happy, but I just can't show the feeling. Can't show. When I'm happy, they think I'm *not* happy."[19]

Defining Religious Beliefs

As social psychologist Nan Sussman explains, people define their self-concepts not only by individual personal attributes, but also by membership in larger groups.[20] For Holocaust survivors after the war, religious affiliation was the most important of these group memberships, and the particular choice of religion became a defining characteristic in the survivor's self-concept. Though choosing and committing to a set of religious beliefs is complex and can develop over a period of many years, all of the witnesses who discuss their beliefs in testimony relate them directly to specific events during the Holocaust. Testimony reveals a range of beliefs, from Orthodox Judaism to ardent humanism, and all those who give testimony are clear: Events witnessed during the Holocaust strongly shaped their religious beliefs. For some witnesses, the stated connection between specific memory and religious belief is straightforward, with the choice of belief remembered as being directly tied to a particular event. For others, the connection is more multifarious, involving interpretation of a collection of remembered events.

Some witnesses interpreted rare instances of good fortune during the Holocaust as miraculous, using these instances as defining events in their development of religious identity. Sabina S. clearly remembers such an event as the source of her religious faith. She and her family were hiding in a bunker, along with several Jewish friends, when they were discovered. Taken by surprise, they quickly escaped, running deep into the woods. With no food and no local people to help, they went to sleep that night convinced that their lives were about to end. Sabina then describes the events of the following day: "And we woke up in the morning, and we walk out and we look. I still can't believe it. The ground was literally covered with mushrooms. Mushrooms! And the people we were with knew that they were not poisonous mushrooms. So it was like manna from heaven!"

Elaborating on her movement toward faith during her years of torment, she says, "Somehow I was helped. And there was like a superpower that helped me." For Sabina S., salvation originally appeared in the form of mushrooms, which exemplify and anchor her strong belief in God.[21]

Morris R. performed slave labor at Czestochowa, making bullets. One day, he was falsely accused of stealing and sentenced to die by hanging. The guards took him up to the gallows, tied his hands, and placed a noose around his neck. As he was about to be hanged, an SS man intervened, saying he was a good worker and that they had apprehended the prisoner who committed the theft. In testimony, Morris says, "I walked down. I walked to the back . . . I don't know what was happening to him. He was an SS man, but at this time something was written up there that I should be privileged to *be*. Thank God." For Morris R., divine intervention seemed a far more plausible explanation for his reprieve than the goodness of the SS.[22]

While doing slave labor in Skarzysko, Sabina G. became sick with typhus, burning with a high fever and experiencing hallucinations. In a fever dream, she saw her father, wrapped in a prayer shawl, offering her an apple. She remembers being parched and desperately wanting a drink:

> And I would say that *Providence* brought my hand down to the end of that bunk. I'm coming to a terrible thing. And there was standing a tin can. The can was usually [filled] with urine. And I must say that I drank it. I drank it not knowing what I'm doing. But I was very thirsty. And it happened to be that that was like a medicine to me. It was maybe the crisis or maybe that *dream* or maybe that drink. I woke up in the morning, and my temperature dropped.[23]

In testimony, Sabina G. attributes her strong belief in God to her specific memory of recovering from typhus during that feverish night in the barracks at Skarzysko.

Other witnesses strongly reject the idea of a supreme being, describing or alluding to specific cruelties that should have been prevented by such a being. Many changed their religious beliefs on this basis. Frania R. says, "I come from an orthodox family. But I cannot believe that there is somebody there and could see all the atrocity that I have seen." In her testimony, Frania tells what she does believe in: "Existence. Presence. Right now. Living for the moment. I don't want to look at the past."[24] At the time she was living through the horrors, Frania rejected her orthodox faith, which in turn led to a loss of faith in the past itself. For Frania, the torment of the past excludes its use, leaving strong faith in the present and hopefulness for the future as her guiding beliefs.

Many survivors embrace a devout and selective form of humanism, exemplified by the succinct testimony of Edith P. "I don't pray to God," Edith says, "I pray to my father."[25] Frieda J. elaborates on this form of humanism. As a young child, Frieda witnessed the hanging of her father, survived a near fatal attack by a German Shepherd, and was eventually captured and transported to Bergen-Belsen where she subsisted for many months, engulfed by starvation and atrocity. After such extensive suffering, Frieda is resolute in her belief that there was nothing at all redeeming during the Holocaust and just as resolute that redemption can be found in simply surviving:

I'm too much of a product of man's inhumanity to man, so I had to learn to turn that around and say but there has got to be something redeeming. And the fact that I'm *here* is a redeeming factor. And because I came out of it and I was able to put my life together, something good had to have happened to me along the way.

Frieda focuses her humanism on the Jewish people who were killed and on those who lived on after the Holocaust. She reinterprets her memory of the hundreds of dead and dying people she witnessed in the ghetto and during her many months in Bergen-Belsen. The events that took place after the Holocaust, though distinct from Holocaust memory, provided a basis for reinterpreting earlier Holocaust memories and for developing a new belief system:

What's come out of it, for me, over the years, is that my faith and my belief has translated itself into the strongest possible belief in the *Jewish people*. I can't begin to describe how this metamorphosis turned out, because I began to see that instead of being sheep, and instead of being just very weak-willed people who really had no wish to live or to fight or to conquer, that the fact that some of us *did* remain and that the state of Israel

was a byproduct of that from this horrible massacre—this Holocaust—made me feel that *this* is something to believe in.[26]

Memories of the horrors witnessed during the Holocaust are too
alien to be used to support a belief system in normal life, so many
survivors draw upon their memories of events after the war to reassemble their beliefs. Those who abandon their belief in God still
maintain a strong commitment to Judaism and to the Jewish people.
For child survivors who changed from one temporary identity to another during the war, the resolution of ambiguous and shifting religious identities is achieved through a dedication to something at once
tangible and idealistic: a strong belief in the state of Israel.[27]

Defining Identities

During the war, Rita L. and her mother hid in a convent where
the priest provided formal religious training and obtained baptismal
papers for Rita. "Once I went to the convent," Rita says, "I was a
very ardent Catholic." She recounts her thoughts about religion just
after liberation: "Now that we are free, I don't ever want to be a Jew
again. I am going to . . . convert for real because I am Catholic and
that's all I'm going to ever be for the rest of my life." After the war,
however, Rita was placed with other Jewish refugees, and she partic-
ipated with them in organized youth groups. By gradually assimilating
into this new social group, Rita rebuilt her self, step-by-step, unaware
of the changes taking place in her self-concept. One day, seemingly
suddenly, she recognized a great change in her religious convictions:
"Not only I wanted to be Jew, but I wanted to be a halutz [pioneer]
and go to Israel. So I took *a total turn around* at that point." For many
child survivors, the ambiguity and danger of Jewish identity just before the war, the necessary embrace of Catholicism during the war,
and the disruption of these newly acquired religious beliefs in the DP
camps after the war confused the self-concept, leading ultimately to
the need for an active decision. As Robert Lifton summarizes in *The
Protean Self*, "Conversion delivers one from chaos."[28]

In 1960, after beginning her second marriage, Rita L. chose a different defining group membership. With this marriage, Rita says she
became American. She no longer defines her self-concept in terms of
having survived the Holocaust. She views the world from the present
and looks toward the future, stating, "My life is totally American,

totally part of same life as any one of my neighbors and my friends."
At the time of this active change, when people asked Rita where she
was from, she simply told them "Europe." She says, "I didn't want to
get into Warsaw Ghetto or any of the experiences. It wasn't that it
was so painful. It was just the fact that I wanted to *negate* the whole
past." Rita concludes, "This was a very closed compartment in my
mind. And in my life."[29]

In a similar way, Hilda S. defined her self-concept in opposition to
her past identity and in opposition to being identifiably different from
others around her. During the war, Hilda was sent away from her
family in Germany to hide in an orphanage in Belgium. After the
war, her memories of fear and deprivation while in hiding led her to
reject both the Jewish identity of her family and the European Christian identity she learned in the orphanage. After liberation, Hilda's
primary motivation was to assimilate, to define a self that never experienced terror and loss—identical to the selves she perceived in her
new, normal world of the United States. "When I came to America,"
she asserts, "my main ambition was to be like everybody else. I didn't
want to be German. I didn't want to be Jewish. I didn't care what I
was, as long as . . . it was like everybody else. My dream was not to
have an accent." As with other survivors, Hilda defines her self-
concept in terms of group membership, but in Hilda's case, the group
is not characterized by family or by religion or by surviving the Holocaust. Rather, Hilda defines her self-concept by being American.[30]

While living in Czechoslovakia after the war, Nadia R. similarly
reconstructed her self-concept. For Nadia, hiding her Jewishness sig-
naled well-being. "It was totally buried in me," she says, "and I felt
that is a good thing. *That*, I thought, was my *proof* how well I came
across the whole trauma." During the twenty-three years that Nadia
lived in Czechoslovakia after the war, her closest friends did not know
she was Jewish.

After immigrating to the United States, Nadia redefined her self-
concept. She chose to accept her Jewishness, and with that acceptance, her former self-concept returned—a self defined immediately
after liberation from the concentration camp of Terezin and one
laden with fears and anxiety. Accepting this former Jewish self, allowing this self to come out of hiding, Nadia also allows the horrors of
the past to coexist with memories just after the war and with her
present life. She does not try to sequester her memories in a closed
compartment. In fact, to "balance" her unpleasant associations with

Jewishness after the war, Nadia R. is now actively involved in Holocaust remembrance, talking to students in high schools, which presents the opportunity for publicly stating her defining group membership: "I am Jewish."[31]

Though the specifics differ, the underlying goal is the same for Rita L. and Hilda S. as it is for Nadia R.: to define the self in terms of membership in a social group. Such a definition connects the individual self and the collective self, encouraging the development of a sense of well-being.[32] Assimilation into a larger collective such as the United States has the same underlying motivation as participating in gatherings of Holocaust survivors or joining Jewish organizations—with different results in one's self-concept. Nadia redefines her self-concept by rejoining Jewish organizations, by placing herself back into the community of Holocaust survivors and of Jewry. Rita and Hilda compartmentalize their confused selves of childhood, selves that hid from the Nazis and assumed different religions. In this way, they redefine their self-concepts through membership in the culture of the safe present, rather than the traumatized past.

Splitting Selves

In her discussion of self-knowledge, Robyn Fivush states that the function of autobiographical memory is to organize knowledge of one's definition of self: "It is the sense of self that makes the memories cohere as a life history that expresses the essence of who we are."[33] Prolonged atrocity, however, redefines the relationship between autobiographical memory and the concept of self. The difference for almost all survivors is that autobiographical memories during the Holocaust stand apart from one's working definition of self, forming an island of remembered experiences, isolated from one's definition of self in normal life. In Fivush's terms, the essence of who we are is divided—a division that can be apparent even at the time memories are formed. Today, many witnesses state that they live a double existence. They view their past lives as separate, yet not separate; their memories as closed, yet open and ever-present.

Prolonged atrocity splits the extended self, with one self functioning in the normal world, guided by expectations from other people, and the other existing in the consuming memories of horror. Those who lived through the terrors of the Nazi ghettos and camps speak explicitly of these two selves. After describing her escape to Prague during a death march from Gross-Rosen to Bergen-Belsen, Beatrice S. admits in her testimony that her children do not know the "real me," conceding that she is playing the part that is expected of her: "You put on a smile and you go. You just become an *actress*." Recalling her time in Auschwitz, Violet S. advances a similar view: "Many times, people that don't know me, they look . . . they have *no idea*. Because all of us survivors, we survived. But part of us is . . . not what you call normal." That part which is not normal is the remembered self from the camps.[34]

As described in the previous chapter, when survivors adapt to chronic torment, they transform into organisms of survival. While traumatized and in this numbed state of adaptation, if prewar memories return, these memories can offer the survivor a glimpse of the humanness that defined the normal self before the war, leading to a reexperiencing of the prewar self. Bessie K. remembers just this kind of brief reawakening. Sick and starving, living in wretched conditions, Bessie performed slave labor, digging ditches and repairing trains. She remembers painting train cars and noticing a small bed inside one of the cars: "It was so strange to me. It's like I never had a bed. I never was a human being. I never knew nothing. I was like an animal. But I was so glad to see it. Made me feel good. This was the first time I felt good inside. That I see something, that there's still *somebody* there." After seeing the small bed, Bessie briefly experienced her prewar self as it washed over her consciousness, momentarily submerging her labor camp self. While recalling her response, Bessie reveals a common fear of those subsisting during extended trauma—that the former self is gone forever, permanently replaced by the victimized self.[35]

So complete is the adaptation to the deprived life of daily survival that memories of one's former life rarely have the strength to reassert their influence over the victimized self. Only after liberation from protracted captivity and only after assimilation into normal life can new memories be used to reconstruct a self that can function within the normal world. With each step of recapturing a normal life—getting married, finding work, raising children, and participating in the community—the reconstructed self grows stronger, supported by new activities and by recent memories resulting from these new activities. Along with the reconstructed self, however, core memories of the Holocaust live on, their images still focused, their strength undiminished, forming a Holocaust self that remains intact throughout one's life. Two segregated groups of memories, one from the Holocaust and one from normal life, lead to the coexistence of dichotomous selves.

Many years after World War II, while living her second life in the United States, Irene W. saw *The Auschwitz Album*, a book of photographs taken during the initial selections of the deportees. She happened to find herself in one of the photographs and was surprised by "the reality of it," saying, "Even to us that whole place and time seems like another world." Irene later presents a contradiction familiar to survivors: "Since the camps, I find myself feeling and relating much differently from my friends and others and yet at the same time putting that into a compartment and integrat[ing] one's life, so that one can function at the same time. But *that* is always there." For Irene, *The Auschwitz Album*, a clear depiction of the past physical self, revived the reality of the remembered horrors, reasserting the victimized self and dominating the postwar self of normal life.[36]

As a child in Bratislava, Renee H. was not quite six years old when the Germans invaded. In Bratislava, she witnessed the daily brutality of family and friends being loaded onto cattle cars. After hiding for a time on a farm near the Tatra Mountains, Renee returned to Bratislava and was eventually deported, traveling eight days and nights in a cattle car to Bergen-Belsen, where she subsisted for more than a year. Renee explicitly addresses the split in her self before and after the war.

> What is left is . . . *two* separate units in one's experience. And so there is the *me* that is the wartime and pre-wartime me and me that is the post-wartime. It's like having an era *before* and *after*. And that—while they are all connected in myself—they are *not* reconcilable. And it took me a long, long time to realize that not only are they not reconcilable, I don't *want* them to be reconcilable. That I wanted them to be separate.[37]

Psychologist Edward Reed writes of the normal duality that is part of our everyday experience of memory: "Reminiscence," according to Reed, "requires two selves and a bridging process that unites them without identifying them." Reed points out that in normal life, the self "can be separated and yet not completely divided . . . dual but not dichotomous." He cites as examples *empathy* and *shame*. In empathy, one self feels someone else's emotion while another self is aware of that feeling. In shame, one self has performed an act that is regrettable, while another self, in the role of judge, condemns the act. In the case of shame, the dual self is unsettling, yet reconcilable. The influences and choices that led to the shameful act can be interpreted and even understood by the person experiencing shame.[38] In stark contrast, survivors of the Holocaust embody dichotomous selves, with each self consisting of distinct and separate defining memories and wholly different systems of judgment. The present self cannot fairly interpret the Holocaust self because of the separation between present and past, a separation exacerbated by the dependable failure of language to serve as a bridge.

When telling others about memories of horror, the act of translating experience into language serves as a persistent reminder of the split self. As Hilda S. recalls her mother's deportation, she discovers the gap between her words and the reality she remembers, her halting testimony conveying the futility of trying to reach across this gap:

> Again, by some fluke, she was one of the last to be————. (She pauses.) To be picked up, if that's the word. To be sent to camps by the————. I'm always amazed at how difficult it is to speak about these events. The language doesn't really exist. "Arrested." When you talk about arresting someone, it usually means a criminal. So I have trouble with that word. "Picked up." "Sent away." Nothing describes the actual events. . . . How does one describe what happened in those years?[39]

The accepted words do not represent the specific experiences, and *semantic memory*—memory for concepts—only accentuates the separation of the two selves in memory. In his analysis of autobiographical memory, Ulric Neisser distinguishes between memory for "a unique and particular past event" and memory for a "repeated and familiar routine" that can be described with a word or a phrase. Both kinds of memory contribute to the *extended self*, which, in Neisser's words is a "cumulated total of such memories: the things I remember having done and the things I think of myself as doing regularly."[40]

Within memory, it is normal and necessary to distinguish between the label for a category of experience and the particular event that exemplifies that category. It is far from normal, however, when profound suffering opens this distinction into an unacceptable semantic schism. In *Days and Memory*, Charlotte Delbo writes of this schism, citing "thirst" as an example of a word that cannot refer both to her experience of thirst at Birkenau and to one's experience of thirst in the normal world.[41] The word "thirst" represents our general schema—our memory for a repeated and familiar experience. But the schema breaks apart before it can be stretched to accommodate Delbo's specific experience of thirst at Birkenau, and the label itself is rendered impotent.

In his cross-cultural exploration of the self, noted social psychologist Harry Triandis states, "Some aspects of the self may be universal. 'I am hungry' may well be an element with much the same meaning worldwide, and across time." For the Holocaust survivor, however, "I am hungry" connects to deeply traumatic memories that create a meaning irreconcilably different from the meaning of the phrase in normal usage. Though the statement of Triandis is generally accurate, its very accuracy emphasizes the permanently alienating semantic schism in the memory of Holocaust survivors.[42]

For some survivors, memory is so vivid that the past horrors seem more real than the present world, and the reality of the present self is in doubt. At the end of her testimony, after describing slave labor at Skarzysko and Czestochowa, after speaking of murderous anti-Semitism after the war, Rose W. concludes:

Thank God, I say, I have children, thank God. And grandchildren. . . . But sometimes I say—I look at my children—and I say maybe it's *not* reality. Because I can———. Sitting there in the camps, I wouldn't believe that I still go out and have married and have a husband and children and grandchildren. And I say, "No, that's not me."[43]

Henry S., who lived through Auschwitz, Gross-Rosen, and Dachau, agrees:

Even as I speak to you now . . . it's like a fantasy world. Because if somebody told me fifty, fifty-one years ago that they guarantee me five years of life, and then I will die, I would have taken it without any question. Five years, that was. And now I'm sitting now with you *fifty* years later. And to me it's still something which is unbelievable.[44]

Guilt

There is considerable discussion and disagreement about guilt in those who have survived widespread catastrophes.[45] From the oral testimony in this study, it is clear that Holocaust survivors experience guilt for extended periods of time, usually beginning shortly after liberation and sometimes continuing until the present day. More than half of the witnesses in this study talked about current feelings of guilt. Guilt, as described by the Holocaust witness, assumes several forms, with multiple causes and different developmental paths, and is not the unitary concept from our normal lives.

Many witnesses evince a questioning, retrospective "why me" guilt, most often thought of as *survivor guilt*. Menachem S. was one of only two children out of possibly 4,000 who survived his concentration camp; all the others were killed. As a result, Menachem experiences this questioning guilt, which he expresses in its most concise form: "You ask yourself the questions: Why? Why did I survive?" In Sweden after the war, Nina S. looked in a mirror for the first time in several years, and she was frightened by what she saw: not her own face but the face of the horrors she endured. She says, "And, of course, a terrible depression set in—and *guilt*. Why are *we* the ones to live? And so many wonderful people did not survive?"[46]

Michael G. lost his family during the Holocaust, and memories of the events that led to his family's murder continue to imprison and interrogate him:

> To live with it and to justify your living. I feel, at many times, I feel guilty. I live with the guilt. And it's not because I've done anything wrong. It's just a guilt there: *why*. I've lived with that guilt for a long time. I ask myself many times when I do certain things and I say, well, I could have helped . . . *if*. If *whatever*. So to tell you that I am free . . . like a bird being free, I'm *not*. I'm surrounded many times in pain and————. But things like that come back and it just works on you. And it's not that easy . . . you're living with a constant question mark about a lot of things that's taken place.[47]

For some witnesses, guilt arises from their memory of having lived at the expense of others who were murdered. The testimony of Chana B. provides an example of this malevolent contract. At Auschwitz,

Chana was selected to die and sent to the block of prisoners awaiting the gas chamber. When the time came for the prisoners in Chana's block to be killed, the guards mistakenly took another group of prisoners instead, and Chana was saved. She says, "For a while I felt extreme responsibility . . . and my children are telling me—especially my oldest—it's not my fault, that you were left alone . . . so it's a great conflict."[48]

Eva L. understands the impossible conditions that killed others in her family, yet her feelings of guilt persist. In the Lodz Ghetto, Eva lay in a coma for five weeks with typhus before finally reviving. To aid her recovery, Eva's father sold his food ration for medicine, and she credits him for saving her life. Soon after, her father died of starvation. She says, "He swell up, and he died. And I could not help him. I couldn't do anything for him." Earlier in her testimony, after describing her father's death, Eva reveals a resolution of her underlying feelings of helplessness: "It was *meant* for me to live. Because under such circumstances, nobody can survive." But Eva also describes the persistent, lingering effects of her family's death: "Sometimes I feel like guilt. Why am I the one, that I am here? . . . And the rest of my family is not?" She laments, "I can never push it away. I can never chase it away."[49]

Psychologists Mardi Horowitz and Steven Reidbord explain the general etiology of feeling simultaneously guilty and not guilty. When a person is victimized by overwhelming trauma, the trauma destabilizes the person's normal experience of a single self-concept. In order to accommodate the traumatic events, the normally coherent sense of self splits into multiple self-concepts, and these multiple selves then permit people to process the traumatic events along "several parallel streams." The result many years later of these parallel streams of encoding is the experience of simultaneous conflicting emotions.[50]

Some survivors have learned to resolve the conflict of living at the expense of others by emphasizing the concept of destiny, excluding the concept of choice. Samuel B. explains:

This stupid feeling of guilt. . . . How is this: If I am alive, that somebody died because of me? Because I was supposed to be alive? All these things were very, very heavy somewhere sitting in me. And it took me years and years to understand, to liberate myself somehow from all this. It was a very crippling feeling. Trying to understand that nothing of all that was my own personal choice. It was all imposed on me by some games of destiny.[51]

After years of inner conflict, many witnesses ultimately realize that responsibility lies with those who imposed the desperate conditions and not with their own responses that may have seemed cowardly or selfish. As with Samuel B., Clara L. shed her conflict and replaced it with a strong belief in destiny. She says, "I was one of those who was destined to survive. And I feel no guilt feelings. I did whatever I could for my parents. I did whatever I could for my sister. And whoever was around me. More I could not do. So I don't feel guilty about it to remain alive."[52]

In some cases, guilt assumes a form that many observers can imagine: an intense regret for failing to prevent the deaths of others. After the brother of Abe L. escaped the ghetto, Abe rescued his brother's young daughters but was unable to save his brother's two sons—ages six and seven. Abe confesses: "These two boys, I can't get over it, until this moment. Day and night, I can't go over it. Not being melodramatic, these two boys are killing me."[53] Memory of one's failure to prevent the deaths of loved ones activates and maintains concepts of the self as weak and helpless. Unable to prevent the atrocities, some survivors incorporate as a permanent part of their self-concept the idea that they contributed to the demise of their families.

Yael Danieli suggests that this type of survivor guilt is, in part, an unconscious attempt to prevent oneself from remembering the absolute helplessness experienced during the Holocaust. According to Danieli, guilt presupposes choice and the ability to decide one's fate. The unyielding pain of guilt is thus more acceptable to the survivor's belief system than the experience of intolerable passivity and helplessness, and guilt serves to defend against the memory of a nightmare world devoid of choice.[54]

For those who were eyewitnesses to the murder of their own families, undying memories create a guilt that splits these witnesses for the rest of their lives. In an episode referred to earlier in this chapter, Beatrice S. describes such an atrocity, as she recalls hiding with her family to avoid capture by the Gestapo:

It was before Pesach. It was very cold and dark and my brother started crying and my mother said "Because of him we'll all get killed." So she went out with him and she covered us. She covered the top up in the cellar, so they wouldn't see there's an opening. And she went to our next door neighbor, who was Christian—Polish, and the Gestapo shot her. And my brother was wounded. And I saw through the little window there, and my father put his hand on my mouth (she gestures), I shouldn't scream. . . . And he was wounded, and the Gestapo came with his boots and just stepped on him.

As a result, Beatrice says, "It's like there are two of me. There's one that wants to have a zest for life, wants to live and enjoy. And there's another part of me that I have guilt feelings."[55]

Kochevit P. relates a similar atrocity for which she claims partial responsibility, consequently suffering overwhelming guilt. As a young child, Kochevit was taken in by a neighbor who saw the SS coming with dogs looking for Jews. Kochevit tells what she witnessed from her neighbor's cellar: "And I saw the family—my mother, my brother, my grandmother, and my aunt, and they shoot them down, on the place." She later explains how she saw the murders:

I was in the cellar and I saw through a small window. (She gestures, ducking her head down and peering out.) And my brother was begging, "Please." And he tried to run away. He said, "Please. Don't shoot me." And he put his————. (She gestures with her right hand in front of her head, then stops talking.) I can't speak about this.

Kochevit then struggles to finish her account:

Was a very long————. It took me a very long time to believe what happened. I was a little girl. I said that they shot them, but they will never come back? And I saw this with my eyes! (She looks down and pauses.) I suffered a lot after this. I was very sorry that I run away, as a child. Because I was blaming myself that everybody is dead. Only I am alive. I was very much disturbed.[56]

For these survivors, the vividness of memory does not diminish, the images of murder do not fade. The normal self reconstructed later in life must coexist with these images, associated with feelings of responsibility and helplessness. For those who were eyewitnesses to their own family's demise, the schema of destiny fails because of the persistent memory of useless proximity.

Some survivors feel guilt for what they consider to be their own unfairness to other victims. Edith P. confesses intense guilt about a single insulting comment she made to an inmate at Auschwitz, an older woman who shoved Edith as they entered their barracks. After years of suffering, after extreme deprivation, brutal beatings, and daily humiliations, Edith refers to this brief insult as "One of my most painful episodes from Auschwitz." Zezette L. tells of the death march out of Auschwitz to Ravensbruck, with the SS guards shooting those who fell. Zezette clearly remembers walking through a wheat field and then escaping. After her escape, she soon realized that another inmate had followed close behind her, and she grew angry at this woman for following her. Zezette says, "I hid behind a wall, and that part I remember very clearly. And I probably do because I feel very guilty about it."[57] An offense that in normal times might demand an apology intensifies into an enduring insult, with Holocaust survivors interpreting their thoughtlessness or selfishness as contributing to the misery of their fellow victims, however excusable and transitory. The interpretation of the insult alters their self-concept by placing these survivors in the role of victimizer, along with its associated characteristics.

Similarly, witnesses express guilt for not having shared their scarce food with others. In some cases, this guilt is not disclosed, a fact revealed in the testimony of those who returned to the Fortunoff Video Archive a second time. Though these witnesses use very similar words to describe previously told episodes about obtaining food, there is one change: A new ending admits guilt that was not described earlier. In testimony given in 1980 and again in 1988, Renee G. tells of receiving two scrambled eggs as a birthday present while in hiding, cooked by the Polish woman who protected Renee's family. In her first testimony, Renee tells the story concisely, with no mention of guilt, concluding the story by saying, "I will never forget those were the best tasting scrambled eggs I've ever had in my life." In her second testimony eight years later, she relates the same episode, but with an additional ending:

I had two scrambled eggs. . . . The only thing is I couldn't really enjoy it because there were all these people around me, watching me eat those two scrambled eggs. And to this day, I still keep dreaming about all those people watching me eating those two scrambled eggs. . . . I see eyes looking at me . . . as if . . . I should have shared with them."[58]

Jolly Z. exhibits the same pattern of remembrance in relating a moving story about sharing extra soup with her mother in Auschwitz. To receive the extra ration, Jolly volunteered to pick up hundreds of corpses and throw them into mass graves. For this labor, she was rewarded with a bowl of soup at the end of the day. Jolly wanted to share the soup with her mother, but her mother initially refused, saying Jolly should have it. Though her mother finally relented, she took only tiny spoonfuls to allow Jolly to have more, and Jolly reciprocated, also taking tiny helpings. They soon realized that they were accomplishing nothing, so they devised a solution: They would feed each other. "She was feeding me and I was feeding her," Jolly says. She concludes the episode by saying that the bowl of soup saved their lives because in two days they were liberated.

In later testimony, Jolly gives virtually the same account about the extra ration of soup, taking turns with her mother, feeding each other the soup. This time, however, Jolly reveals more. She ends her remembrance of the episode by stating that she failed to share the soup with the other inmates who were also dying, referring to her act as "a limited sharing." Jolly remembers experiencing, "terrible guilt not to share it with the rest of them." She says, "Side by side with this beautiful story, there was still this *guilt* of not sharing it with others."[59]

REASONS FOR SILENCE

One nearly universal response of Holocaust survivors is silence. Beginning shortly after liberation and lasting more than thirty years, most survivors actively remained quiet about their memories of the Holocaust. Oral testimony provides several overlapping reasons for the decades of silence, for the profound reluctance of those witnesses who gave testimony recently, and for the continued suppression of those who remain quiet.

After the war, some survivors completely avoided describing their experiences, focusing instead on finding family and rebuilding their lives. Others tried to tell about the atrocities of the Nazi ghettos and camps but were met with an impressive assortment of disapproval from potential listeners. Some of these survivors clearly remember a single, brief admonishment that discouraged them from talking for decades. Or they remember that after several attempts to recount the events, they were simply not believed. Contributing to the survivors' active silence is the clear knowledge that describing the events in detail means experiencing the pain of core memory, whereas avoiding detailed recall allows distractions to take time away from the painful images. Some survivors are willing to bear their own emotional pain, but they discover that it is too distressing for their listeners—especially loved ones. So they too remain quiet.

The Elusiveness of Understanding

For all the survivors who eventually gave testimony, underlying the stated reasons for not talking is the clear knowledge that even if listeners believe, they cannot fully understand. Celia K. elaborates:

> Even American people, well-educated people, who are constantly working with the Holocaust survivors, I think, even you. It's hard for you to comprehend what it is, really, to go through and feel what we went through . . . It is hard for a person who didn't experience it to really put it in the proper perspective.[60]

Nina S., convinced of the improbability of effective communication, says, "Nobody can understand who wasn't there . . . Even now, which I'm sitting here and telling to you, I don't know if you know what I'm saying." There is too much to tell, the extent of shame and grief too great, the ghettos and the camps too alien for others to imagine. An infinite horror demands impossibly infinite time and effort to convey, as Leo G. explains: "If you want to record the Holocaust, [it's] not just numbers—in the thousands, in the hundreds, in the millions. You can focus almost on one family, on one person, on one particular day. If you go through the details, it's just enough for a lifetime."[61]

Similarly, Edith G. avoids talking not because people refuse to listen, but because language cannot bring about an emotional understanding. According to Edith, when survivors give testimony, words find memories and then expose the emotions within the memories, even though the words themselves cannot adequately convey these emotions to the listener:

It makes no sense to talk about it because nobody understands. Nobody understands the feeling . . . to be frightened, to be scared. Not to know what will *be* tomorrow. Not to know what to *do* tomorrow. Not have a home. Not to know where to sleep, where you put your head down. Not to trust your neighbor. You don't understand and nobody will understand. And that's the reason why people don't like to talk about it.

Though Edith tries to convey her past suffering in testimony, after an hour and twenty minutes, she remains convinced that people cannot understand because, she says, "There are not words enough to bring the situation back and relive."[62]

Inhabiting the normal world for many years and internalizing its perspective, survivors themselves have difficulty believing what they endured so many years ago. Looking back, many survivors know their memories are accurate, while simultaneously experiencing them as impossible. They know the memories represent real events, but they no longer believe that such torment could be inflicted and that anyone could survive. They wonder aloud how others could possibly believe their memories if they do not believe their *own* memories.

More than an hour into his testimony, Leon H. says, "Who will believe? Nobody believes it because I don't believe myself—that this kind of a thing could happen. I don't believe it. How could you?" Similarly, Jolly Z. says, "It's unimaginable. You know what? Sometimes I don't believe it anymore. I sometimes ask myself, was it possible? How can anybody believe it, if I question it?"[63] Eva L. agrees, saying her own disbelief convinces her of the disbelief of others:

I cannot believe that I was part of all this. . . . That's why I never like to talk to anybody. People ask me to tell the story, and I refuse, because I don't believe . . . and my imagination cannot absorb it. That I was able to live through such a horror. How can somebody, an outsider, visualize? And believe that a human being is able to go through this—six years of such horror. Six years. Which every day was a lifetime of horror, of the most terrible horror. . . . How could anybody believe that this is possible if I *myself*, being through, cannot absorb that it is possible for a human being to survive in such conditions and to be here?[64]

In *The Remembered Self*, Daniel Albright states that memory needs to be grounded "in sensorium" with a "biophysical presence," that memory involves the presence of the rememberer at a certain time in a particular place, and that without this remembered presence, the word "memory" does not apply.[65] When Holocaust survivors remember past atrocities, they are able to summon their own biophysical presence in the original events, but it is a presence that they experience as separate from their current physical self. They do not doubt that they were in the horrors; they doubt that the person who was traumatized by these horrors and the person remembering that traumatized self are one and the same.

The Discouragement of Others

After recovering in the DP camps and immigrating to their new homeland, some survivors possessed a fierce motivation to talk, but the responses of the potential listeners extinguished this motivation. When Ernest R. first arrived in the United States after the war, survivors who arrived before him issued a warning:

> You're not supposed to talk about your war times. Because if you going to tell them really what happened, first of all, they're not going to believe you and second of all, they're going to tell you that, "We had also hard time. We had to go to New Jersey for cigarettes." Or, "We had meat rationing." So, we really never talked about it.[66]

The unbridgeable distances between specific memories of suffering and general schemas of normal existence discourage survivors from putting their experiences into words so that others may understand. In testimony, Max B. conscientiously tells of his twelve dreadful days inside a train transport to Bergen-Belsen; how he moistened his parched, cracked lips with rags soaked in urine; how he became so desperately hungry that he cut the liver out of a corpse and ate it to prevent starving to death. When Max tried describing this suffering after the war, he says people would respond by saying, "We had hard times, too. . . . We couldn't eat meat. We had to eat chicken." His conclusion is barely audible: "No use to talk."[67]

In some cases, a single instance of reproach endured in memory, discouraging survivors from talking for decades. Martin S. immigrated to the United States after the war and attended yeshiva. During the first few months, he wanted to inform everyone around him about his enslavement at Skarzysko, the murder of his father, and his time at Buchenwald, earnestly telling everything he could to the rabbi and to his fellow students. One day when things were quiet, a boy turned to Martin and said, "Why don't you tell one of your bullshit stories?" Martin says from that day on, he did not say a word about the Holocaust for more than thirty years. Though Martin was asked to give testimony in the early 1980s, he decided against it because of the lesson he learned after the war: "People don't give a damn"—a lesson that threw him "into a cocoon." Martin does not want to talk about the Holocaust because of the responses of others, fearing that if he tells, he will "lose credibility."[68]

After arriving in the United States as a fifteen-year-old, Renee H. heard the same message as Martin, though in a more polite form. Renee remembers trying to tell her American family about her struggles during the Holocaust, taking care of her deaf sister, witnessing the brutality of the transports, running in terror from Nazi officials, and eventually experiencing the horrors of Bergen-Belsen. Her adopted family was very religious, according to Renee, and when she began to talk, they firmly instructed her to move her experiences into "a general expression" of the Jewish people, which Renee interpreted as meaning they did not want to hear about her experiences during the Holocaust. Renee then chose to express herself quietly in writing.[69]

Avoiding the Pain of Memory

Many survivors avoid talking about the Holocaust to protect themselves from additional emotional pain. The statement of Michael G. is typical of those who fear the release of guarded emotion: "Every time I sit down to do a tape, I get choked up. I can't." Zezette L. says, "I don't want to think about it because I can't *bear* to think about it." Edith G. emphasizes that there are clear images that survivors always think about but that talking about the past forces them to confront other painful images that they do not normally think about. As survivors engage in extended recall, they relate episodes below the level of conscious awareness, episodes that are recalled only because they are directly connected to those that are immediately accessible.[70]

Some survivors elude disclosure by avoiding details, talking about their lives in cryptic labels. Ruth A. first encountered this avoidance of detail during initial contact with survivors after the war:

Nobody spoke. Nobody said————. The only question was, "Where were you during the war?" "I was in a concentration camp." That's it. "I was in the partisans." That's it. "I was hiding in the—some place." That's it. Nobody spoke any details. It seems that the people wanted to block it out from their mind. They did not want to talk about it, just vaguely question: "What is your name? Where did you live before the war? Where were you during the war?" And that was the whole conversation.[71]

Some survivors do not want to admit the self of the traumatized past into their present set of self-concepts. Explaining her reasons for not talking, Bessie K. says, "I was alone, within myself. And since that time I think all my life I have been alone." Bessie says she is *alone within herself* because of the absolute depth of the split in her two selves. In an effort to avoid confrontation with the shameful past, Bessie K. killed her traumatized self: "To me, I was dead. I died and I didn't want to hear nothing. I didn't want to *know* nothing and I didn't want to *talk* about it. And I didn't want to admit to myself that this happened to me."[72]

Some survivors remain silent out of concern for the emotional responses of the listener. In explaining this concern, Leo G. presents the dilemma of disclosure and empathy: "If that person listens and understands it, and if he does, it must have an effect on him. Then I figure, then I feel I put my burden on *him*. And have I got a right to?" To protect others, Sabina S. also prefers not to talk, displaying that preference even with those recording her testimony: "I don't talk about it. If people ask me, yes. I do not want to upset them, so I do not talk about that. And what else would you like to know?"[73]

Within one's family, the dilemma of disclosure and empathy presents a paradox to survivors. If they care about their children, they must tell them about their past. And if they care about their children, they must *not* tell them about their past in order to protect them from emotional pain. When discussing his family, Karl S. struggles to resolve this dilemma, saying, "I wonder which is the right course for me to do, to transmit such values to my children, so they become uneasy with themselves? Or should they live in a dream world, which

I believe it is, and let them enjoy themselves now until something happens?"[74]

The testimony of Violet S. exposes the struggle between shielding one's children and talking to them about the past, between teaching them positive values and exposing them to the details of evil. For many years, her youngest son wondered where his grandparents were, and Violet deceived him as long as she could, telling him they lived far away and could not visit. For Violet and others, it is not only the imparted emotional pain of describing traumatic memory that prevents talking, it is the fundamental difficulty of communicating the inexplicable:

> How can you tell a child? How can I tell my child, my young son? To tell him that another human being *burned* his . . . grandparents. How can you tell such horror? This is why we couldn't speak. They weren't [killed] by gunfire or by natural disaster or something. They were killed by human beings. How can you tell a child something like that, when you [are] teaching them that we are civilized human beings?[75]

To manage the struggle of telling their children about the Holocaust, survivors often assume an incremental approach. Helen L. did not volunteer information, but she did answer questions from her children and her grandchildren: "So we would tell them the truth," she says. "Hitler killed Daddy's parents and Hitler killed my parents. So that's no grandparents. We were telling them not much, a little bit." Ruth A. admits that she talked very little to her children, once in a while telling them a small story. She says, "They feel bad. I can tell the tears in their eyes when I do talk about it." Sabina S. says that she was so conditioned to hide her Jewishness during the war that she translated this strategy to the United States as incremental revelation. "Little by little," she says, "I started to talk a little bit about my experiences." Using identical phrasing, Beatrice S. describes speaking to her son: "Little by little, I always tell him something. But it's really very difficult to tell." Gradually, step-by-step, these survivors pieced together a representation of their past trauma for their children.[76]

Other survivors resolve the dilemma of disclosure and empathy by not talking at all to their children, focusing exclusively on protecting their children from painful knowledge. Josephine B. remembers the one failed attempt shortly after liberation when her mother tried to talk about her experiences during the Holocaust: "My mother started telling the story and at that particular moment my brother started to *cry*. So *much* that—that is the truth and nothing but the truth—we *never* talked about it again."[77]

Clinical psychologists who work with survivors of trauma promote the therapeutic value of talking about the trauma, allowing the victimized to examine their emotions in detail and to regain control of their own individual narratives.[78] For Holocaust survivors, the therapeutic value of speaking their memories is an open question. Witnesses themselves disagree, with some avoiding opportunities to talk and others carefully welcoming the opportunity to communicate the horrors to receptive listeners. Although obvious almost to the point of tautology, if imposed silence is exacerbating emotional disturbance, then talking itself is therapeutic. In such cases, conditions should be set up to allow these survivors to communicate their memories, conditions that would eliminate the social discouragements identified by witnesses in this study, while recognizing and managing the inevitable pain of remembrance.

Depending on the desired audience, survivors could actively seek out environments that are receptive to remembering: family meetings among survivors and their children, mediated by family therapists; official gatherings of Holocaust survivors; instructional programs for teaching young people about the Holocaust; archives for collecting oral testimony. To force the reticent to talk is not helpful. Encouraging them to enter settings that are conducive to talking may be therapeutic.[79]

For Henry S., it took a gathering of Holocaust survivors to summon his motivation to speak his memories:

> I have a boy and a girl. Actually now they're a man and a woman. And I didn't even talk to them for many years after the war. It was actually in '82 we had a big gathering in Jerusalem of survivors, and that was kind of a panacea. Not only for me but for many people from that point on. We *could* express. We could *talk* about it. Before this, we didn't. My children didn't know practically anything about it.[80]

OVERCOMING SILENCE

The social psychologist Harry Triandis outlines the three aspects of self cognitions: private, collective (or familial), and public.[81] Some witnesses report that translating private cognitions into collective cognitions within the family is helpful. When these private cognitions become part of the collective, familial self-concept, then the collective cognitions undergo change. After attending a gathering of Holocaust survivors, Hilda S. began to talk for the first time, with a resulting change in her collective self-concept. She says, "I started telling about it. My husband said he's gotten to know me all over again." In 1992, Marian N. says she began talking *to regain her lost collective self.* She says, "My Jewish consciousness didn't come until much, much later. I would say not really even until I had children, and my son was on the phone once with his grandfather who said something to him about being Jewish. And he said, 'What is that?' And I felt, Oh my God, it's time." Marian says, "It wasn't until then that I started even talking about my background."[82]

For those who are reluctant, actively expressing Holocaust memories within a receptive social environment demonstrates the possibility of talking without harm. After talking, the private self-concepts become more receptive to the presence of traumatic memory—not the traumatic events themselves but the memories of these events. Because many survivors avoid talking about their memories to protect the younger generations, oral testimony may be the most effective and least threatening method of disclosure.[83] In fact, many witnesses perceive oral testimony primarily as a method for communicating with their children and grandchildren and only secondarily as a method for communicating with the interested public.

After an hour and a half of testimony, Karl S. offers a spontaneous observation about the effects of giving testimony. He says, "It makes me feel a little bit contented. Because, until about a year ago, I did not want to discuss those experiences at all. So I feel that maybe I'm opening it up and it might have a beneficial effect on my personal life."[84] Though Karl is appropriately cautious about the expected therapeutic effects, he is aware that giving testimony might open healthy exchanges in the future. Though exhausting and unsettling for all witnesses, the act of giving testimony provides meaning to the recall of traumatic events, meaning that arises not from the content of the traumatic memories but from the recording of these memories.

For those who are willing, translating private memories of horror into the public domain can be powerfully beneficial. Nadia R. has begun speaking to high school students about her experiences during the Holocaust. She refutes the idea that reliving the horrors through speaking memories creates additional pain. She says, "First of all, I am going over it if I am *speaking* about it or not. There is not really *one* day of my life or one night that I don't think about it." Nadia also rejects the dilemma of empathy and disclosure. "I'm not inflicting *pain* on my children or on the students I'm talking to," she says. "I'm just inflicting the *knowledge*."[85]

The child survivor and psychiatrist, Robert K. presents a symposium for high school students every year. In his testimony he asserts, "Nothing that I have ever heard from any psychiatrist or psychoanalyst in the world . . . matches one twenty-minute presentation by one of my survivor panelists in terms of their therapeutic well-being." He explains the source of the therapeutic value: "It is turning the *worst* possible experience . . . a degradation, a mutilation of their souls," into something "constructive." He points out that these survivors have guarded their memories for decades, hiding the memories within themselves or within their families. He then describes the survivors' therapeutic revelation when speaking in public:

> They *discover* that there are five hundred students there who listen to them—and you should see the listening that goes on when they speak. And they see perhaps, perhaps they're doing something with their experience that some of those five hundred will be touched by them, to perhaps make even this much (he holds his thumb and forefinger one inch apart) of a shift in their perception of life, their philosophy. That gives the survivor great hope. And I've seen [them] go through it and get depressed and break down and be in tears and stay depressed for two weeks. And tell me that it was the best day of their lives.[86]

With public disclosure, there is no catharsis. The telling releases painful emotion but does not diminish the emotion. Change occurs in interpreting the function of traumatic memory. Memory is no longer meant to be hidden. It is meant to bring to life those who perished and to educate those who were not there. Holocaust memories remain, in part, to preserve the existence of those who were murdered. Therefore, it is not appropriate to have survivors put their traumatic memories behind them, but rather to encourage the survivors to accept the role of part-time guardian of their family's legacy rather than full-time guardian."[87] Transmission of memory to receptive listeners for the purpose of teaching is profoundly therapeutic to the survivors, giving meaning not to the memories themselves but to the act of recalling—an act that formerly provided only torment. In the blunt words of Robert K., "It's turning shit into gold."[88]

PRESCRIPTIONS OF MEMORY

Toward the end of the testimonies, many witnesses speak about their memories for the purpose of instructing the listener. Once testimony is given, once specifics of memory have been recorded and the videotape assumes the responsibility of documenting remembered history, expressing the meaning of Holocaust memory takes on increased urgency. Most witnesses end their testimony by articulating general observations abstracted from their specific Holocaust memories. All the witnesses who returned to the Fortunoff Archive to give testimony a second time speak of the profound importance of leaving behind the lessons of memory. Jolly Z. is one such witness who returned for additional testimony. She speaks of the "frustrations" with her earlier testimony, saying, "It focused too much—or *tried* to focus too much—on the objective level, on factual things." Her reason for returning to record Holocaust memory is clear. "We all know about the atrocities—or *now* we do," she says. "But what are some of the lessons?"[89] Chapter 6 describes the profound importance of these lessons to the witnesses and characterizes the content of the lessons themselves.

NOTES

1. Testimony reveals many examples of the prevalence and specificity of the connections between memory and behavior. In Tape HVT-641, Martin S. elaborates on specific fears linked to remembered deprivations many years earlier. He asserts, "I will always have my tank full of gas." He pauses; then he explains: "I'm always ready to *run away*, always ready, just in case." While performing slave labor as a child at Skarzysko, from the time he awoke in the dark of the early morning until the time he collapsed from exhaustion at night, Martin had to be vigilant, staying very busy while trying to avoid beatings. Connected to these memories of hypervigilance at Skarzysko is Martin's fear and avoidance of general anesthesia, which he explains in later testimony: "That is a direct response to what happened as a child. I must always have control." (Refer to Tape HVT-1091.) Lenore Terr, in *Unchained Memories*, documents this same fear in those who have been victims of incest (New York: Basic Books, 1994).

Painful memories of deprivation and hunger lead to the present fear in normal life of not having enough food and supplies, which in turn leads to conscientious efforts to conserve. In describing his singular desire after the war, Alfred F. reveals the specific memory that fuels his elemental motivation to conserve today: "I remember when I was liberated, I had one wish in life: to be able to eat *potatoes. Every day.* Only potatoes, that's what I wanted. If I could have *that*, I would be happy" (Tape HVT-2762, testimony of Alfred F., 1995).

The testimony of Clara L. is representative of the fear of dogs: "Ever since that time, I cannot go near a dog. I'm so afraid—even if I walk in the *neighborhood* of a dog." Isabella L. reveals the source of her fear of dogs in her description of the SS officer who supervised the transport from her home town in Hungary to Auschwitz: "He came with a silver pistol, a German Shepherd—which I am forever fearful, I'm terrified of German Shepherds— and he came to call out the names, prepare them for the next day's deportation" (Tape HVT-1850, testimony of Clara L., 1993; Tape HVT-1270, Isabella L., 1989).

Bessie K. speaks of the connection between her Holocaust memories and her fear of snow: "When the snow comes, I hit the ceiling. I'm petrified. As old as I get, I have to work at it." She explains that in a camp in Estonia, she was a slave laborer: "And we shoveled the snow. They took us in the fields . . . empty fields with only the sky and the snow. And this did it for me: the snow. I wasn't in contact with nobody. I was alone, only the snow and the sky" (Tape HVT-206, Bessie K. in the testimony of Jacob and Bessie K., 1983).

Renee G. responds today to her confinement as a youth, hiding from the Nazis for fifteen months in a pit underneath a manure pile. Because of her confinement many years ago, unable to stand up straight, unable to breath fresh air, Renee now requires open space, including a house with many windows. "Big windows," she says. Inside her own room, she always keeps her door open, "ready to run." Her husband has an office without windows. "I don't go in there," she says. "I stand in the door" (Tape HVT-976, Renee G., 1988).

Menachem S. describes a unique episode of lasting fear. Menachem's parents worked in the labor camp of Oskar Schindler during the war, and Menachem tells of meeting Schindler during his visits to Israel many years after the war. He observes, "The interesting thing was, that everyone was still afraid of him" (Tape HVT-152, testimony of Menachem S., 1979).

2. Tape HVT-3260, testimony of Nina S., 1996.

3. Tape HVT-220, testimony of Jolly Z., 1983; Tape HVT-1091, Martin S., 1988.

4. Tape HVT-641, testimony of Martin S., 1986.

5. Tape HVT-72, testimony of Beatrice S., 1982; Tape HVT-3132, Nadia R., 1995.

6. Tape HVT-1, testimony of Eva B., 1979; Tape HVT-897, Ernest R., 1987; Tape HVT-36, Celia K., 1980.

7. Tape HVT-1270, testimony of Isabella L., 1989.

8. Mardi J. Horowitz and Steven P. Reidbord, "Memory, emotion, and response to trauma," in *The Handbook of Emotion and Memory: Research and Theory*, edited by Sven-Åke Christianson (Hillsdale, N.J.: Erlbaum, 1992), 350.

9. Tape HVT-3132, testimony of Nadia R., 1995.

10. Tape HVT-152, testimony of Menachem S., 1979.

11. The passages in the text are from the following testimonies: Tape HVT-3261, testimony of Solomon L., 1996; Tape HVT-3260, Nina S., 1996; Tape HVT-2188, Samuel Z. in the testimony of Samuel and Wolf Z., 1993; Tape HVT-854, Sol F., 1992. Other representative descriptions are in the testimony of Sabina S., Hanna G., and Jacob K. Sabina S. says, "Right after the liberation, I used to wake up crying, dreaming, after nightmares that the Germans were chasing me. This was for quite a long time I used to wake up crying, because of those nightmares." Hanna G. says, "Nights. Most of the nights are still during the war, seeing Mom, and everybody, and horrors. Many, many nights, constantly screaming. That I'm being followed or threatened, and I wake up in a sweat." She adds, "And you are afraid you are going to be taken away." Jacob K. says, "I still have dreams . . . how to conduct myself in case there's another evacuation." (Tape HVT-623, testimony of Sabina S., 1985; Tape HVT-136, Hanna G., 1982; Tape HVT-206, Jacob K. in the Jacob and Bessie K., 1983.)

12. Tape HVT-284, testimony of Alan Z., 1984.

13. Tape HVT-2854, testimony of Aladar M., 1995; Tape HVT-1850, Clara L., 1993.

14. Tape HVT-3380, testimony of Henry S., 1996.

15. Nan M. Sussman, "The Dynamic Nature of Cultural Identity Throughout Cultural Transitions: Why Home Is Not So Sweet," *Personality and Social Psychology Review* 4 (2000): 355–373.

16. Tape HVT-3380, testimony of Henry S., 1996.

17. Tape HVT-2148, testimony of Hilda S., 1993; Tape HVT-1537, Jacqueline R., 1986.

18. Tape HVT-71, testimony of Eva L., 1982.

19. Tape HVT-2045, testimony of Alina Z., 1993.

20. Sussman, "The Dynamic Nature of Cultural Identity Throughout Cultural Transitions," 355–373.

21. Tape HVT-623, testimony of Sabina S., 1985.

22. Tape HVT-1897, testimony of Morris R., 1992.

23. Tape HVT-287, testimony of Sabina G., 1984.

24. Tape HVT-115, testimony of Frania R., 1979.

25. Tape HVT-974, testimony of Edith P., 1987.

26. Tape HVT-191, testimony of Frieda J., 1980.

27. One universal conviction emerges from the memories of atrocity: a devout commitment to Israel, interpreted—as at Yad Vashem—as the chapter following the Holocaust in the story of the Jewish people. In testimony, Claude Lanzmann articulates this personal devotion to Israel: "The destruction of Israel would be, for me, something even worse than the Holocaust, the Shoah. I would kill myself. This, I am sure of this. I cannot imagine going on living as a Jew, without this country. As if Israel would have been only a periphrase [circumlocution] in the history of the Jews" (Tape HVT-700, testimony of Claude L., 1986).

Many witnesses perceive Israel as a savior, convinced that there would have been no Holocaust had there been an Israel. The connection to Israel moves beyond political passion to personal attachment. Karl S. says that during the 1956 Sinai War, he was physically ill for three days because he is "part of the organism called Jewry." Many witnesses talk of their devotion to Israel and their personal suffering when Israel is attacked (Tape HVT-173, testimony of Karl S., 1980).

28. Robert Jay Lifton, *The Protean Self: Human Resilience in an Age of Fragmentation* (New York: Basic Books, 1993), 171.

29. Tape HVT-2256, testimony of Rita L., 1993.

30. Tape HVT-2148, testimony of Hilda S., 1993.

31. Tape HVT-3132, testimony of Nadia R., 1995. Nadia then explains her reasoning for attending synagogue services after immigrating to the United States. Aware of her debilitating anxiety with Jewishness, she wanted to "balance it out" afterward with an active decision: "I tried to make this *by choice* rather than a happening." Making this response a theme in her life, Nadia and her husband then put their daughter in an Orthodox Jewish school because they could, not for religious reasons. In *The Protean Self*, Robert Lifton asserts that there are two tendencies in developing one's self-definition: to open up (the *protean self*) and to shut down (the *constricted* or *fundamentalist* self). (Lifton, *The Protean Self*, 81–82.) A person who has lived through great suffering usually does both, while avoiding the extremes. Nadia now accepts her Jewish identity, yet she is clear that she does not want to be a "professional survivor," reacting to those, she says, who define themselves predominantly in terms of their Holocaust identity.

32. Sussman, "The Dynamic Nature of Cultural Identity Throughout Cultural Transitions," 355–373.

33. Robyn Fivush, "The Functions of Event Memory: Some Comments on Nelson and Barsalou," in *Remembering Reconsidered,*" edited by Ulric

Neisser and Eugene Winograd (New York: Cambridge University Press, 1988), 277.

34. Tape HVT-72, testimony of Beatrice S., 1982.; Tape HVT-1650, Violet S., 1991.

35. Tape HVT-206, Bessie K. in testimony of Jacob and Bessie K., 1983.

36. Tape HVT-65, testimony of Irene W., 1982.

37. Tape HVT-50, testimony of Renee H., 1979.

38. Edward S. Reed, "Perception Is to Self as Memory Is to Selves," in *The Remembering Self: Construction and Accuracy in the Self-narrative*, edited by Ulric Neisser and Robyn Fivush (New York: Cambridge, 1994), 283, 287–289. An alternative interpretation is that the unified self is a reified concept, inappropriate for an in-depth analysis of self concepts and especially unsupportable in a discussion of those who have survived extended atrocity. That is, there are not different (or split) selves, but rather different kinds of knowledge that contribute to culturally nourished definitions of self. In the case of Holocaust survivors, there exist simultaneously two irreconcilable sets of knowledge. Although this interpretation may engender a more elaborated account of self-knowledge, it is not consistent with the actual language of the witnesses. It is the witnesses who speak of the concept of a unified self—in contrast to their own experience of irreconcilably split selves. When witnesses engage in self-analysis, their testimonies reveal the phenomenal experience of *two* different selves.

39. Tape HVT-2148, testimony of Hilda S., 1993.

40. Ulric Neisser "Five Kinds of Self-knowledge," *Philosophical Psychology* 1 (1988): 35–59.

41. Charlotte Delbo, *Days and Memory*, translated by Rosette Lamont (Marlboro, Vermont: Marlboro Press, 1990), 4.

42. Harry C. Triandis, "The Self and Social Behavior in Differing Cultural Contexts," *Psychological Review* 96 (1989): 507.

43. Tape HVT-657, testimony of Rose W., 1986.

44. Tape HVT-3380, testimony of Henry S., 1996. More than forty years after the war, Martin S. began experiencing this reversal of past and present in his sleep: "I have a new dream. That I am back in the camp, and everything I enjoyed in the U.S. was a dream." In this dream, he says, "the reality is the camp" (Tape HVT-641, testimony of Martin S., 1986).

45. From the testimony, it is clear that the connections between events in the world and the resulting guilt feelings are too particular and too diverse to be assessed with a quantitative analysis. Nevertheless, it is feasible to identify and categorize the different sources of guilt. In a general way, Leo G. elaborates on the difficulty of evaluating suffering, focusing on the impossible pain within families:

> In the whole story of the Holocaust, you always talk about, so many died: thousands, hundreds of thousands, millions. The bigger tragedy, if anybody can visualize this, is dehumanization, degradation, and

agonization . . . for the ones that lived and the ones that didn't live, or how they died, how some died. Dying . . . suffering in separate, was not as horrible, not even ten percent as horrible as when the orders took place with kinfolk near each other. Can you even visualize? Mothers and children, of course, it's been documented. . . . If it comes in front of a relative and a close one—kin, the spiritual part of a human being disintegrates to a point beyond describing (Tape HVT-158, testimony of Leo G., 1980).

Robert K. bluntly rejects common beliefs about this kind of survivor guilt. He is disdainful of what clinical psychology and psychiatry have done to misconstrue concepts concerning Holocaust survivors: "The only survivors . . . that I know who have guilt are those who were looking after a close relative who died in their arms and they thought perhaps they could have done or should have done something else. And even *they* know they couldn't have" (HVT-318, testimony of Robert K., 1984).

46. Tape HVT-152, testimony of Menachem S., 1979; Tape HVT-3620, Nina S., 1996.

47. Tape HVT-1880, testimony of Michael G., 1992.

48. Tape HVT-92, testimony of Chana B., 1980.

49. Tape HVT-71, testimony of Eva L., 1982.

50. Mardi J. Horowitz and Steven P. Reidbord, "Memory, Emotion, and Response to Trauma," in *The Handbook of Emotion and Memory: Research and Theory*, edited by Sven-Åke Christianson (Hillsdale, NJ: Erlbaum, 1992), 353.

51. Tape HVT-618, testimony of Samuel B., 1995.

52. Tape HVT-1850, testimony of Clara L., 1993.

53. Tape HVT-1394, testimony of Abe L., 1990.

54. Yael Danieli, "Treating Survivors and Children of Survivors of the Nazi Holocaust," in *Post-Traumatic Therapy and Victims of Violence*," edited by Frank M. Ochberg (New York: Brunner/Mazel, 1988), 278–294.

55. Tape HVT-72, testimony of Beatrice S., 1982.

56. Tape HVT-85, testimony of Kochevit P., 1979.

57. In the testimony of Edith P., a woman inmate, described by Edith as having beautiful red hair, shoved Edith in the barracks, and Edith responded spitefully: "Don't push me. By the way, you are not a redhead." To this day, her rudeness haunts her, and every year at Yom Kippur, Edith asks forgiveness from the woman (Tape HVT-974, testimony of Edith P., 1987; Tape HVT-100, Zezette L., 1980).

58. Tape HVT-5 and Tape HVT-976, testimony of Renee G., 1980; 1988.

59. Tape HVT-34, testimony of Jolly Z. and Rosalie W., 1979; Tape HVT-972, Jolly Z., 1988.

60. Tape HVT-36, testimony of Celia K., 1980.

61. Tape HVT-3260, testimony of Nina S., 1996; Tape HVT-158, Leo G., 1980.

62. Tape HVT-571, testimony of Edith G., 1985.

63. Tape HVT-628, testimony of Leon H., 1985; Tape HVT-972, Jolly Z., 1988.

64. Tape HVT-71, testimony of Eva L., 1982.

65. Daniel Albright, "Literary and Psychological Models of the Self," in *The Remembering Self*, edited by Ulric Neisser and Robyn Fivush (New York: Cambridge University Press, 1994), 19–40.

66. Tape HVT-897, testimony of Ernest R., 1987.

67. Tape HVT-94, testimony of Max B. in Max and Lorna B., 1980.

68. Tape HVT-641, testimony of Martin S., 1986.

69. Tape HVT-50, testimony of Renee H., 1979.

70. Tape HVT-1880, testimony of Michael G., 1992; Tape HVT-100, Zezette L., 1980; Tape HVT-571, Edith G., 1985.

71. Tape HVT-2678, testimony of Ruth A., 1994.

72. Tape HVT-206, Bessie K. in testimony of Jacob and Bessie K., 1983.

73. Tape HVT-158, testimony of Leo G., 1980; Tape HVT-623, Sabina S., 1985.

74. Tape HVT-173, testimony of Karl S., 1980.

75. Tape HVT-1650, testimony of Violet S., 1991.

76. Tape HVT-2853, testimony of Helen L., 1995; Tape HVT-2678, Ruth A.,1994; Tape HVT-623, Sabina S., 1985; Tape HVT-72, Beatrice S., 1982.

77. Tape HVT-869, testimony of Josephine B., 1992.

78. Questions remain in clinical psychology about the treatment of those victimized by prolonged and widespread trauma. Many prescribed approaches for treating PTSD appear insufficient for victims of prolonged atrocity. In fact, some clinical strategies for effectively alleviating the pain and disturbance of circumscribed traumatic events are not feasible with Holocaust survivors. In a seminal article, Ronnie Janoff-Bulman describes four effective strategies for coping with post-traumatic stress following circumscribed victimization. The first such strategy, "redefining the event," is not appropriate for Holocaust memories because it involves "creating hypothetical worse worlds; construing benefit from the experience." The second strategy, "finding meaning," is similarly inappropriate because it involves "the attempt to make sense of one's experience, to search for meaning in the victimization." The third clinical strategy, "changing behaviors," involves taking specific actions to prevent similar victimization. A victim of criminal assault might, for instance, take formal training in self-defense, diminishing the self-concept of victim and promoting a self-concept in control. As described earlier, Holocaust survivors do take precautions with events in normal life associated with traumatic events in the past, but because the trauma

suffered is unprecedented and unrepeated, there is no evidence of therapeutic value other than avoiding anxiety-provoking situations, such as dogs, trains, people in uniforms, personal trust in neighbors, and the languages of their past tormentors. The fourth proposed strategy of Janoff-Bulman has proved to be effective with Holocaust survivors: seeking the resonant influence of social support. (Refer to Ronnie Janoff-Bulman, "The Aftermath of Victimization: Rebuilding Shattered Assumptions," in *Trauma and Its Wake*, edited by Charles R. Figley [New York: Brunner/Mazel, 1985], 15–35).

One conclusion is clear: The delineation of post-traumatic stress disorder (PTSD) in DSM-IV is too limited and too focused on discrete events to apply uncritically to victims of widespread and prolonged atrocity. Nearly a decade ago, Judith Herman noted that the diagnostic formulation of PTSD, based primarily on circumscribed events, does not account for the manifestations of prolonged and repeated trauma, especially the distinctive experience of surviving national efforts of genocide. For further elaboration, refer to Judith Herman, "Sequelae of Prolonged and Repeated Trauma: Evidence for a Complex Posttraumatic Syndrome (DESNOS)," in *Posttraumatic Stress Disorder: DSM-IV and Beyond*, edited by Jonathan Davidson and Edna Foa (Washington, D.C.: American Psychiatric Press, 1993), 213–228.

79. James Pennebaker and his colleagues have presented evidence for the therapeutic value of talking and writing about profoundly traumatic experiences. In particular, the careful act of writing allows people who have been victimized to organize and control the narratives that describe the core memories. Writing allows expression without immediate judgment (James W. Pennebaker, Steven D. Barger, and John Tiebout, "Disclosure of Trauma and Health among Holocaust Survivors," *Psychosomatic Medicine*, 1989, 51, 577–589). Witnesses do report that writing their Holocaust memories is helpful—even necessary; however it is probably not the case that the trauma will become, in the words of Kent Harber and James Pennebaker, "more fully integrated within the person's network of memories and beliefs" (Kent D. Harber and James W. Pennebaker, "Overcoming Traumatic Memories" in *The Handbook of Emotion and Memory: Research and Theory*, edited by Sven-Åke Christianson [Hillsdale, NJ: Erlbaum, 1992], 359–387).

80. Tape HVT-3380, testimony of Henry S., 1996.

81. Harry C. Triandis, "The Self and Social Behavior in Differing Cultural Contexts," *Psychological Review* 96 (1989): 506–520.

82. Tape HVT-2148, testimony of Hilda S., 1993; Tape HVT-1881, Marian N., 1992.

83. A few witnesses report improvement in nightmares after talking about their Holocaust memories. Zev H. had recurring nightmares for more than thirty-five years after the war, nightmares that revisited the camps and the liquidation of his ghetto, as well as the last few months of the war, "which was the worst," says Zev. In 1975, Zev provided his first oral testimony for

a friend who was working on a Holocaust project. Although he was not able to tell "the whole thing," he says he told "a little bit," and that afterward he felt better for the very first time. About his nightmares, Zev says, "I still have them, but in a lesser form. I am waking up sometimes in the night." He ends his testimony at the Fortunoff Archive optimistically: "And I hope with this telling of story, I have even less. I get it out of . . . my system" (Tape HVT-622, testimony of Zev H., 1985).

When Menachem S. settled into life after the war, he began having nightmares: "Nightmares that were totally abstract, but they were always repeating themselves." For Menachem, the underlying theme was helplessness: A conveyer belt moved him inexorably toward a rolling press that would crush him to death. Unable to move off the conveyor belt, with no power to stop it, he rolled closer and closer to the press. He awoke each night, disoriented and crying violently, unable to stop sweating and shaking, unable to go back to sleep. This nightmare persisted for many years before gradually dissipating, though the memory of the nightmare persisted. When Menachem was initially approached to give testimony, he refused, fearing the return of this nightmare. And after deciding to give testimony, the nightmare *did* return, but with a difference: "Again, the conveyor belt, rolling presses, helplessness, terrible anxiety. And, for the first time in my life, I have *stopped* the conveyor belt." He says he woke up, still feeling anxious but with a "wonderful sense of fulfillment and satisfaction." He adds, "For the first time, I wasn't disoriented" (Tape HVT-152, testimony of Menachem S., 1979). For a few witnesses, exemplified by Zev H. and Menachem S., remembering at length and in detail, though emotionally distressing and exhausting, can diminish the harassment of nightmares.

84. Tape HVT-173, testimony of Karl S., 1980.

85. Tape HVT-3132, testimony of Nadia R., 1995.

86. Tape HVT-318, testimony of Robert K., 1984.

87. Boaz Kahana, Zev Harel, and Eva Kahana, "Clinical and Gerontological Issues Facing Survivors of the Nazi Holocaust," in *Healing Their Wounds: Psychotherapy with Holocaust Survivors and Their Families*, edited by Paul Marcus and Alan Rosenberg (New York: Praeger, 1989), 209.

88. Tape HVT-318, testimony of Robert K., 1984.

89. Tape HVT-972, testimony of Jolly Z., 1988.

CHAPTER 6

BEYOND THE AFTERMATH: LESSONS OF MEMORY

After the war, survivors of the Holocaust struggled to recapture their physical health and began to reassemble their lives, searching for family, marrying, emigrating, working, and raising children. European communities devoted their efforts to recovery. The United States celebrated its hard-fought victory, then moved ebulliently into a period of unprecedented population growth and economic expansion. The popular media, reflecting the mood of the country, remained devoutly uninterested in the miseries of the recent past.

After recovering their health and moving back into normal life, some survivors insisted on remembering the horrors of the Holocaust aloud, desiring to tell an unreceptive world what it apparently did not know—that Hell had been conscientiously constructed on Earth and that they had been there. Those who had not witnessed the Holocaust confronted these talkative witnesses with a patchwork of earnest discouragement: confident disbelief, misplaced camaraderie, impatience, scolding, blame, and untimely indifference. The Nuremberg Trials exposed Nazi perpetrators and elaborated the concept of crimes against humanity. The trials provided an opportunity to discuss justice, morality, and responsibility in the wake of unprecedented atrocity, and nearly two decades later, the Eichmann trial reawakened this discussion, but for most of the thirty years following the war, the air filled with imposed quiet.

In the United States, high school textbooks permitted a sentence or two about concentration camps, inserted in a section on World War II, accompanied by a postage-stamp photograph of liberated inmates at Bergen-Belsen. Though a handful of writers eloquently detailed the horrors they experienced, external memory was scant. Internal memory, blanketed by self-denial and the indifference of others, remained hidden. In the 1960s, more survivors began to publish. More unbelievable stories emerged, supported by documents, photographs, historical analysis, and film footage. A few narrative movies were produced, with the Holocaust as an unseen character in the distant background, influencing the protagonists to behave oddly. Mostly, however, the general public lived in preoccupied complacency, and Holocaust memories remained unspoken.

After thirty years, a confluence of events pushed the Holocaust into the foreground. The oldest survivors retired from their jobs, second families grew up, and children left home. The business of reconstructing lives slowed, and some survivors began talking again. In 1978, the television miniseries *Holocaust* aired in prime time, watched by millions. Large gatherings of survivors convened; more historians began analyzing and organizing the documents of the Nazis. Memorials were planned and constructed—some with considerable difficulty. Survivors spoke in schools, and educators talked about developing curricula to teach students about the Holocaust. Survivors began recording oral testimonies.

By the end of the 1970s in the United States and Europe, scholars and artists had produced a critical mass of work about the Holocaust, large enough to be noticed by the popular culture. Restrained expression grew into a congregation of voices searching for meaning in the rupture of Western civilization. Lessons derived from the Holocaust proliferated, from frequently repeated aphorisms that could fit on bumper stickers to scholarly analyses of the complex events that culminated in unprecedented mass murder—with predictable denials.

Recently, some of the reluctant outpouring of the past two decades has given way to a different kind of quiet, an appropriately ardent caution about making judgments and finding meaning. After three decades of suppression and two decades of prolific writing, filming, and museum building, many people are now taking the time to listen to the messages of those individuals who directly experienced the atrocities of the Holocaust.

In this chapter, the witnesses themselves state the lessons of Holocaust memory. After many years of living in the normal world haunted by memories of another, alien world, these witnesses impart their interpretations. They send messages to cross the vast outer space between two worlds that share nothing except the witnesses themselves. These witnesses are not ethicists; most do not have advanced degrees in history or philosophy or theology. Some of their lessons sound cryptic; some prickly; many unsettling; but they are direct statements based on specific memories of horror, with the perspective of decades between the remembered events and the derived lessons. The lessons of memory transmitted by the witnesses show diversity and commonality, contradiction and agreement—and considerable pessimism.

PURPOSES OF MEMORY

The most powerful message of memory that witnesses convey is the fundamental necessity of remembering itself. All witnesses provide testimony to document the events of the Holocaust. All witnesses externalize their memories to leave behind a permanent record for future generations. For many people, the underlying purpose of memory—to bear witness—was the *raison d'être* during the horrors of the camps. The commitment to remember provided the motivation for survival.

As Aaron S. struggles with the conflict between the pain of memory and the obligation to give testimony, he links the fundamental purpose of memory to his very survival:

> My brother and my mother was gassed. I know that for sure. That's definite. But————. (He pauses.) I never wanted to talk about this. (He cries and then speaks slowly through his tears.) My kids made me do it. That I should leave *something* for the next generation to know what happened there. Otherwise nobody will know what happened there. . . . This is what *kept me alive*. I always thought there's got to be *somebody* who come out here and tell this story, what happened there. That one human being can do this to another human being.[1]

For Alina Z., the horrors of the Holocaust defined her life, just as the message of her memories saved her life. She begins by describing the Warsaw Ghetto uprising as the originating event for the remainder of her days: "That's what started the beginning of the next half of my life," she says, pausing and growing angry. "Murderers! Evil. Evil! (She shakes her head.) It's hard to believe." Alina proceeds to detail the horrendous events in the concentration camps, along with the admission that through all of her suffering, through the relentless physical and emotional pain, the message of memory prevailed, a message that singularly prevented Alina from taking her own life:

The worst part of my being in concentration camp . . . I was pregnant when I came to camp. In the beginning, I didn't know that I was pregnant. But when I find out, that was hard to understand what I went through. Especially the last days when the child was pushing to go out . . . I was afraid . . . they gonna beat me up. I was so afraid because I got twenty-one in Majdanek, and all the time my body was blue. My whole body was blue. I was afraid of beating because I didn't want to be crippled. I said to myself—*something*. Let them shoot me to finish my life because it was very hard to live, very hard. Many times I was thinking to go on the wire and touch it and just finish my————. And in the back of my head was *who gonna tell the world what happened?*[2]

Though the emotional pain of remembrance is of great concern to them, witnesses state that the motivation to make memory public is powerful enough to overcome this concern. At the beginning of his testimony, Marc S. reveals the conflict between his wariness about the painfulness of Holocaust memory and his obligation to record personal memories:

I would like to make one thing clear. It causes any of us who lived through the Holocaust—survivors—a lot of *pain* to talk about it, our personal experiences, as well as the total picture of the Holocaust. The only reason I consented to do it is for future generations. Me, as an eyewitness, to give my account, what I lived through and the way I saw it.[3]

In *Momentous Events, Vivid Memories*, a comprehensive study of personal event memory, the cognitive psychologist David Pillemer introduces the concept of "memory directives," referring to the prescriptive function of specific memories.[4] He observes that cognitive psychology has assigned this prescriptive function primarily to general schematic representations in semantic memory and not to particular remembered instances. The widely accepted view is that schematic knowledge structures represent the meanings of worldly events, along with the prescriptions for applying these meanings. Pillemer recognizes this view and offers a counter proposal: Specific memories themselves provide functional meaning for people's lives. In fact, the testimony of Holocaust witnesses makes it clear that prescription is part of specific memory and is of profound importance to the rememberer. Moreover, the testimony broadens the prescriptive function of traumatic memory to the extended rememberer—those who tell and those who listen to the remembered events. Personal memory functions not only to prescribe beliefs and actions for the individual but also to provide meaning to members of one's family and to the wider community. In turn, carrying out the purpose of specific memory, providing its meaning to others, cycles back to influence the structure of the memories themselves.

At the end of his testimony, Abraham E. reveals that the anticipated pain of speaking his memories prevented him from giving testimony for many years but that the purpose of memory actually mitigated the pain of memory:

> I am very ... proud of myself. Because in the beginning I thought I wouldn't be able to make it. It's very hard. But I thought it is going to be even much tougher. But maybe because of the reason: because I feel I am accomplishing something for *someone else*, not for myself. Maybe this helped me to go through with it.[5]

In his discussion of the prescriptive function of specific memory, Pillemer defines two directives of memory that are of particular relevance in understanding first-hand traumatic memories: *originating events* and *anchoring events*. According to Pillemer, an originating event is a single momentous event that is remembered as "the birth of a set of enduring beliefs or attitudes." Specific memories of originating events function to motivate and reorient a person's beliefs.

An anchoring event validates those beliefs that were engendered by the originating event, strengthening these beliefs and making them more enduring.[6]

When witnesses hear about atrocities in the world that remind them of experiences during the Holocaust, these current atrocities serve as anchoring events for the originating events of the Holocaust. They connect directly to Holocaust memories, drawing out their original meaning and their emotion. In testimony given in 1980, Edith P. ends by saying, "When I learned about Cambodia, I went into a deep depression. It pains me terribly that the world has not learned."[7] The news of contemporary cruelty reinforces the lessons from the originating events of the Holocaust and anchors these lessons at the center of the survivors' beliefs about the hopelessness of preventing depravity. In testimony given in December of 1994, David K. mixes past and present, lamenting the indifference of other nations to the mass murder of European Jews during the Holocaust and connecting this indifference to recent tragedies in Africa and Europe:

Unfortunately, it's very bad to be weak and small. . . . When it happened, the world didn't care, and the world still doesn't care. Whether it is Rwanda or whether it is Bosnia, or whatever. Very same European countries—and in part, the United States—that turned a deaf ear when so many people got killed, admittedly in a different way. There was an organized government-led effort using technology to erase from the face of the world, a whole people. The scale was different, the nature of it was different. But the cruelty, the cold cruelty of people, I think, is the same as it was before.[8]

Leo B. shows the same characteristic hopelessness toward those worldly events that show profound cruelty.

My heart is scarred forever. I'm just speechless, that I have lived. I'm 76 years old now and I'm alive and kicking. And have a family, have two kids, have a grandson. It's wonderful. (He pauses.) But will it ever get better? Will the war ever stop anywhere on this face of the Earth? No way. No place. It's Yugoslavia. It's Middle East.[9]

In this single, brief passage, Leo B. speaks of his heart being "scarred forever," while his life is "wonderful." In this passage, Leo reveals the inconsolable difference between the horrors of his past and the normality of his present life, the dark lessons of the Holocaust accentuated and validated by the news of atrocities elsewhere in the world. These recent events awaken the lessons of the Holocaust as well as the emotions within Holocaust memory, and they intrude on Leo's normal, present life.

News reports of widespread atrocity validate the Holocaust survivor's belief in the potential for profound cruelty in human beings, anchoring this belief and applying it as a general lesson about the fundamental bleakness of human nature. Recent catastrophes are described not as examples of the Holocaust repeated, but as examples of a similar kind of cruelty repeated, unchecked, in other areas of the world. In this study, witnesses refer specifically to the emotional consequences of hearing about bombings in the Middle East, about genocide in Cambodia during the late 1970s, about genocide in Rwanda in 1994, and about widespread, systematic killing in Bosnia and Kosovo in the mid-1990s.

When speaking of recent atrocities, the witnesses do not diminish the individual suffering of the victimized nor the cruelty of the criminals. They choose to understand and to empathize with the recently victimized through their memories of the Holocaust, but not to judge the level of suffering. The witnesses associate other atrocities but do not compare. They do not view the events through the lens of the Holocaust, but rather possess an increased sensitivity for detecting cruelty, spiritual malignancy, and oppression.

HOPELESSNESS AND CHOICE

During my study, I did not record a single witness stating the phrase, "Never again" as an important prediction to leave behind in recorded testimony. Specific memories of the Holocaust simply do not provide that prescription. In fact, Holocaust memory leads many witnesses to predict that the organized mass murder of Jewish people could happen again—given desperate economic conditions, rising nationalism, and charismatic demagogues. Emphasizing the historical persistence of anti-Semitism in Europe, Chaim E. believes that mass murder of Jews will happen again, saying that it could be 100 years from now or even 500 years. He says, "It's not a question of *if*, it's a question of how long." His expectation that "it could happen again" fuels his advice: "If you hear something, react to it."[10]

Toward the end of his testimony, Leon H. displays a sharp rise in energy, issuing a similar warning, both personal and public: "To tell the Jewish people. To tell the whole world. They should tell the world. That *this* Jew today is not the one they used to know. Hit back, very hard! Before you *get* hit! (He shouts.) Don't wait! Don't ever wait. . . . Please. Because you going to get hit and be too late."[11] Leon's testimony, forty years after the end of World War II, conveys a lesson with disquieting immediacy—as if the remembered horrors happened only recently. The lesson begins in specific, personal memory and floods into the larger community.

Many witnesses openly reject the possibility of preventing widespread atrocities in the future. Meir V. states bluntly, "Sometimes I even think that much as we try to make the world not forget, not to repeat a calamity like this again, it doesn't work." Nina S. says, "I personally have a *very* strong suspicion that it *might* happen again. Not that it might; that it *could* happen again." Though Ernest R. believes in the necessity of testimony, he agrees that all the efforts of the survivors cannot prevent another Holocaust.[12]

Pessimism about the prevention of future atrocities pervades even the most energetic and generative witnesses. Hilda S. speaks to Jewish groups and to young people at high schools. She explains her motivation: "The hope, of course, is that by our existence or by having lived through it, we can *teach* others, or *warn* others, or *educate* others not to allow anything like that to happen. But I have very little hope."[13] Embedded in specific memories of horror, the concept of hope remains forever contaminated by its failure in the past.

Karl S. was a young child during the war, hiding from the Nazis. He speaks of the pessimism of his father, who managed to live through numerous horrors. In testimony, Karl quotes his father's appraisals of the future for the Jewish people: "We are hated and disliked by everyone." "There's no place we can run away." "The United States can turn into a Germany." "There's no protection any place." "The world never learns a lesson." Karl wonders aloud whether these bleak proverbs are inappropriately unhopeful or simply realistic. He summarizes his own pragmatic advice to his eleven-year-old son, based on a childhood spent avoiding capture by the Nazis: "I don't believe in fighting, but I do not believe in retreating."[14]

Jolly Z. describes watching the birth of a baby to an inmate in a slave labor camp in Hamburg. She finishes her account with a vivid depiction of the SS man who took the baby, held its head down in a sink, and drowned it, saying, "Here you go little Moses, down the river." After remembering that episode, Jolly says, "For a long time, it was difficult to have hope after that." Though this episode might lead some witnesses to an unconditional loss of hope, that is not the lesson that Jolly ultimately conveys. The drowning of the infant is superseded by a specific memory that serves as an originating event in support of Jolly's lesson that the perpetrators were able to choose their actions. Jolly describes this memory. Under guard by the SS, she and several other inmates were trying desperately to push a heavy carriage stuck in some oily mud, but they failed to dislodge it. One SS man commanded another: "Why don't you beat these Jews! That's the way they will work." So, the SS man beat them with a whip, but according to Jolly, not very forcefully. The SS man who initially gave the order proclaimed, "You don't know how to hit Jews." Jolly then describes the resulting carnage: "He took the whip and started to really, really hit us. Kick us. And that night many of us went home with broken ribs and bloody faces. It was a terrible, terrible sight." The next morning, the other SS man told Jolly that he was ashamed to be a German. From this memory, Jolly formed one of her fundamental lessons: "Even within that system, even under those circumstances, they had choices where they could be brutal or could still help us and thereby enable us to survive."

In her second testimony, Jolly Z. extends the lesson of human choice to the victims of Nazi atrocities as well as the perpetrators, a controversial message anchored by other memories, which Jolly summarizes: "Side by side with these atrocities, I saw love, courage, fortitude . . . I saw sisters fighting over a piece of bread, but I saw sisters dying for each other." She then offers the general lesson arising from these memories. "Beast or angel, we have a choice," she says. "In the shadow of the gas chambers, I found my faith in the *potential* of man because I realize that we all have the potential for both extremes: of good and evil." While not blurring the distinction between the perpetrators and the victims ("beast or angel"), Jolly offers a basic lesson of human nature linked to specific memories.[15]

COMING FORWARD WITH MEMORY

The underlying purpose of traumatic memory, bearing witness, does not diminish with time. As the reasons for silence fall away, as children encourage their aging parents to speak, the purpose of memory asserts itself even more strongly, and witnesses who have not talked for many years come forward to record their testimony. In this testimony, witnesses provide three overlapping reasons for their decision to speak: the fear that time is running out, the desire to fill in details that they have not revealed to anyone, and the obligation to counteract those who would deny or diminish the horrors of the Holocaust.

Many of those who provided testimony for the first time more than a half century after the Holocaust state that the immediate reason for recording memory is the fear that time is running out for passing on their memories. Nina S. lived through the Lodz Ghetto, through Auschwitz and Bergen-Belsen, yet remained silent about her Holocaust experiences for fifty years. In 1996, she explains what made her decide to give testimony: "I'm getting older. My husband is gone already. And I just feel that it's my obligation. Because before they all died, they said, 'Don't forget to tell the world what they doing to us.' And I feel *now* is my time." For those who were young children during the Holocaust, the desire to leave a record is especially urgent. Their reason is clear: to tell their memories before it is too late. The testimony of Ernest R. is representative of child survivors: "Unfortunately, after we are gone—probably I am one of the youngest ones who can talk about it—it will be only history books. It will be an old story." His goal is to "leave a legacy" to his children, "that they should remember that it did happen." Rita L. also expresses this concern: "We must come out with this. Because if we don't, that's it. We're the last generation. There's no one left. So now I talk about it."[16]

In a recent essay, Lawrence Langer recognizes this concern while also stating what witnesses tacitly acknowledge by giving testimony: the archived testimony alleviates this concern. The impact of survivors' narratives will remain as long as testimony is preserved and as long as it is studied, just as other historical events—he cites the American Civil War—have not diminished in historical significance or personal immediacy after the last witnesses died.[17] For survivors, however, the clear directive of traumatic memory overrides this knowledge: *Tell now or it will be too late.* Memories nearly sixty years old convey the message that not informing family and friends, not telling the wider community, leads to disastrous consequences. Though conditions today are clearly different, the meaning attached to silence still applies. Silence indicates indifference, and indifference can be fatal. Hilda S. refers to this lesson as a moral obligation:

"Sometimes the need to do the right thing is so compelling that it acquires a primacy over all other fears and possibilities that could happen."[18]

Near the close of the twentieth century, many survivors had talked to their families about the Holocaust, but not in detail. Over the years, these survivors had been encouraged by their families to give testimony in order to leave a full record of their memories, to fill in detail that they had not revealed to anyone. The fiftieth anniversary of liberation in 1995 provided a clear reminder that it was time to fill out the stories, that it was time to provide detail. As Hubert W. explains: "All my children know about it. . . . I am sure I told my wife, but we never—we never *elaborate* on it. It was my daughter who, many years ago, said to me, 'Dad, you should either write a book or put it on tape.' So, that's why I'm here today, fifty years later."[19]

Many witnesses state that their testimony is motivated by concerns for family: Testimony given in the early to mid-1980s is for the children; in the 1990s, for the grandchildren. Though the stated audience is immediate family, the recalling of personal memory for public archiving suggests a belief that the testimony will be of value to a broader audience and a belief in the permanence of recorded memory. A public record of personal memory suggests that, despite the universal doubts about the listener's ability to understand, the witnesses retain hope for the usefulness of testimony.

A final reason for providing the lessons of memory is the desire to counteract those who seek to deny or diminish the reality of their Holocaust memories. In 1995, Nadia R. came forward to give testimony for this very reason. She says, "I feel very strongly about the growing deniers movement. And that is *so* perverse to me . . . I feel such a strong urge to fight as much as I can do. So it's only fifty years, and already are there people who say it wasn't. What will happen when we won't be here anymore?" To create a living history, when Nadia speaks at schools, she tells the students to tell their grandchildren that a real human being went through the Holocaust and talked about it. In her testimony, Nadia elaborates a quixotic optimism:

The ultimate goal is to prevent. But I'm not so naive with the——. Looking back into the human history, can we really prevent another genocide? Or another Holocaust like this? But at least, if nothing else, at least *try*. So these people would be witnesses and not to have this six million just forgotten. Because then the job will be really done. And that's why I'm doing it. So the deniers will not succeed in their efforts to have this totally blotted out.

Although Nadia believes her Holocaust experiences are painful to her children's generation, this belief does not deter her from speaking out: "You speak about it, and this happens. And some people *don't* speak about it, and it happens." She admits that speaking about the Holocaust has created fearfulness in her daughter, instilling a "shtetl mentality," and she admits that telling young people about the Holocaust causes them pain, but she makes it clear that the crime is the atrocity perpetrated by the Nazis, not the decision on the part of survivors to speak.[20]

Henry S. is also concerned about denial, believing that time is running out: "After the last one of us is gone. And that's only a few years hence. More and more literature will be written and lectures will be given that the Holocaust never existed."[21] Similarly, Marc S. emphasizes that testimony is important now:

Especially at a time when they [are] even trying to whitewash the whole thing and say that it never happened, that six million Jews didn't even perish. To me, it's just like killing the six million once over again. And for that reason, I believe [it is] the obligation of every survivor to give his personal account.[22]

To some observers, the goal of refuting Holocaust denial may seem outdated, even paranoid, but the existence of such denial continues to be reinforced—and even anchored—by memorable events in the news. In April 2000, for example, after the testimony of Nadia R., Henry S., and Marc S., a decision was handed down in a highly publicized libel case brought by British writer David Irving against Holocaust scholar Deborah Lipstadt. Mr. Irving charged that Professor Lipstadt libeled him in her book *Denying the Holocaust* when she called him a dangerous advocate of Holocaust denial. Though the court decision went resoundingly against David Irving, concurring with and extending Professor Lipstadt's conclusions that Irving engaged in willful distortion of historical fact in order to deny the Holocaust, the lawsuit itself supported the reality that prominent people can publicly deny the memories of Holocaust survivors.[23]

The directives of memory are immovable because they are rooted in a specific remembered reality. Although the directives can take the form of general principles, the source of these directives is traumatic memory—memory that does not fade, fueled by emotion that does not abate. Moreover, without evidence to refute the directive of an originating event, the directive endures as part of memory.

RESOLVING THOUGHTS OF REVENGE

The coexistence of malignant memories of horror and fundamental schemas of decency and justice creates a powerful desire for some form of retribution. Though witnesses reveal thoughts of revenge, nearly all of them state that they rejected the opportunity to act on these thoughts. One witness, Celia K., fought with the partisans, and she admits killing people in raids against the Nazis and their collaborators, but when presented with an opportunity to exact revenge, she did not follow through:

> There was one incident. They caught a young German soldier and they brought him to me. I was the only Jewish girl in . . . this section. They said, "He's all yours. Do with him whatever you want to do." A young kid, maybe nineteen years old. I don't know, maybe I'm ashamed to tell this. He had a wounded knee. I could not kill him. I fixed his knee. I bandaged him. I don't *know* what got into me. I could not hurt him. I fixed up his knee. He was a young fellow, with blue eyes, a blond little thing, dirty, skinny, disheveled.

She concludes, "I hated myself for the weakness."[24]

David Pillemer identifies the memory directive of the *turning point*, which is a specific, remembered event that changes one's perspective, altering an important goal in one's life.[25] Some witnesses, such as Celia K., report no such turning point in their lesson about revenge. Though Celia refused revenge when given an easy opportunity, she interprets this as a mistake, an anomalous event not to be used to anchor a lesson. Such a lesson contradicts her self-concept at the time as that of a fighter, able to kill for her cause. Many other witnesses do report turning points in their attitudes about revenge, remembering a single event that redirected their original lesson to carry out revenge. With these witnesses, the turning point results from a deep conflict between wanting to punish the perpetrators and wanting to recover their nascent self-concept of decency. For these witnesses, the return from degradation to normalcy, rebuilding the body and reconstructing the self-concept, prevailed over revenge.[26]

Leo G. remembers a specific incident that functioned as a turning point in his search for revenge—a still, small voice reaching back to his fragile prewar self:

> I don't know if you should record this, not that I put something on myself. The first instinct was, get me something, anything to kill somebody. . . . Knocked at one door . . . can hear a woman crying and a baby crying, crying from the other side of the door. And that was enough to stop us, emotionally. . . . If it would have been a man in there, I think—I don't know what we would have done.[27]

Some witnesses remember instructions from other people as a turning point. Shortly after liberation, a sergeant asked Zoltan G. what he would do if he had power over the Germans, and Zoltan replied angrily, "For five years up, I would kill them all. I wouldn't let them live, no one of them." He remembers the sergeant telling him that he must show the Germans a better way of living. For Zoltan, the message of showing others a humane way of responding ultimately carried, and Zoltan concludes, "He was right. I was wrong."[28]

Other recently liberated inmates were simply too weak to do anything but try to recover their physical selves. Aaron S. remembers that just before he was liberated, the SS ripped off their uniforms and escaped into the forest, leaving their prisoners and their weapons behind:

> They were stupid enough to throw the guns away. There was a lot of revenge there. (He speaks slowly.) But———. (He cries.) I couldn't do it. They gave me gun. I said, "I can't shoot nobody." Some people did it. I said I can't do it. (He composes himself.) They were running after them. And the Army came down . . . and for the first two hours that's all I did is cry. I had a blanket over me. I didn't know what to say, what to do.[29]

In a similar situation at liberation, Daniel F. was approached by an American soldier with three captured German soldiers. The American soldier gave Daniel a gun and told him he could shoot one of the German soldiers, but Daniel did not. He says his only goal was to regain his health.[30]

For some witnesses, revenge itself provided the turning point away from punishing the perpetrators and toward reconstructing the self. Alan Z. remembers his strong desire for revenge, and he remembers witnessing violent retribution after liberation. "I said somehow I want . . . to live through this and see the Germans defeated. My only wish was to see a German, to kill him right there, cut him to pieces even. I wish, and I lived it through. I saw it. Because when Bergen-Belsen was liberated . . . gruesome things happened." For three full days after liberation, Alan reports that the inmates of Bergen-Belsen were free to do what they wished. He witnessed vengeance against the captured SS guards and approved of this vengeance but found he could not participate:

> They set up a tribunal . . . sentenced every SS man to different deaths. But I cannot, I couldn't watch that. One thing I saw, which I run away from it, I couldn't see it anymore. They take an SS man, was the worst one, and they sentenced him to death. While they sentencing him to death, they put him in a cement sidewalk, stretched out, with the hands tied to the back and the feet. And three Russians and one Pole lifted up a cement block, a very heavy one, and put it on his head and squashed him while he alive. And I said, this is the end of this. I don't want to see any more. They did all these things to them. All kinds of different deaths they gave them. This is good. But I don't want to see any more.[31]

Alan Z. recognized the value of punishing the perpetrators but realized that carrying out revenge would prevent recovery of his prewar self.

Hanna F. remembers exacting a limited revenge. While the Russian Army advanced, the Germans kept Hanna not far from Dresden, where she stayed until April 1945. After a barrage of bombing by the Allied forces, her German captors became disorganized about what to do with their prisoners. When they arrived in Prague, Hanna managed to escape captivity and find a Czech family who took her in for two weeks, until liberation. One day, Hanna remembers seeing soldiers marching by, and she left the house. She says, "I just sat out in the gutter. Didn't have the strength to even to stand." She realized then that the soldiers marching toward her were surrendered Germans, and she remembers saying to herself, "I'm going to kill one. I have to kill one. I'm going to kill one." She then tells of her revenge:

> They were coming closer. I got my full strength. I got up. And picked my right arm up and I hit one in the face. He didn't know what hit him. The blood start running. (She pauses.) I felt such a relief. I just sit down in the gutter and cried. Everybody was applauding, but I couldn't even get up.... That was the revenge I took."[32]

Near the end of his testimony, Nat G. tells of spontaneous revenge. At ninety-five years of age, Nat is the oldest witness in this study. Nearly fifty years old when World War II ended, Nat possessed more prior knowledge of inhumanity than other survivors, remembering the First World War as well as earlier programs. His anger at the Nazis appears more infused with comparisons to other crimes against humanity, crimes that were massive and brutal, but dwarfed by the systematic, relentless cruelty of the Nazis. At the end of the war, after being imprisoned at Narva, Nat and the remaining inmates were loaded onto boats in the Baltic Sea and abandoned with no food and no water for three days and nights. Nat managed to survive, and after liberation, he regained his strength. Shortly afterward, while riding in a jeep from Feldafing, Nat and another inmate came upon a German factory:

> And we made a regular program over there. I brought over 140 watches. This watch came from over there. (He shows the one he is wearing and laughs.) And on the way back, we were so excited, we were so *mad*, that on the way back, a boy was driving ... two Germans were walking, a road. A man and a woman. He went right through them, right through them. He killed them right away. And the jeep was loaded with watches. Locks, watches, everything. We were so mad. That's what they did to us. For what? For what reason?[33]

Hanna F. and Nat G. took their revenge, which served as a turning point to move on with the rebuilding of their lives.

Violet S. reveals her remembered thoughts as a turning point in rejecting revenge:

> It wasn't just a mess of . . . hoodlums . . . These were the top intelligence, scientifically, who *planned* to burn our children alive. I never, never forgive them. Never. I tried. And then you say, revenge. Now what will we do? What could we have done? The same thing they have done to us? Then we wouldn't have been any better.[34]

Most survivors do remember making an active decision about their desire for revenge, often many years after the events. In her first testimony in 1980, Edith P. epitomizes the witnesses' struggle with their attitudes toward the Germans. Edith wants to know: Should she hate them? Should she forgive them? In her second testimony eight years later, Edith says she has resolved her dilemma: she *ignores* them.[35]

Almost all survivors do eventually translate revenge into the rebuilding of their lives with family and work: Each child is a miracle and each child a defeat of Nazism; each professional accomplishment a brace supporting normalcy and a blow against Nazi perversion. A few witnesses, however, remember no such turning point. Without resolution, without a turning point in the lesson of revenge, the conflict between memories of past atrocities and present schemas of retributive justice can generate thoughts of revenge that continue to smolder. Ernest R. concisely describes this dormant desire: "I thought at one time that I would like to take vengeance. And that vengeance is possibly still deep inside. In me."[36]

FRAMES OF EXPRESSION

After the war, many survivors externalized their memories quietly in journals. After Holocaust archives were set up several decades later, survivors were able to express their memories aloud in the form of oral testimony, presenting a combination of factual description, emotional expression, moral lessons, and historical instruction. Some survivors expressed their memories in art and music.

In the disjointed flow of testimony, witnesses often use figurative language to convey their memories of atrocity—figures of speech that help connect their memories of atrocity to the listener's imagination of the horrors. In particular, witnesses use metaphor and simile, metonymy, understatement, paradox, humor, irony, and rhetorical questioning. Most jarring are the rare instances of humor embedded within the factual descriptions of events in oral testimony—humor that provides a glimpse of the horrors while maintaining emotional distance. In some cases, sardonic humor was evident even at the time of the events. Herbert L., for example, describes the ignorance of Red Cross observers at Theresienstadt by telling a dark joke. He describes how the inmates at Theresienstadt prepared for the inspection by the Red Cross:

> We beautified the camp for at least a month before they came. And since there were too many bodies—people—around, I think one-third of them were sent into the gas chambers in Auschwitz to make it appear better. And then these dummies from the Red Cross came, and the joke circulated that one of the dummies asked, "How do you like it in Theresienstadt?" And the answer was, "I must say very good." That was the joke, with the emphasis on *must*.[37]

Even more bleak is the reported comment that deportees made to those who stayed behind in the Nazi ghettos. "See you on the shelves," they would say to each other, meaning that the next time they encountered one another, they would be in the form of products on the shelves of a store.

Similarly, Leon H. uses irony to avoid detail while emphasizing the life-and-death necessity of standing *appell* at Auschwitz: "God forbid, you were lost. You had to be killed. Not lost." Midway through her testimony, Barbara T. mocks herself and her tormentors by saying, "If I sound bitter, it's only because I am." Sabina S. provides a glimpse of the absolute loss of freedom during the Holocaust by juxtaposing descriptions of past horrors with self-effacing observations about the inconsequential in her present life: "So it felt good that I'm alive. I'm in a free country and I'm worried that my nail polish doesn't match my lipstick. Isn't that great?" Witnesses use this kind of humor to condense ineffable complexity into an accessible phrase that communicates some of their torment.[38]

The open-endedness of oral testimony permits witnesses to tell memory in detail, without imposed time limits. Witnesses speak those memories that come to mind, without a plan and without an outline.[39]

Magda F. summarizes succinctly: "I did not read notes. It came just by itself, the way I remember it." In testimony, witnesses freely and spontaneously recall the events of the Holocaust, though they acknowledge there is more to tell. Testimony ends after the witnesses have completed what they consider to be their story, but it does not end because memory is exhausted. Leo B. ends his efforts to reveal the scarring lessons of memory through the use of rhetorical questioning: "Will this ever end? It's still not. Never end. Has the world ever learned? Have *we* learned?"[40] After finishing the recall of episodes, many witnesses end their testimony abruptly, stopping not because they have no more to say but because of their anticipation of incapacitating emotional pain.

After more than an hour of testimony, Eva V. begins to talk about her children, and as she does so, she breaks down and cries. She looks at the camera and says, "Thank you. I do it enough." Eva then raises her hand to shield her face from the camera. At the end of his testimony, Alfred F. talks about his "wonderful" wife and two children, then shakes his head with grief, fighting tears for the first time during his testimony. He looks at the camera and says, "I think I've told my story." Getting up quickly from his chair, he leaves while the camera is still filming. After three hours of testimony, Meir V. says simply, "I'm also glad that I got it over with." When he notices the camera still filming, he adds forcefully, "You can stop now."[41]

Knowing there is more to say, some witnesses encounter difficulty ending the testimony.[42] Aaron S. suffered through more than two years in Auschwitz, followed by a death march in the winter of 1945 to Gleiwitz, then Gross-Rosen, then Dachau, and finally Muhldorf. After describing liberation, Aaron says, "I guess this is my story. There are some things maybe more to say, but I guess I'll leave it for somebody else to say it." After realizing there is no apparent end to his memories, Aaron seeks to close his testimony. The interviewers each thank Aaron, and his testimony appears to be over. As the camera is about to be turned off, Aaron interjects, "I didn't want to come, for a long time." The camera then goes off, the screen goes dark, and the testimony is over. Or so it seems. The camera soon comes back on again, and Aaron begins to talk of non-Jewish people being killed at Auschwitz, trying to establish a sense of completeness to his story. He then concludes: "I happened to be there from the beginning to the end, so I happened to see all this. But, I don't know. I guess I'm going to————. We're going to talk about this as long as we're alive."

He tries again to close his testimony with words, but fails. Instead, he reaches into a file to retrieve photographs of himself as a little boy, and photographs of his mother and father and his brother and sister, all of whom were murdered. He presents these photographs to be recorded as part of his testimony, the portraits accomplishing what words could not: closure on describing the infinite.[43]

Those survivors with talents in the visual arts express the emotion of traumatic memory in images, bypassing the limitations of words. In testimony, Samuel B. describes one of his general strategies as a visual artist:

> I certainly do not make illustrations of the things that have happened. I do it all in a very symbolic way, in a way which only gives a sense of a world which was shattered, of a world which was broken. Of a world that exists again through enormous effort to put everything together when it is absolutely impossible to put it together. Because the broken things can never become whole again. But we still can make something that *looks* as if it was whole. And live with it. More or less this is the subject of my painting. Whether I paint still lifes or people or landscapes, there is always something of that moment of destruction there.[44]

Judith G. also records personal history through her art. She describes one of her collages that depicts what appears to be an abstracted landscape:

> When you look at it right now, it looks colorful, and one cannot really see its content. But I saw my plants as half human. Each plant has an image, a human image. Also, if you look at what's growing: Limbs are growing. All these are limbs. All over. Also, the image I saw underneath the grass, I saw people. And even those who have rotted away, I still see legs and children and faces.

She explains the presence of both the moon and the sun in the collage. "Everybody was there. Everybody watched. The trees watched. The sun watched. The neighbors heard. And nobody did a thing."[45]

Remembering the specific events that lay waste to the myth of human decency, survivors convey an underlying tenet of their lives, the inescapable uncertainty that results from mass destruction. Those who lived through the Holocaust inhabit this realm of uncertainty. They wonder about what was, what might have been, and what will be. Their message strives to be heard over what Milan Kundera refers to as "the noisy foolishness of human certainties."[46] Leo B. interrogates the intolerable unknown of his family's death: "Perished. How? What way? I don't know." After nearly three hours of testimony, David K. questions the aborted future of all the victims: "Who knows what talents could have developed if these children had grown up?"[47] The artwork of Judith G. represents this uncertainty in the plants made from legs and hands, plants that stand for the amputated lives of the murdered children. The relentless speculation feeds back and activates vivid memories of loss.

After the war, the failure of others to recognize the unprecedented enormity of the Holocaust and the unwillingness to believe the specific cruelties cannot be underestimated. For thirty years, the world was uninterested in simply hearing about the miseries of the victimized. As a result, the survivors' memories of the atrocities remained imprisoned and unvalidated.

Living through the most extreme deprivations, denied personal bonds that join us during times of normalcy, survivors are left with the inescapable view of human beings as distinct, isolated entities. Stripped of the veneer that covers people in normal life, survivors clearly perceive the simultaneous presence of individual perspectives. They know that each life story is but one set of experiences and that many survivors must contribute to the overall personal history. They are acutely aware of the limited and varied perspectives of individuals, and this is one of their universal lessons.[48]

Always aware of another possible world, survivors convey their fundamental unease with normal life. Insistent memories of horror form a self that permanently inhabits a world only they know. Heda K., a survivor of Auschwitz, acknowledges this fact with a general lesson drawn from her own individual experience: "Everyone who survived the way I did, we sort of don't feel at home in this world any more. . . . You never forget, you never get rid of it, but you learn to live with it. And that sets you apart from other people."[49] Survivors communicate their memories with force and clarity, but also with a sense of hopeful futility. After raising families, building careers, and contributing to their communities, memories of unprecedented horror endure. Throughout the survivors' postwar lives, insurgent memories continue to vivify an unearthly past. Perceived memories split the self and leave behind dichotomous human beings who live in the present world as tormented guests.

NOTES

1. Tape HVT-1533, testimony of Aaron S., 1991.
2. Tape HVT-2045, testimony of Alina Z., 1993. Alina then tells of the dreadful birth of her son and the perverse hopefulness of the inmate who delivered the baby.

> And the baby was born. And she said, "You have a boy." And she took away the boy. And 'til today, I don't know where is the boy. I beg her, crying. And I ask her to give me the baby . . . I said I don't want to live. I want to die with my baby. I can't fight anymore. I want to die. And she look at me and she sit down and she beg me to quiet down. And she said, "He's so beautiful. We gonna find your husband. You gonna have children." . . . I said I can't live any more. I want to die.

3. Tape HVT-176, testimony of Marc S., 1982.
4. David B. Pillemer, *Momentous Events, Vivid Memories* (Cambridge, Mass.: Harvard University Press, 1998), 63–98.
5. Tape HVT-579, testimony of Abraham E., 1985.
6. Pillemer, *Momentous Events, Vivid Memories*, 70, 71, 74.
7. Tape HVT-107, testimony of Edith P, 1980.
8. Tape HVT-2741, testimony of David K., 1994.
9. Tape HVT-2680, testimony of Leo B., 1994.
10. Tape HVT-756, testimony of Chaim E., 1986.
11. Tape HVT-628, testimony of Leon H., 1985.
12. Tape HVT-1892, testimony of Meir V., 1992; Tape HVT-3260, Nina S., 1996; Tape HVT-897, Ernest R., 1987.
13. Tape HVT-2148, testimony of Hilda S., 1993.
14. Tape HVT-173, testimony of Karl S., 1980.
15. Tape HVT-34, testimony of Jolly Z. and Rosalie W., 1979; HVT-220, Jolly Z., 1983.
16. Tape HVT-3260, testimony of Nina S., 1996; Tape HVT-897, Ernest R., 1987; Tape HVT-2256, Rita L., 1993.
17. Lawrence L. Langer, in "Reflections," *Newsletter of the Fortunoff Video Archive for Holocaust Testimonies*, Spring 2000, 4–5.
18. Tape HVT-2148, testimony of Hilda S., 1993.
19. Tape HVT-2809, testimony of Hubert W., 1995.
20. Tape HVT-3132, testimony of Nadia R., 1995.
21. Tape HVT-3380, testimony of Henry S., 1996.

22. Tape HVT-176, testimony of Marc S., 1982.

23. Deborah E. Lipstadt, *Denying the Holocaust* (New York: The Free Press, 1993). News story reported in the *New York Times*, Sarah Lyall, April 12, 2000, p. A1.

24. Tape HVT-970, testimony of Celia K., 1987.

25. Pillemer, *Momentous Events, Vivid Memories*, 76.

26. Leo B. was born in Sosnowiec, Poland, in 1918. After liberation, he walked back to Sosnowiec, in frigid weather. He details his decision not to seek revenge when he had the opportunity:

> I stopped on the road and one family, I'll never forget this as long as I———. It was four generations Germans, and I begged them to give me something warm to warm up my insides because it was cold. I was still wearing prisoner's clothes. And I had a good sense of smell. They wouldn't give me anything but coffee and I know they got something in the oven. And they took out bread because they didn't want the bread to burn. And they wouldn't offer me any. And that's all I had to do, go out. A hundred feet away, there were Russians. If I would have told them that, they would have killed them all. And we had the right for three days to go to kill every German we saw, but I never had the heart to kill anybody. So, when I walked out, there was a Russian woman on a truck and she had a pig, but this was already baked, and it didn't bother me. I ate it. (Tape HVT-2680, testimony of Leo B., 1994.)

27. Tape HVT-158, testimony of Leo G., 1980.

28. Tape HVT-35, testimony of Zoltan G., 1979.

29. Tape HVT-1533, testimony of Aaron S., 1991.

30. Tape HVT-978, testimony of Daniel F., 1988.

31. Tape HVT-284, testimony of Alan Z., 1984.

32. Tape HVT-971, testimony of Hanna F., 1987.

33. Tape HVT-1637, testimony of Nat G., 1991.

34. Tape HVT-1650, testimony of Violet S., 1991.

35. Tape HVT-107, testimony of Edith P., 1980; Tape HVT-974, Edith P., 1987.

36. Tape HVT-897, testimony of Ernest R., 1987.

37. Tape HVT-2830, testimony of Herbert L., 1995.

38. Tape HVT-628, testimony of Leon H., 1985; Tape HVT-780, Barbara T., 1986; Tape HVT-623, Sabina S., 1985.

39. In the summer of 1994, I was in the control room with a witness's son watching the recording of testimony. The son had in his hand what looked like an outline. As his father began to give testimony, the son grew tense. Within minutes, he became agitated, saying, "This is not what we

came to tell about. Why is he talking about this?" Shaking his head, he folded the paper and placed it in his pocket. He rested his chin on his hand and just watched.

40. Tape HVT-1185, testimony of Magda F., 1989; Tape HVT-2680, Leo B., 1994.

41. Tape HVT-2254, testimony of Eva V., 1993; Tape HVT-2762, Alfred F., 1995; Tape HVT-1892, Meir V., 1992.

42. Joanne Rudof, the archivist at the Fortunoff Video Archive, says, "The end comes many times" (Personal communication, November 1998).

43. Tape HVT-1533, testimony of Aaron S., 1991.

44. Tape HVT-618, testimony of Samuel B., 1995.

45. Tape HVT-1879, testimony of Judith G., 1992.

46. Milan Kundera. Interview by Philip Roth. In *Shop Talk: A Writer and His Colleagues and Their Work*, edited by Philip Roth (New York: Houghton Mifflin, 2001), 90-100.

47. Tape HVT-2680, testimony of Leo B., 1994; Tape HVT-2741, David K., 1994.

48. The testimonies of David K. and Leo G. exemplify the view of multiple perspectives. After describing the concentration camp at Gross-Rosen, David K. says, "I'm giving you *my* impressions. I'm sure that of the 4,000 people that come there, you get other impressions." Leo G. says, "The tragedy of the Holocaust will never be really known in spite of the hundreds and hundreds of books." He says that each book "reflects only one person at a particular place at a particular time" (Tape HVT-2741, David K., 1994; Tape HVT-977, Leo G., 1988).

Sabina S. espouses this view about her rescuers, while maintaining the validity of statistical facts. After describing how she was helped by one Ukrainian family, she says, "So there are always exceptions to the rule. That's why I never generalize. Like I cannot say *all*. I mean I would say that the *majority* of the Ukrainians were horrible, yes, but that's not *all*. There's always an exception to the rule . . . so you cannot generalize" (Tape HVT-623, Sabina S., 1985).

49. Tape HVT-99, testimony of Heda K., 1980.

APPENDIX

SELECTION OF THE TESTIMONIES

A total of 129 separate testimonies from 125 witnesses contributed to the findings in this book. These testimonies totaled more than 200 hours of recorded recall. Table A.1 lists the testimonies in order of their archive number; Table A.2 lists the witnesses in alphabetical order according to the last name. As shown in Table A.1, 117 of the testimonies consisted of one witness each; the remaining twelve testimonies included more than one witness. Eighty-five testimonies were identified in the published records of archived testimonies at the Fortunoff Video Archive: forty-seven of these were chosen from the *Guide to Yale University Library Holocaust Video Testimonies* and thirty-eight were chosen from the Yale University on-line records available through ORBIS. Fifteen testimonies were sampled from Lawrence Langer's *Holocaust Testimonies*. Twenty-nine testimonies came from the set of witnesses who gave testimony more than once.

Two sets of witnesses in this study were chosen within defined categories. One category consisted of testimonies from Jewish survivors who were interviewed more than once. A total of fourteen people were in this group, with twelve providing testimony once in 1979 or

1980 and then again seven to nine years later in 1987 or 1988. (Two of these twelve people provided three testimonies, with an intervening testimony given in 1983.) Of the two remaining witnesses, one gave testimony in January 1986 and May 1988; the other gave testimony in 1980 and in 1985. This distinctive group provided information on the efforts of giving testimony and on constancy and change in Holocaust memory over time. A second category consisted of thirty-two witnesses who were young children during the Holocaust, born between 1931 and 1940. These witnesses ranged in age between infancy and eight years old when World War II began. Four of the child survivors were also in the category of witnesses interviewed twice and twenty-eight were chosen from the *Guide to Yale University Library Holocaust Video Testimonies* and the on-line records available through ORBIS.

For the entire sample of 125 witnesses, the witnesses ranged in age when giving testimony from forty to ninety-five years old, with the oldest being forty-three years old when World War II began (born in 1896). Descriptive statistics for the overall sample are as follows: The mean age in 1945 was 19.7 years old; the mean age when providing testimony was 60.9 years old; standard deviations were 8.25 and 10.06, respectively. There were sixty-six women and fifty-nine men. Testimonies were provided between May 1979 and July 1996.

SAMPLING PROCEDURES IN OTHER STUDIES

When studying people who have lived through mass destruction, standard procedures for choosing participants are often not feasible or even appropriate. Consider some examples of valid and comprehensive research efforts that show the range of difficulties in sampling a devastated population of human beings. In a study of PTSD, Klaus Kuch and Brian Cox chose 124 Holocaust survivors "out of 145 applicants for German compensation."[1] In their study of memory of Holocaust survivors, Willem Wagenaar and Jop Groeneweg obtained data from the previously collected testimony of seventy-eight witnesses chosen in different ways from the criminal trial of De Rijke at Camp Erika in the Netherlands. These investigators clearly described the complexity of obtaining participants and the difficulty of controlling the sampling process. They stated that, "The major part of the interviews were haphazard and unsystematic" and that "from the protocols it was not always clear how the witnesses were found."[2]

James W. Pennebaker, Steven D. Barger, and John Tiebout studied thirty-three people who happened to be in a group of fifty-six survivors interviewed as part of an archive project in the Dallas, Texas area.[3] In a study of coping behavior in survivors of Nazi concentration camps, Joel E. Dimsdale stated that, "Survivors were located through rabbis, word of mouth, and the assistance of an organization of concentration camp survivors."[4] In his seminal study of survivors of Hiroshima, Robert Lifton used two groups of survivors: "one consisting of thirty-three chosen at random from the lists kept at the Hiroshima University Research Institute for Nuclear Medicine and Biology" and a second group "consisting of forty-two survivors especially selected because of their general articulateness and particular prominence in atomic bomb problems."[5] Though these methods for choosing participants are not the methods employed with undamaged populations, they are effective for studying survivors of widespread atrocity. In terms of culture, educational level, socioeconomic status, and age, the participants are diverse.

The studies listed above clearly communicate their sampling procedures. Though there are unique difficulties with gathering representative samples, it is important to specify sampling procedures, with detailed information about the participants. Many studies, however, provide less than complete descriptions. In fact, some studies do not describe their sampling procedures at all and do not even specify the number of participants. One research group that follows traditional methods for sampling participants is that of Boaz Kahana, Eva Kahana, and Zev Harel. Their extensive work has examined the psychological well-being of Holocaust survivors through the use of structured questionnaires.[6]

ORAL TESTIMONY AND ACCURACY

In the 1980s, the Yale Archive gathered repeated testimony from fourteen Jewish survivors of the Holocaust. With ten of these survivors, a period of seven to nine years passed between the first testimony and the second. I studied these testimonies in an effort to assess constancy and change in Holocaust memory. In particular, I analyzed episodic recall and noted those episodes that witnesses described in both of their testimonies. I then compared the descriptions of these repeated episodes for each of the witnesses. This comparison revealed that for all of the discrete episodes that I recorded, important details were described in a similar manner and the gist was the same across both testimonies. In no cases were there direct contradictions. This comparison also showed identifiable categories of difference in the descriptions of the same episodes. Differences occurred in (1) the specific information about the events and (2) emphasis and wording. The most apparent distinction in the first category (specific information) involved details about the events themselves versus personal observations about one's reaction to the events. When the episodes in the first testimony were more elaborated, the additional information tended to involve more description of the events themselves. When episodes in the second testimony were more elaborated, there was more description of emotions and more observations about the memories. An example of this pattern is shown in the testimony of Daniel F., with the second testimony given eight years after the first. In both testimonies, Daniel describes waiting in the barracks to die after being selected for the gas chamber at Auschwitz. In the first testimony, he describes the events in more detail, including his eventual escape from the barracks. In the second testimony, he elaborates more on his thoughts and emotions while waiting to die.[7]

With regard to the second category (emphasis and wording), it is not surprising that there were differences in testimony given eight years apart. Witnesses do not memorize their episodic recall like actors with a script. However, I detected no systematic changes in emphasis or wording across the fourteen witnesses I studied. The testimony of Jolly Z. presents a distinctively strong example of changes in emphasis and wording. Jolly describes an episode in which she and other inmates tried to push a carriage out of some oily mud under guard by two SS men. One SS man ordered the other to beat the women. In the initial testimony, Jolly recalls that the first SS man struck the women, but not forcefully. In the second testimony, Jolly recalls that he did not strike the women but simply shouted at them to work harder. This difference is as close to a contradiction as I found, but within the context of the entire episode, it is more accurately interpreted as a change in emphasis concerning the first SS man's effort to avoid brutalizing the women. In both testimonies, the second SS man took a whip and beat the women badly.

Jolly's description of the beating by the second SS man illustrates a change in wording. In the first testimony she says, "That night many of us went home with broken ribs and bloody faces." In the second testimony she says, "That day many of us went home with broken cheek bones and arms, and bloody faces." Although some of the words are different, the gist is the same: Many of the women returned to their barracks with their bones broken and their faces bloodied.

The testimony of Jolly Z. also provides an example of a change in the specifics of remembered conversation. In the first testimony, Jolly tells of an SS man who drowned an infant. She remembers the SS man saying "There you go little Moses," as he held the infant down in a sink filled with water. In the second testimony, Jolly quotes the SS man as saying, "Here you go little Moses, down the stream."[8] As with nontraumatic memory, Holocaust memory does not preserve conversation verbatim. The wording of the comments is similar but changed; the gist is identical.

Table A.1
Testimonies Listed in Order of Archive Number

1. Eva B. T-1
2. Eva B. T-1, second
3. Leon W. T-2
4. Sally H. T-3
5. Renee G. T-5
6. William R. T-9
7. Hanna F. T-18
8. Jolly Z. and Rosalie W. T-34, daughter and mother
9. Zoltan G. T-35
10. Celia K. T-36
11. Dori L. T-46
12. Paul D. T-48
13. Renee H. T-50
14. Dori K. T-59
15. Irene W. T-65
16. Hillel K. T-69
17. Eva L. T-71
18. Beatrice S. T-72
19. Henry F. & Chana F. T-81, husband and wife
20. Kochevit P. T-85
21. Bronia L. and Nathan L. T-89, mother and son
22. Chana B. T-92
23. Max B. and Lorna B. T-94, husband and wife
24. Heda K. T-99
25. Zezette L. T-100
26. Edith P. T-107
27. Frania R. T-115
28. Millie W. (Malka D.) T-134
29. Hanna G. T-136
30. Rachel G. T-139
31. Emina N. and Miriam W. T-144, sisters
32. Walter S. T-146
33. Menachem S. T-152
34. Daniel F. T-153
35. Albert K., Gena K., & Kurt K., T-154, parents and son
36. Leo G. T-158
37. Pincus S. and Sylvia S. T-163, husband and wife
38. Karl S. T-173

39. Marc S. T-176
40. Frieda J. T-191
41. Klara A. and Donald W. T-201, mother and son
42. Bessie K. and Jacob K. T-206, wife and husband
43. Alex H. T-210
44. Adele W. T-213
45. Jolly Z. T-220, second
46. Salomon M. T-253
47. Mary E. T-260
48. Alan Z. T-284
49. Hanna H. T-285
50. Sabina G. T-287
51. Baruch G. T-295
52. Myra L. T-299
53. Robert K. T-318
54. Arnold C. T-363
55. Moses S. T-511
56. Edith G. T-571
57. Abraham E. T-579
58. Dori L. T-593, second
59. Samuel B. T-618
60. Zev H. T-622
61. Sabina S. T-623
62. Leon H. T-628
63. Martin S. T-641
64. Rose W. T-657
65. Claude L. T-700
66. Abraham P. T-738
67. Chaim E. T-756
68. Barbara T. T-780
69. Sol F. T-854
70. Nathan L. T-856
71. Josephine B. T-869
72. Ernest R. T-897
73. Annette G. T-933
74. Dori K. T-969, second
75. Celia K. T-970, second
76. Hanna F. T-971, second
77. Jolly Z. T-972, third
78. Edith P. T-974, second
79. Renee G. T-976, second
80. Leo G. T-977, second
81. Daniel F. T-978, second
82. Martin S. T-1091, second
83. Eva B. T-1101, third
84. Ruth J. T-1104
85. Anna K. T-1115
86. Max B. T-1125, second
87. Lorna B. T-1126, second
88. Sally H. T-1154, second
89. Magda F. T-1185
90. Isabella L. T-1270
91. Clemens L. T-1315
92. Abe L. T-1394
93. Aaron S. T-1533
94. Jacqueline R. T-1537
95. Nat G. T-1637
96. Aranka S. and Violet S. T-1649
97. Violet S. T-1650
98. Clara L. T-1850
99. Judith G. T-1879
100. Michael G. T-1880
101. Marian N. T-1881
102. Meir V. T-1892
103. Morris R. T-1897
104. Alina Z. T-2045
105. Hilda S. T-2148

106. Michael M. T-2149
107. Samuel Z & Wolf Z. T-2188, twins
108. Eva V. T-2254
109. Rita L. T-2256
110. Ilse K. T-2258
111. Rena C. T-2293
112. Lea I. T-2330
113. Peter S. T-2337
114. Esther W. T-2609
115. Ruth A. T-2678
116. Leo B. T-2680
117. David K. T-2741

118. Irena D. T-2756
119. Alfred F. T-2762
120. Hubert W. T-2809
121. Herbert L. T-2830
122. Al B. & Joseph B. T-2833, brothers
123. Helen L. T-2853
124. Aladar M. T-2854
125. Nadia R. T-3132
126. Nina S. T-3260
127. Solomon L. T-3261
128. Henry S. T-3380
129. Martha S. T-3531

Table A.2
Witnesses Listed in Alphabetical Order

1. Klara A. T-201
2. Ruth A. T-2678
3. Al B. T-2833
4. Chana B. T-92
5. Eva B. T-1; T-1101
6. Joseph B. T-2833
7. Josephine B. T-869
8. Leo B. T-2680
9. Lorna B. T-94; T-1126
10. Max B. T-94; T-1125
11. Samuel B. T-618
12. Arnold C. T-363
13. Rena C. T-2293
14. Irena D. T-2756
15. Paul D. T-48
16. Abraham E. T-579
17. Chaim E. T-756
18. Mary E. T-260

19. Alfred F. T-2762
20. Chana F. T-81
21. Daniel F. T-153; T-978
22. Hanna F. T-18; T-971
23. Henry F. T-81
24. Magda F. T-1185
25. Sol F. T-854
26. Annette G. T-933
27. Baruch G. T-295
28. Edith G. T-571
29. Hanna G. T-136
30. Judith G. T-1879
31. Leo G. T-158; T-977
32. Michael G. T-1880
33. Nat G. T-1637
34. Rachel G. T-139
35. Renee G. T-5; T-976
36. Sabina G. T-287

37. Zoltan G. T-35
38. Alex H. T-210
39. Hanna H. T-285
40. Leon H. T-628
41. Renee H. T-50
42. Sally H. T-3; T-1154
43. Zev H. T-622
44. Lea I. T-2330
45. Frieda J. T-191
46. Ruth J. T-1104
47. Albert K. T-154
48. Anna K. T-1115
49. Bessie K. T-206
50. Celia K. T-36; T-970
51. David K. T-2741
52. Dori K. T-59; T-969
53. Gena K. T-154
54. Heda K. T-99
55. Hillel K. T-69
56. Ilse K. T-2258
57. Jacob K. T-206
58. Kurt K. T-154
59. Robert K. T-318
60. Abe L. T-1394
61. Bronia L. T-89
62. Clara L. T-1850
63. Claude L. T-700
64. Clemens L. T-1315
65. Dori L. T-46; T-593
66. Eva L. T-71
67. Helen L. T-2853
68. Herbert L. T-2830
69. Isabella L. T-1270
70. Myra L. T-299
71. Nathan L. T-856
72. Nathan L. T-89
73. Rita L. T-2256
74. Solomon L. T-3261
75. Zezette L. T-100
76. Aladar M. T-2854
77. Michael M. T-2149
78. Salomon M. T-253
79. Emina N. T-144
80. Marian N. T-1881
81. Abraham P. T-738
82. Edith P. T-107; T-974
83. Kochevit P. T-85
84. Ernest R. T-897
85. Frania R. T-115
86. Jacqueline R. T-1537
87. Morris R. T-1897
88. Nadia R. T-3132
89. William R. T-9
90. Aaron S. T-1533
91. Aranka S. (and Violet S.) T-1649
92. Beatrice S. T-72
93. Henry S. T-3380
94. Hilda S. T-2148
95. Karl S. T-173
96. Marc S. T-176
97. Martha S. T-3531
98. Martin S. T-641; T-1091
99. Menachem S. T-152
100. Moses S. T-511
101. Nina S. T-3260
102. Peter S. T-2337
103. Pincus S. T-163
104. Sabina S. T-623

105. Sylvia S. T-163
106. Violet S. T-1650; T-1649
107. Walter S. T-146
108. Barbara T. T-780
109. Eva V. T-2254
110. Meir V. T-1892
111. Adele W. T-213
112. Donald W. T-201
113. Esther W. T-2609
114. Hubert W. T-2809
115. Irene W. T-65

116. Leon W. T-2
117. Millie W. (Malka D.) T-134
118. Miriam W. T-144
119. Rosalie W. T-34
120. Rose W. T-657
121. Alan Z. T-284
122. Alina Z. T-2045
123. Jolly Z. T-34; T-220; T-972
124. Samuel Z. T-2188
125. Wolf Z. T-2188

NOTES

1. Klaus Kuch and Brian J. Cox, "Symptoms of PTSD in 124 Survivors of the Holocaust," *American Journal of Psychiatry* 149 (1992): 337–340.

2. Willem A. Wagenaar and Jop Groeneweg, "The Memory of Concentration Camp Survivors," *Applied Cognitive Psychology* 4 (1990): 77–87.

3. James W. Pennebaker, Steven D. Barger, and John Tiebout, "Disclosure of Traumas and Health among Holocaust Survivors," *Psychosomatic Medicine* 51 (1989): 577–589.

4. Joel E. Dimsdale, "The Coping Behavior of Nazi Concentration Camp Survivors," in *Survivors, Victims, and Perpetrators*, edited by Joel E. Dimsdale (New York: Hemisphere Publishing, 1980), 163–174.

5. Robert Jay Lifton, *Death in Life: Survivors of Hiroshima* (New York, Random House, 1967), 6.

6. Refer to the following studies: Zev Harel, Boaz Kahana, and Eva Kahana, "Psychological Well-being among Holocaust Survivors and Immigrants in Israel," *Journal of Traumatic Stress* 1 (1988): 413–429. Boaz Kahana, Zev Harel, and Eva Kahana, "Predictors of Psychological Well-being among Survivors of the Holocaust," in *Human Adaptation to Extreme Stress*, edited by John P. Wilson, Zev Harel, and Boaz Kahana (New York: Plenum Publishing, 1988); Zev Harel, Boaz Kahana, and Eva Kahana "Social Resources and the Mental Health of Aging Nazi Holocaust Survivors and Immigrants," in *International Handbook of Traumatic Stress Syndromes*, edited by John P. Wilson and Beverley Raphael (New York: Plenum Press, 1993), 241–252.

7. Tape HVT-153, 1980; Tape HVT-978, 1988, testimony of Daniel F.

8. Tape HVT-220, 1983; Tape HVT-972, 1988, testimony of Jolly Z.

SELECTED BIBLIOGRAPHY

Albright, Daniel. "Literary and Psychological Models of the Self." In *The Remembering Self*, edited by Ulric Neisser and Robyn Fivush, 19–40. New York: Cambridge University Press, 1994.

American Psychiatric Association. *Diagnostic and Statistical Manual Volume 4*. New York: American Psychiatric Association, 1994.

Appelfeld, Aharon. *The Iron Tracks*. Translated by Jeffrey M. Green. New York: Schocken Books, 1998.

Bauby, Jean-Dominique. *The Diving Bell and the Butterfly*. Translated by Jeremy Leggatt. New York: Knopf, 1997.

Block, Gay, and Malka Drucker. *Rescuers: Portraits of Moral Courage in the Holocaust*. New York: Holmes & Meier Publishers, 1992.

Boder, David P. *I Did Not Interview the Dead*. Urbana, Ill.: University of Illinois Press, 1949.

Brewer, William F. "What Is Autobiographical Memory?" In *Autobiographical Memory*, edited by David C. Rubin, 25–49. New York: Cambridge University Press, 1986.

Brewin, Chris R., Tim Dalgleish, and Stephen Joseph. "A Dual Representation Theory of Posttraumatic Stress Disorder." *Psychological Review* 103 (1996): 670–686.

Brown, Roger, and James Kulik. "Flashbulb Memories." *Cognition* 5 (1977): 73–99.

Buber, Martin. *Between Man and Man*. Translated by Ronald Gregor Smith. New York: Macmillan, 1965.

———. *Hasidism and Modern Man*. Translated and edited by Maurice Friedman. New York: Harper & Row, 1966.

Carocci, Giampiero. *The Officers Camp*. Translated by George Hochfield. Evanston, Ill.: Northwestern University, 1997.

Christianson, Sven-Åke, ed. *The Handbook of Emotion and Memory: Research and Theory*, Hillsdale, N.J.: Erlbaum, 1992.

Coles, Robert. *The Spiritual Life of Children*. Boston: Houghton Mifflin, 1990.

Delbo, Charlotte. *Days and Memory*. Translated by Rosette Lamont. Marlboro, Vt.: Marlboro Press, 1990.

Dershowitz, Alan M. *Chutzpah*. Boston: Little, Brown and Company, 1991.

Dimsdale, Joel E., ed. *Survivors, Victims, and Perpetrators: Essays on the Nazi Holocaust*. New York: Hemisphere Publishing, 1980.

Figley, Charles R., ed. *Trauma and Its Wake*. New York: Brunner/Mazel, 1985.

Fivush, Robyn. "The Functions of Event Memory: Some Comments on Nelson and Barsalou." In *Remembering Reconsidered*, edited by Ulric Neisser and Eugene Winograd, 277–282. New York: Cambridge University Press, 1988.

Fogelman, Eva. "The Psychology Behind Being a Hidden Child." In *The Hidden Children*, by Jane Marks, 292–307. New York: Fawcett Columbine, 1993.

Fortunoff Video Archive. *Guide to Yale University Library Holocaust Video Testimonies*. 2nd ed., New Haven, Conn.: Yale University Library, 1994.

Friedman, Carl. *Nightfather*. Translated by Arnold Pomerans and Erica Pomerans. New York: Persea Books, 1994.

Gilbert, Martin. *Atlas of the Holocaust*. New York: William Morrow and Company, 1993.

Gold, Paul E., "A Proposed Neurobiological Basis for Regulating Memory Storage for Significant Events." In *Affect and Accuracy in Recall*, edited by Eugene Winograd and Ulric Neisser, 141–161. New York: Cambridge University Press, 1992.

Goldhagen, Daniel Jonah. *Hitler's Willing Executioners: Ordinary Germans and the Holocaust*. New York: Knopf, 1996.

Greene, Joshua M., and Shiva Kumar. *Witness: Voices from the Holocaust*. Old Westbury, N.Y.: Joshua M. Greene Productions, 1999. Film.

Greenspan, Henry. *On Listening to Holocaust Survivors: Recounting and Life History*. Westport, Conn.: Praeger Publishers, 1998.

Harber, Kent D., and James W. Pennebaker. "Overcoming Traumatic Memories." In *The Handbook of Emotion and Memory: Research and*

Theory, edited by Sven-Åke Christianson, 359–387. Hillsdale, N.J.: Erlbaum, 1992.

Harel, Zev, Boaz Kahana, and Eva Kahana. "Psychological Well-being among Holocaust Survivors and Immigrants in Israel." *Journal of Traumatic Stress* 1 (1988): 413–429.

———. "Social Resources and the Mental Health of Aging Nazi Holocaust Survivors and Immigrants." In *International Handbook of Traumatic Stress Syndromes*, edited by John P. Wilson and Beverley Raphael, 241–252. New York: Plenum Press, 1993.

Hartman, Geoffrey H. *The Longest Shadow: In the Aftermath of the Holocaust*. Bloomington, Ind.: Indiana University Press, 1996.

Hartman, Geoffrey H., ed. *Holocaust Remembrance: The Shapes of Memory*. Cambridge, Mass.: Blackwell Publishers, 1994.

Hass, Aaron. *The Aftermath: Living with the Holocaust*. New York: Cambridge University Press, 1995.

Helmreich, William B. *Against All Odds: Holocaust Survivors and the Successful Lives They Made in America*. New York: Simon & Schuster, 1992.

Herman, Judith Lewis. *Trauma and Recovery*. New York: Basic Books, 1992.

———. "Sequelae of Prolonged and Repeated Trauma: Evidence for a Complex Posttraumatic Syndrome (DESNOS)." In *Posttraumatic Stress Disorder: DSM-IV and Beyond*, edited by Jonathan Davidson and Edna Foa, 213–228. Washington, D.C.: American Psychiatric Press, 1993.

Hilberg, Raul. *Perpetrators, Victims, Bystanders: The Jewish Catastrophe 1933–1945*. New York: Harper Collins, 1992.

Hirsch, Edward. *The Night Parade*. New York: Knopf, 1989.

Hoffman, Alice, and Howard Hoffman. "Reliability and Validity in Oral History: The Case for Memory." In *Memory and History*, edited by Jaclyn Jeffrey and Glenace Edwall, 107–130. Lantham, Md.: University Press of America, 1994.

Horowitz, Mardi J. "Psychological Response to Serious Life Events." In *Human Stress and Cognition*, edited by Vernon Hamilton and David M. Warburton, 235–263. Chichester, Great Britain: Wiley, 1979.

Horowitz, Mardi J., and Steven P. Reidbord. "Memory, Emotion, and Response to Trauma." In *The Handbook of Emotion and Memory: Research and Theory*, edited by Sven-Åke Christianson, 343–358. Hillsdale, N.J.: Erlbaum, 1992.

Howe, Mark L., and Mary L. Courage. "The Emergence and Early Development of Autobiographical Memory." *Psychological Review* 104 (1997): 499–523.

Hubbell, Sue. *Waiting for Aphrodite*. New York: Houghton Mifflin, 1999.

Janoff-Bulman, Ronnie. "The Aftermath of Victimization: Rebuilding Shattered Assumptions." In *Trauma and Its Wake*, edited by Charles R. Figley, 15–35. New York: Brunner/Mazel, 1985.

Jeffrey, Jaclyn, and Glenace Edwall. *Memory and History: Essays on Recalling and Interpreting Experience*. Lanham, Md.: University Press of America, 1994.

Kahana, Boaz, Zev Harel, and Eva Kahana. "Clinical and Gerontological Issues Facing Survivors of the Nazi Holocaust." In *Healing Their Wounds: Psychotherapy with Holocaust Survivors and Their Families*, edited by Paul Marcus and Alan Rosenberg, 197–211. New York: Praeger, 1989.

Katz, Steven T. *The Holocaust in Historical Context*. New York: Oxford University Press, 1994.

Klee, Ernst, Willi Dressen, and Volker Riess, eds. *"The Good Old Days": The Holocaust as Seen by Its Perpetrators and Bystanders*. Translated by Deborah Burnstone. New York: Free Press, 1991.

Koriat, Asher, Morris Goldsmith, and Ainat Pansky. "Toward a Psychology of Memory Accuracy." In *The Annual Review of Psychology*, Volume 51, edited by Susan T. Fiske, Daniel L. Schacter, and Carolyn Zahn-Waxler, 481–537. Palo Alto, Calif.: Annual Reviews, 2000.

Kotre, John. *White Gloves: How We Create Ourselves Through Memory*. New York: Free Press, 1995.

Kovner, Abba. *Scrolls of Fire*. Paintings by Dan Reisinger. Translated by Shirley Kaufman with Dan Laor. Jerusalem: Keter Publishing House, 1981.

Kraft, Robert N. "Holocaust Memory: Persistent Recall of Extreme Trauma." In *Viewing Psychology as a Whole*, edited by Robert R. Hoffman, Michael F. Sherrick, and Joel S. Warm, 375–398. Washington, D.C.: American Psychological Association, 1998.

Kuch, Klaus, and Brian J. Cox. "Symptoms of PTSD in 124 Survivors of the Holocaust." *American Journal of Psychiatry* 149 (1992): 337–340.

Langer, Lawrence L. *Holocaust Testimonies: The Ruins of Memory*. New Haven, Conn.; Yale University Press, 1991.

———. *Admitting the Holocaust: Collected Essays*. New York: Oxford University Press, 1995.

———. *Preempting the Holocaust*. New Haven, Conn.: Yale University Press, 1998.

Lanzmann, Claude. *Shoah: An Oral History of the Holocaust*. New York: Pantheon Books, 1985.

Laub, Dori, and Nanette C. Auerhahn. "Failed Empathy—A Central Theme in the Survivor's Holocaust Experience." *Psychoanalytic Psychology* 6 (1989): 377–400.

LeDoux, Joseph E. "Emotion as Memory: Anatomical Systems Underlying Indelible Neural Traces." In *Handbook of Emotion and Memory*, edited by Sven-Åke Christianson, 269–288. Hillsdale, N.J.: Erlbaum, 1992.

Leitner, Isabella, and Irving A. Leitner. *Isabella: From Auschwitz to Freedom*. New York: Anchor Books, 1994.

Levi, Primo. *Survival in Auschwitz* and *The Reawakening.* Translated by Stuart Woolf. New York: Summit Books, 1985.

———. *Moments of Reprieve.* Translated by Ruth Feldman. New York: Penguin Books, 1987.

———. *The Drowned and the Saved.* Translated by Raymond Rosenthal. New York: Vintage Books, 1989.

Lev-Wiesel, Rachel, and Marianne Amir. "Secondary Traumatic Stress, Psychological Distress, Sharing of Traumatic Reminisces, and Marital Quality among Spouses of Holocaust Child Survivors." *Journal of Marital and Family Therapy* 27 (2001): 433–444.

Lifton, Robert Jay. *The Protean Self: Human Resilience in an Age of Fragmentation.* New York: Basic Books, 1993.

Lifton, Robert Jay, and Eric Markusen. *The Genocidal Mentality.* New York: Basic Books, 1990.

Linton, Marigold. "Ways of Searching and the Contents of Memory." In *Autobiographical Memory,* edited by David C. Rubin, 50–67. New York: Cambridge University Press, 1986.

Lipstadt, Deborah E. *Denying the Holocaust.* New York: The Free Press, 1993.

Loftus, Elizabeth. "The Reality of Repressed Memories." *American Psychologist* 48 (1993): 518–537.

Marcus, Paul, and Alan Rosenberg, eds. *Healing Their Wounds: Psychotherapy with Holocaust Survivors and Their Families.* New York: Praeger, 1989.

Marks, Jane. *The Hidden Children: The Secret Survivors of the Holocaust.* New York: Fawcett Columbine, 1993.

McGaugh, James L. "Involvement of Hormonal and Neuromodulatory Systems in the Regulation of Memory Storage." *Annual Review of Neuroscience* 12 (1989): 255–287.

Miller, Judith. *One, by One, by One: Facing the Holocaust.* New York: Simon and Schuster, 1990.

Moskovitz, Sarah. *Love Despite Hate: Child Survivors of the Holocaust and Their Adult Lives.* New York: Schocken Books, 1983.

Nahem, Sam. *Looking into the Face of Evil.* Columbus Ohio.: Columbus Holocaust Video Project, 1995. Film.

Neisser, Ulric. "Five Kinds of Self-knowledge." *Philosophical Psychology* 1 (1988): 35–59.

Neisser, Ulric, ed. *Memory Observed: Remembering in Natural Contexts.* San Francisco: W. H. Freeman, 1982.

Neisser, Ulric, and Robyn Fivush, eds. *The Remembering Self: Construction and Accuracy in the Self-narrative.* New York: Cambridge University Press, 1994.

Neisser, Ulric, and Eugene Winograd, eds. *Remembering Reconsidered: Ecological and Traditional Approaches to the Study of Memory.* New York: Cambridge University Press, 1988.

Newman, Judith Sternberg. *In the Hell of Auschwitz*. West Kingston, R.I.: Judith Sternberg Newman, 1963.

Ozick, Cynthia. *Metaphor & Memory*. New York: Knopf, 1989.

Pennebaker, James W., Steven D. Barger, and John Tiebout, "Disclosure of Trauma and Health among Holocaust Survivors." *Psychosomatic Medicine* 51 (1989): 577–589.

Pillemer, David B. *Momentous Events, Vivid Memories*. Cambridge, Mass.: Harvard University Press, 1998.

Rae, Stephen. "John Mack." *New York Times Magazine*, 20 March 1994, 30–33.

Reed, Edward S. "Perception Is to Self as Memory Is to Selves." In *The Remembering Self: Construction and Accuracy in the Self-narrative*, edited by Ulric Neisser and Robyn Fivush, 278–292. New York: Cambridge, 1994.

Reyna, Valerie F. "Fuzzy-Trace Theory and False Memory." In *Memory Distortions and Their Prevention*, edited by Margaret Jean Intons-Peterson & Deborah L. Best, 15–27. Mahwah, N.J.: Erlbaum, 1998.

Reyna, Valerie F., and Allison L. Titcomb. "Constraints on the Suggestability of Eyewitness Testimony: A Fuzzy-Trace Theory Analysis." In *Intersections in Basic and Applied Memory Research*, edited by David G. Payne and Frederick G. Conrad, 157–174. Mahwah, N.J.: Erlbaum, 1997.

Rosenberg, Blanca. *To Tell at Last: Survival under False Identity, 1941–45*. Urbana, Ill.: University of Illinois Press, 1993.

Rubin, David C., ed. *Autobiographical Memory*. New York: Cambridge University Press, 1986.

———. *Remembering Our Past: Studies in Autobiographical Memory*. New York: Cambridge University Press, 1995.

Sarbin, Theodore R. "The Narrative as a Root Metaphor for Psychology." In *Narrative Psychology: The Storied Nature of Human Conduct*, edited by Theodore R. Sarbin, 3–21. New York: Praeger, 1986.

Schacter, Daniel L. "Implicit Memory: History and Current Status." *Journal of Experimental Psychology: Learning, Memory, and Cognition* 13 (1987): 501–518.

———. "The Seven Sins of Memory: Insights from Psychology and Cognitive Neuroscience." *American Psychologist* 54 (1999): 182–203.

Segev, Tom. *The Seventh Million: The Israelis and the Holocaust*. Translated by Haim Watzman. New York: Hill and Wang, 1993.

Semprun, Jorge. *Literature or Life*. Translated by Linda Coverdale. New York: Penguin Books, 1997.

Siegel, Daniel J. "Memory, Trauma, and Psychotherapy: A Cognitive Science View." *Journal of Psychotherapy Practice and Research* 4 (1995): 93–122.

Silberman, Charles E. *A Certain People: American Jews and Their Lives Today.* New York: Summit Books, 1985.

Singer, Isaac Bashevis. *Reaches of Heaven: A Story of the Baal Shem Tov.* Illustrated by Ira Moskowitz. New York: Farrar Straus Giroux, 1980.

Singer, Jefferson A., and Peter Salovey. *The Remembered Self.* New York: The Free Press, 1993.

Spiegelman, Art. *Maus: A Survivor's Tale.* New York: Pantheon, 1986.

Spiegelman, Art. *Maus II: A Survivor's Tale: And Here My Troubles Began.* New York: Pantheon, 1991.

Sussman, Nan M. "The Dynamic Nature of Cultural Identity Throughout Cultural Transitions: Why Home is Not So Sweet." *Personality and Social Psychology Review* 4 (2000): 355–373.

Tec, Nechama. "A Historical Perspective: Tracing the History of the Hidden-Child Experience." In *The Hidden Children* by Jane Marks, 273–291. New York: Fawcett Columbine, 1993.

Terr, Lenore. *Unchained Memories.* New York: Basic Books, 1994.

———. "True Memories of Childhood Trauma: Flaws, Absences, and Returns." In *The Recovered Memory/False Memory Debate*, edited by Kathy Pezdek and William P. Banks, 69–80. San Diego: Academic Press, 1996.

Tolman, Deborah L., and Mary Brydon-Miller, eds. *From Subjects to Subjectivities: A Handbook of Interpretive and Participatory Methods.* New York: New York University Press, 2001.

Triandis, Harry C. "The Self and Social Behavior in Differing Cultural Contexts." *Psychological Review* 96 (1989): 506–520.

Unterman, Alan. *Dictionary of Jewish Lore and Legend.* London: Thames and Hudson, 1991.

van der Kolk, Bessel A. "The Body Keeps the Score: Memory and Evolving Psychobiology of Posttraumatic Stress." *Harvard Review of Psychiatry* 1 (1994): 253–265.

van der Kolk, Bessel A., Alexander C. McFarlane, and Lars Weisaeth, eds. *Traumatic Stress: The Effects of Overwhelming Experience on Mind, Body, and Society.* New York: Guilford Press, 1996.

Wagenaar, Willem A., and Jop Groeneweg. "The Memory of Concentration Camp Survivors." *Applied Cognitive Psychology* 4 (1990): 77–87.

Weimer, Walter B. "Psycholinguistics and Plato's Paradoxes of the Meno." *American Psychologist* 28 (1973): 15–33.

Weinberg, Jeshajahu, and Rina Elieli. *The Holocaust Museum in Washington.* New York: Rizzoli International, 1995.

Wiesel, Elie. *A Jew Today.* Translated by Marion Wiesel. New York: Vintage Books, 1979.

———. *One Generation After.* New York: Pocket Books, 1978.

————. *Night*. Translated by Stella Rodway. New York: Bantam, 1982.

————. *The Forgotten*. Translated by Stephen Beckers. New York: Summit Books, 1992.

Williams, Linda Meyer. "Recall of Childhood Trauma: A Prospective Study of Women's Memories of Child Sexual Abuse." *The Journal of Consulting and Clinical Psychology* 62 (1994): 1167–1176.

Winograd, Eugene, and Ulric Neisser, eds. *Affect and Accuracy in Recall: Studies of "Flashbulb" Memories*. New York: Cambridge University Press, 1992.

Young, James E. *The Art of Memory: Holocaust Memorials in History*. New York: The Jewish Museum, 1994.

INDEX

Albright, Daniel, 146, 159 n.65
Anger, 36, 67
Anne Frank, xiv, xv
Anniversary effect, 124
Anti-Semitism, 95, 96, 127, 137,
    169–170
Appell, 84, 89 n.60, 110, 112, 180
Artistic expression of Holocaust
    memory, 182–183. *See also*
    Forms of expression
Atrocity
    coexisting with, 110–115
Attention during trauma
    distortions of, 101–103
The Auschwitz Album, 135
Auschwitz-Birkenau
    arrival at, 20–21, 32, 96–98, 101–
        105, 113–114
    Canada Kommando, 19
    death march from, xiv–xv, 142
    selections, 113, 138–139

slave labor, 84
survival, 97, 111, 112–115, 134
torture, 108
transport to, 47, 95–96, 99–100,
    102

"Back There," 21–23, 26
Banks, William, 117 n.24
Barger, Steven, 160 n.79, 189, 195
    n.3
Bauby, Jean-Dominique (*The Div-
    ing Bell and the Butterfly*), 6–
    7, 15 n.18
Bearing witness, 165–166, 171–172
Behavioral consequences of trau-
    matic memory, 121–124, 153–
    154 n.1. *See also* Fears
Bergen-Belsen, xv, 103–104, 108–
    110, 114, 130, 177
Birthday effect, 66
Boder, David P. (*I Did Not Inter-

view the Dead), 67, 87 n.24, 116 n.6
Bodily memory, 21
Borges, Jorge, 33
Bosnia, 168–169
Breznitz, Shlomo, 68, 88 n.27
Brewin, Chris R., 50 n.22, 51 n.25
Brown, Roger, 24, 51 n.24
Brydon-Miller, Mary, 16 n.30
Buber, Martin, 6, 15 n.17, 92
Buchenwald, 63

Cambodia, 10, 41–42, 168–169
Camp Erika, 14 n.1, 51–52 n.30, 52 n.33, 188
Cannibalism, 104, 109, 146
Carocci, Gampiero, 7, 15 n.20
Catharsis
  absence of, 38, 152
Catholicism, 73–74, 131
Chelmno, 95, 110
Child survivors, 57–86. *See also* Hidden children
  conflation of thoughts and memories, 74–76
  confusions within memory, 78–82
  delayed effects of trauma, 64–67
  developing concepts of self, 61–74
  differences in testimony from older survivors, 86
  early maturation, 65–66
  first memories, 59–61
  games, 70–72
  mistakes in memory, 76–79
  mourning the loss of childhood, 63–66
  periods of personal memory, 58–61
  separation, 68–74
  silence, 83–85
Christianson, Sven-Åke, 53 n.51, 93, 116 n.4, 155 n.8, 158 n.50, 160 n.79

Clampitt, Amy, 5, 15 n.11
Common memory, 22, 25
Constructive memory, 24
Core Memory, 25–27, 51 n.28, 76–78
Courage, Mary L., 50, n.18
Cox, Brian J., 188, 195 n.1
Czechoslovakia, 124, 132, 177

Dalgleish, Tim, 50 n.22, 51 n.25
Danieli, Yael, 140, 158 n.54
Deep memory, 22–23, 25
Delbo, Charlotte (*Days and Memory*), 137, 157 n.41
Destiny, 139–140
Deutschkron, Inge, 88 n.35
Dimsdale, Joel E., 189, 195 n.4
Disbelief, 3–5, 144–147
Dissociation, 92, 100–101, 117 n.24
Diversity of viewpoints, 183, 186 n.48
Dogs, 32, 60, 123, 130, 153–154 n.1
DP (displaced persons) camps, 74, 146
DSM-IV, 115 n.2, 160 n.78
Dual beliefs, 105, 118 n.33
Duality of memory, 22–29

Eichmann Trial, xv, 163
Emotion, 53 n.51, 55–56 n.83, 94
  in child survivors, 81
  difficulty showing, 128
  during testimony, 34–37, 54 n.59
  in memory, 2, 34–38
  triggers, 122–124
Encoding of traumatic events, 91–93

Fears, 122–123, 153–154 n.1. *See also* Behavioral consequences of traumatic memory
Figley, Charles R., 160 n.78

Films about the Holocaust, xv
Fiske, Susan T., 14 n.1
Fivush, Robyn, 50 n.15, 83, 89
    n.58, 133, 156 n.33, 157
    n.38, 159 n.65
Flashbulb memory, 24, 51 n.24
Forms of expression, 5–6, 179–184
    art, 182–183
    figurative language, 5–6, 179–180
Fortunoff Video Archive for Holo-
    caust Testimonies, xv, xvi, 9–
    10
Fuzzy-trace theory
    verbatim versus gist memory, 25,
    51 nn.27, 28

General Motors, xiv
Gestapo, 123, 140–141
Goeth, Amon, 109
Gold, Paul E., 93, 116 n.4
Goldsmith, Morris, 14 n.1
Groeneweg, Jop, 14–15 n.1, 51–52
    n.30, 52 n.33, 188, 195 n.2
Guilt, 121, 138–143, 158 n.57
    and no guilt, 139–140
    not measurable, 157–158 n.45
    reasons for
        inability to save loved ones,
        140–142
        living at the expense of others,
        138–140
        not helping others, 142–143
        "why me?," 138, 158 n.45
    survivor guilt, 138, 158 n.45

Haden, Catherine, 83, 89 n.58
Harber, Kent D., 53 n.51, 160 n.79
Harel, Zev, 161 n.87, 189, 195 n.6
Hartman, Geoffrey H., xix n.3, 11,
    16 n.31
Herman, Judith Lewis, 160 n.28
Hidden children, 57, 67–72, 142–
    143

Hirsch, Edward, xiii
Hoffman, Alice, 9, 15–16 n.24
Hoffman, Howard, 9, 15–16 n.24
Hoffman-Fischel, Hana, 88 n.35
Holocaust (1978 television minise-
    ries), 85, 164
Holocaust denial, 173–175
Holocaust remembrance, 133, 151–
    153
Holocaust Testimonies, 21, 22, 50
    nn.13, 16. See also Lawrence
    L. Langer
Hopelessness, 168, 169–171
Horowitz, Mardi J., 139, 155 n.8,
    158 n.50
Howe, Mark L., 50 n.18
Hubbell, Sue, 16 n.29
Humiliation, 32, 105
Humor, 180
Hunger, 95, 106–108, 153–154 n.1

Implicit memory, 25
Interview procedure, xvi–xvii, 9
Irving, David, 174
Israel, 131, 156 n.27

Janoff-Bulman, Ronnie, 159–160
    n.78
Joseph, Stephen, 50 n.22, 51 n.25

Kahana, Boaz, 161 n.87, 189, 195
    n.6
Kahana, Eva, 161 n.87, 189, 195
    n.6
Koriat, Asher, 14 n.1
Kosovo, 169
Kotre, John (White Gloves), 26, 51
    n.29
Kraft, Robert N., 56 n.87, 88 n.46
Krakow, 59, 61
Kuch, Klaus, 188, 195 n.1
Kulik, James, 24, 51 n.24
Kundera, Milan, 186 n.46

Langer, Lawrence L., 21, 22, 50 nn.13, 16, 172, 184 n.17
Language
  analysis of, 48–49
  limitations of, 7, 32–33, 136–137, 144–145
Lanzmann, Claude, 5, 91, 156 n.27
LeDoux, Joseph E., 93, 116 n.4
Levi, Primo, 33, 41, 53 n.48, 55 n.73
Liberation, 5, 98–99, 116 n.6
Life Is Beautiful (1998 film), xv, 70
Life review, 55–56 n.83
Lifton, Robert Jay, 117–118 n.33, 131, 156 nn.28, 31, 189, 195 n.5
Linton, Marigold, 16 n.29, 37, 54 n.62
Lipstadt, Deborah E., 174, 185 n.23
Lodz Ghetto, 8, 45–47, 106–107, 139
Loftus, Elizabeth F., 50 n.20
Luck, 111, 118 n.52

Majdanek, 110
Marks, Jane (*The Hidden Children*), 87 n.25
Markusen, Eric, 118 n.33, 189, 195 n.5
McGaugh, James L., 93, 116 n.4
Memory for traumatic events
  accuracy, 14 n.1, 88 n.43, 189–191
  Balkanization of, 2
  and current events, 41, 168–169
  divided, 24–29
  episodic elements and structure, 17–18, 30
  increasing painfulness with age, 43–45
  mistakes, 27–29, 76–79
  organization of, 29–34
  persistence of, 1–2, 38–45
  physiological effects of, 123–124
  purposes of, 3, 165–169
  retrieval of, 41–42
  taxonomy of, 11–13
  temporal, 28, 99–100
  for thoughts, 7–8
  validation, 78–82
  visual, auditory, and olfactory images, 18–21, 39–41.
  See also Core memory; Dissociation; Duality of memory; Memory directives; Narrative memory; Repression
Memory directives, 167–168
  anchoring events, 167–168
  originating events, 167–168
Mengele, Josef, 2, 40
Metamemory, 12, 37–38
Moral principles
  violation of, 106–107
Moskovitz, Sarah, 88 n.35

Narrative memory, 25–27, 51 n.28
Narrative organization, 5, 17, 30–32
Neisser, Ulric, 14 n.1, 22, 50 n.15, 52 n.36, 116 n.4, 136, 157 nn.33, 38, 40, 159 n.65
Nightmares, 39, 84, 125–126, 155 n.11, 157 n.44, 160–161 n.83
Numbness, 92, 96–101, 116 n.10

Oral testimony
  beginnings, 34
  distinctive characteristics of, xv–xviii, 7–10, 33–34, 185–186 n.39
  emotional effects of, 37–38
  endings, 33–34, 180–182
  reasons for, 150–153, 165–166, 171–175
  studying, 5, 10–13

transitions in, 30–32
warnings in, 169–170
ORBIS, xv, 187

Panic attacks, 42, 123
Pansky, Ainat, 14 n.1
Paradox of learning (Plato), 3–5
Pennebaker, James W., 53 n.51,
    160 n.79, 189, 195 n.3
Perception
    denial and distortion of, 92, 103–
    105
Pessimism and optimism, 169–171,
    181
Physiology of traumatic memory,
    93–94
Pillemer, David B. (*Momentous
    Events, Vivid Memories*), 56
    n.86, 88 n.39, 167, 175, 184
    nn.4, 6, 185 n.25
Plaszow, 109
Post-traumatic stress disorder
    (PTSD), 23, 115 n.2, 159–
    160 n.78
Predictions, 169–171
Psychotherapy, 87 n.8, 150, 159–
    160 n.78, 160 n.79, 161 n.87

Qualitative research, 10–13, 48–49,
    16 n.30

Rage, 36, 67
Reasons for giving testimony, 151–
    153, 165–166, 171–175
    bearing witness, 165–166, 171–
    172
    for children and grandchildren,
    173
    countering Holocaust deniers,
    173–175
    time is running out, 172–173
Recall, 29–34
    chronological, 29–32

chronological and geographic,
    30
and the imposition of continuity,
    30–31
incompleteness of, 33–35
non-narrative, 21–23, 26
pain of, 165–167
as strings of episodes, 29–30
Reed, Edward S., 135–136, 157
    n.38
Reese, Elaine, 83, 89 n.58
Reidbord, Steven P., 139, 155 n.8,
    158 n.50
Repeated testimony, 36–38, 74–76,
    142–143, 187–188
Religious beliefs, 128–131, 156 n.31
    conversion and identity, 72–74,
    131–133
    humanism, 130–131
    miracles, 128–129
    suppression of, 131–133
Repression, 54–55 n.63, 66, 100–
    101, 117 n.24
Rescuers
    naiveté of, 116 n.6
Research methods, xviii, 10–13, 48–
    49, 187–188
Revenge, 175–179, 185 n.26
    limited, 177–179
    as motivation, 114–115
    turning points, 175–178, 185
    n.26
Reyna, Valerie F., 25, 51 n.27. *See
    also* Fuzzy-trace theory
Robinson, John A., 53 n.51
Roth, Philip, 186 n.46
Rubin, David C., 16 n.29, 53 n.51,
    54 n.62, 89 n.58
Rudof, Joanne, 186 n.42
Rwanda, 10, 168–169

Sabotage, 32, 112
Safer, Martin A., 53 n.51

Sampling procedures, xv–xvi, 187–189
Schacter, Daniel L., 14 n.1, 51 n.26
Schindler's List (1993 film), xv, xvii
Schindler, Oskar, 84, 154 n.1
Selections, 105, 113, 138–139
Self-concepts
  altered, 126–137
  in child survivors, 61–74
  split, 2, 133–137, 148, 157 n.38
Semprun, Jorge, 7, 15 n.19
Shoah (1985 film), 5, 91
Siegel, Daniel J., 50–51 n.23, 51 n.26
Silence, 164
  in child survivors, 83–85
  overcoming, 150–153, 167, 171–175
  reasons for, 143–150
    avoiding the pain of memory, 147–148
    discouragement of others, 146–147
    dilemma of disclosure and empathy, 6, 148–150
    elusiveness of understanding, 144–146
Skarzysko, 8, 18, 19, 31, 62, 63, 100, 112, 129
Sobibor, 95, 108
SS (Schutzstaffel), 28, 32, 35–36, 39, 46–47, 80–81, 103, 113, 129, 141, 171, 176–177, 190–191
Survival schemas, 105–110
Sussman, Nan M., 128, 155 nn.15, 20, 156 n.32
Swiss banks, xiii–xiv

Teaching the Holocaust, 94–95
Tec, Nechama, 87 n.25

Terezin (Theresienstadt), 80–81, 132, 180
Terr, Lenore (*Unchained Memories*), 22, 50 n.17, 115 n.2, 153 n.1
Tiebout, John, 160 n.79, 189, 195 n.3
Titcomb, Allison, L., 51 n.27
Tolman, Deborah L., 16 n.30
Transports, 9, 47, 95–96, 99–100, 102
Triandis, Harry C., 137, 150, 157 n.42, 160 n.81

Uncertainty, 2, 111, 113–114
United States Holocaust Memorial Museum, 9, 16 n.25
Ustaša, xiii

Van der Kolk, Bessel A., 50 n.21, 93, 116 n.4
Vichy, xiv
Vilna, 59
Volkswagon, xiv

Wagenaar, Willem A., 14–15 n.1, 51–52 n.30, 52 n.33, 188, 195 n.2
Warsaw Ghetto, 30, 99, 132
Weimer, Walter B., 15 n.10
Westerbork, 63, 69
Wiesel, Elie, 106
Williams, Linda Meyer, 117 n.24
Winograd, Eugene, 14 n.1, 52 n.36, 116 n.4, 157 n.33
Witnessing the killing of one's family, 123, 140–142

Yad Vashem, 9, 156 n.27

Zahn-Waxler, Carolyn, 14 n.1

About the Author

ROBERT N. KRAFT is Professor of Cognitive Psychology and Chair of the Department of Psychology at Otterbein College.